ACHIEVING EXCELLENCE IN FUND RAISING

Henry A. Rosso
and Associates

Foreword by Robert L. Payton

ACHIEVING EXCELLENCE IN FUND RAISING

*A Comprehensive Guide
to Principles, Strategies,
and Methods*

Jossey-Bass Publishers · San Francisco

Jossey-Bass books and products are available through most bookstores. To contact Jossey-Bass directly, call (888) 378-2537, fax to (800) 605-2665, or visit our website at www.josseybass.com.

Substantial discounts on bulk quantities of Jossey-Bass books are available to corporations, professional associations, and other organizations. For details and discount information, contact the special sales department at Jossey-Bass.

For sales outside the United States, please contact your local Simon & Schuster International Office.

Manufactured in the United States of America.

JACKET DESIGN BY WILLI BAUM

Library of Congress Cataloging-in-Publication Data
Rosso, Henry A., date.
    Achieving excellence in fund raising: a comprehensive guide to principles, strategies, and methods / Henry A. Rosso and associates. — 1st ed.
       p.   cm. — (The Jossey-Bass nonprofit sector series)
    Includes bibliographical references and index.
    ISBN 1-55542-387-6
    1. Fund raising.   I. Title.   II. Series.
HG177.R67 1991
658.15'224—dc20   91-16609

HB Printing   10 9 8 7   FIRST EDITION

The Jossey-Bass
Nonprofit and Public Management
Series

Contents

Foreword

This book will be known as *Rosso*. People will turn to it the way others have turned to *Samuelson* in economics or to *Osler* in medicine or (at the University of Chicago, at least) to "McKeon's *Aristotle*." *Rosso* will sit alongside *Seymour* on your shelf of the indispensable works on fund raising.

This is a solid handbook and guide to the field of philanthropic fund raising. It is rooted in practice and experience. It is an example of what the Greeks called *phronesis*, "practical wisdom," distilled as it is from tens of thousands of hours of thinking about how good works get done.

"Rosso" is Henry A. Rosso, a name by which even his wife would not know him. He is *Hank* Rosso, as unaffected and direct as his nickname, one of the great teachers by the standards of any field, and probably the greatest teacher the field of fund raising has ever known.

Hank has gathered together in this book the substance of his own teaching from The Fund Raising School, writing many of the chapters himself and enlisting the aid of some of his peers (Phil Brain, for example) and a new generation (Kay Sprinkel Grace, for example).

Hank speaks of fund raising as an art form, and in some ways it is a language art. Hank's contributions in these pages reveal his own great joy in language. He is a living reminder that behind every really good businesslike approach there is humane sensitivity and social awareness. That is one of the lessons of this book.

There are many other lessons along the way. Some you will know because the authors strive to be very clear and specific in what they are saying. Other insights will catch you unaware: Gene Tempel's passing reference to "the affirmation of mission"; Kay Grace's comment that "systems liberate." Hank Rosso on language, Art Frantzreb on values, Kim Klein on "grass roots"; your vision, both focal and peripheral, will be sharpened and expanded on every page.

There is also much on fund raising's received wisdom in this book, sometimes referred to by several authors drawing from a common well of tradition; for example: *People don't give to causes; people give to people with causes.* Such whispered advice will quietly echo and reverberate through you semi-consciously for years to come. It becomes part of the sediment of knowledge tested by your own experience from which you will eventually dredge up your own view of how the philanthropic world works.

The test of what you have learned will not only show up in your performance, it will be most vividly revealed (betrayed?) when you become a teacher yourself. Serious practitioners are always serious teachers. In fund raising, most of the knowledge flows that way, through channels carved out by such books as this one.

All of the authors are practitioners. As Hank Rosso indicates in his introduction, *Achieving Excellence in Fund Raising* is but one of a growing number of efforts that are developing a profession of fund raising. There is clearly more practical than academic learning here, although many of the authors (Tempel and Fogal, for example) draw on scholarly research in the social sciences to fashion their own frame of reference. (Education in business management and public administration has proceeded along the same path.) In time, the practical wisdom of this book will seep into the epistemic writings of the academy. Increasingly, the study of fund raising will benefit from the constructive criticism of the academy as well as from a wider and deeper empirical knowledge base. *Rosso II*, another book in the making, will show more signs of seepage in both directions. Scholars and practitioners, and practitioner-scholars, have much to learn from each other. (If only my colleagues in the liberal arts would read this book—how much stronger the liberal arts would be.)

This book is based directly on the teachings of The Fund Raising School, which Hank Rosso founded seventeen years ago. It is still another reminder of Vince Lombardi's best advice: Never stop working on the fundamentals. As one who has spent thirty years in and around fund raising for higher education, I have been humbled by how much I learned from my own participation in The Fund Raising School's Course 101—and now, again, from *Rosso*.

There is much to argue with in this book. Every application of a principle is a test of the principle. You will challenge some of the principles here, just as "101" students do. Hank will applaud your determination to be skeptical and tough-minded and down-to-earth. *Achieving Excellence in Fund Raising* offers a larger worldview than that, however; it (and Rosso himself) testify to values and attitudes and conviction. The world of fund raising is a world of noble aspiration confronted with the demands of mundane technique. Neither makes sense without the other.

Without ever giving a lecture on ethics, Hank Rosso's ethical sensitivity permeates every lecture he gives, every word of advice he offers, every generous gift of his time to help his students serve the cause he has served so well.

This book is another such gift from Rosso. Learn from him and his friends and colleagues. And then practice what you preach: Pass along what you've learned.

Indianapolis, Indiana Robert L. Payton
September 1991

Preface

In the five decades since the end of World War II, the structure and strategies of fund raising have changed significantly. Fund raising has come to be accepted as a discipline with both dignity and rigorous requirements for attention to the details that make it the productive servant to philanthropy that it is.

In the contemporary period, the planning, directing, and implementing of fund raising plans are more the responsibility of an in-house practitioner than they have ever been in the past. External professional counsel is still available to provide full-time direct program management or time-limited consulting guidance to the professional in-house staff. The phenomenon of program management by in-house staff is increasingly apparent and will continue to be so into the future. These practitioners — some beginning their experience, some technically trained in the mechanics, others more learned in the overall dynamics of the form — are part of what is still an emerging profession.

Advancement from an emerging to a learned profession will be slow-paced and will not be formalized until such time as a body of professional knowledge has been expanded and verified through valid research by qualified investigators. At that time, finally, the practitioner will be certified or accredited as a learned professional on the basis of the results of a written examination on the content of this knowledge base, as well as on the proof of performance through actual fund raising experience.

Then, and only then, will the professional fund raising person be able to walk in dignity and in companionship with accountants, attorneys, physicians, and others who are considered learned professionals. At that time, fund raising will be accepted more universally as honorable and the profession of fund raising as noble. Learning technical and mechanical aspects of fund raising will not be enough. Understanding philanthropy's role in the advancement of a society and fund raising's servant role to this advancement will be the key to this accomplishment.

The purpose of this book is to add to the existing body of knowledge. Its further purpose is to demonstrate that fund raising is multifaceted and multidimensional by defining and expanding the principles pertaining to the facets and to the dimensions. It seeks to foster an understanding of the elements and to promote an acceptance of the relationships and the inter-dependence of the elements that support the practice of fund raising.

In addition, this book is intended as a comprehensive text on the concepts, principles, techniques, and disciplines of ethical fund raising. It is designed to meet the varied needs of various people who might approach this subject from a variety of perspectives. For example:

1. The fledgling fund raising practitioner might want to understand this fascinating art form in its larger dimensions and perhaps can learn from a review of the concepts offered on the pages that follow.
2. The skilled professional can benefit by an occasional revisiting of many of the old and some of the new principles that justify and bring an excitement to the process.
3. The senior management team should understand that to deploy re-sources — a management function — one must direct creative energy to the gathering of resources — also a management function — and further understand that it is wise for senior managers to know more about the gathering process.
4. The trustees are the primary stewards of organizations of the indepen-dent sector, and as such should accept and support fund raising in the important role that it plays in providing the human and financial capital necessary to the functioning of these organizations.
5. Any other person — philanthropist, volunteer, employee, or government official — can be helped to understand that there is moral justification, dignity, and an ethical base for fund raising that give back a spiritual value to all who are associated with it.

The book is organized into six domains of knowledge that are sup-ported by chapters that relate the concepts and principles pertinent to each domain. The chapters reflect the broad experience and the professional competence of the participating authors.

The reader can follow the chapters sequentially. This will lead to a better understanding of the integrated nature of the fund raising process and the relationships and interdependence of the elements within each domain. Conversely, the reader may wish to read individual chapters out of sequence for a detailed study of selected principles and techniques.

Part One provides the reader with an overview of fund raising. The central theme is developed around a cycle to demonstrate that fund raising functions as a continuum, with each piece in its logical place on that continuum and each piece essential to the whole. A philosophy for fund raising is a serious expression of the worth of this process and testimony to the effect that it does possess a dignity, a worth, and a set of values. No one should ever apologize for being part of an ethical fund raising undertaking.

Part Two focuses on institutional readiness, or the preparedness of the organization to expose itself to public scrutiny by embarking on a fund raising program. Does it understand that it must function within an environment that can be supportive, or competitive, or hostile, or turbulent? Does the organization know the makeup of its constituency? What is the organization's mission? Is its definition of a mission a true statement of values, a philosophical expression of the needs it is serving, or is it a technical listing of the goal it intends to serve? What difference does any of this make to the fund raising process?

Part Three dissects the various fund raising "vehicles," a bit of jargon within the profession that refers to the techniques that are used to raise money. The authors examine each of the vehicles in terms of its application, requirements, and connection with other vehicles. For example, what is the purpose of direct mail, and what impact will a successful mail campaign have on the development of major gifts and planned-gift prospects? What is the meaning and importance of a base of contributors?

Part Four dwells on the principle that fund raising is a management process and, as such, must rein in the top echelons of the organization. Do the trustees have any responsibilities for fund raising? How is the chief executive officer involved? The program staff? The support staff? Is each entity an integral part of the program? By the same token, how important is the information? What kind of information is needed and how is it used strategically? What role does the external fund raising consultant play in serving the organization? How is the consultant selected, and how can this service be used effectively to serve the needs of the organization?

Part Five offers a discourse on standards and ethics for fund raising, as well as an analysis of the resources necessary and available for strengthening the diverse skills of the professional practitioner. *Standards*, *morals*, and *ethics* are common expressions in conversations among professionals in this age. There is an awareness of the importance of continuing discourse on the subject. There is an equal awareness of the necessity for the professional, no matter how practiced, to hone the skills that transcend technical aptitudes to ensure continuing professional proficiency in an increasingly turbulent environment.

Part Six concludes with a definitive statement of the integrated fund raising process, the strategy of creating a consciousness about the totality of the organization's financial needs and focusing the organization's creative energy to resolve those needs through an intelligently conceived and thoughtfully executed fund raising program.

Many individuals have played a role in bringing this book to reality.

Some have been the goad to the compilation of the principles and techniques of fund raising into a single text. I acknowledge with gratitude the urgings of Robert L. Payton, director of the Center on Philanthropy, Indiana University; Eugene R. Tempel, vice-chancellor for external affairs, Indiana University at Indianapolis; and Charles A. Johnson, vice-president for development of the Lilly Endowment. Their frequent reminders that the publication of the book was overdue provided a disquieting, albeit effective, form of motivation.

There were the quiet but ever-so-persistent prods of individuals who attended sessions of The Fund Raising School. The questions were always the same: "When do we get your book?" To each of these, my thanks for the continuing encouragement that spurred this project to completion.

Special thanks are due to each of the authors who contributed chapters to the book. Each was cooperative and understanding whenever it was necessary to return the manuscript for revisions. I hope that this final text will live up to their expectations and to the professional standards that they espouse.

A very special expression of gratitude is due to two very special people: first, to my wife, Dottie, who offered invaluable assistance both for ensuring proper manuscript preparation for the final copy of this book and for working energetically and ably during the formative years of The Fund Raising School by typing, revising, printing, and hauling study guides, and processing, cajoling, and nurturing enrollees almost beyond the point of fatigue. Without her dedication, inspiration, and assistance, the founding and development of the school would never have been possible; second, to Linda Schraufnagl Rosso, our daughter-in-law, who cooperated so willingly to apply her extensive editing skills to ensure coherence in much of the text.

The principles and techniques that constitute the content base were originally formulated for the study guide that has been used as the instructional text for The Fund Raising School's comprehensive course offerings. Permission has been granted by The Fund Raising School and by the Center on Philanthropy of Indiana University to expand those concepts in narrative form for use in this book. I am grateful for their support.

Two individuals gave so much of themselves to assist in the founding of The Fund Raising School in 1974: Joseph R. Mixer, at that time special assistant to the chancellor, University of California, Berkeley; and Lyle M. Cook, at that time vice-president for university relations, University of San Francisco. Both contributed significantly to the development of the base of professional knowledge that supported the teachings of the school over the years. I am grateful for the energy, the talent, and the time that they directed to the embryonic effort.

San Rafael, California   Henry A. Rosso
September 1991

The Authors

Henry A. Rosso is founding director and director emeritus of The Fund Raising School, a program of the Indiana University Center on Philanthropy at Indianapolis. Before founding the school in 1974, Rosso was a senior vice-president and member of the board of directors of G.A. Brakeley and Company, Inc., a national fund raising consulting firm. He is the first consultant to be elected as an associate member of the American Association of Fund-Raising Counsel, Inc.

He is a magna cum laude graduate of Syracuse University (1949) and a member of Phi Beta Kappa Society. He was awarded an honorary doctor of laws degree by Pacific Union College in 1988.

At the 1985 International Conference of the National Society of Fund Raising Executives, Rosso was presented the Outstanding Fund Raising Executive of the Year Award. In 1990, Indiana University recognized Rosso's contribution to philanthropy by creating the Henry A. Rosso Award for Lifetime Achievement in Ethical Fund Raising. The first recipient was Henry A. Rosso. He is a past president of the Development Executives Roundtable, a member of the Golden Gate chapter of the National Society of Fund Raising Executives, The American Society for Training and Development, and the American Management Association.

Rosso has conducted classes in the fund raising process throughout the United States and in Australia, Canada, and New Zealand.

Phyllis A. Allen has been a fund raising executive with Sharp HealthCare in San Diego for the past four years. She began her career as a copywriter and broadcaster in Medford, Oregon, in 1957, where she remained for eight years. After working in advertising and public relations, she became the executive director for Akron General Development Foundation in 1973. She joined Children's Hospital in San Francisco in 1980, moving to San Diego in 1983 to be with Scripps Memorial Hospitals Foundation.

Bonita M. Bergin pioneered the concept of service dogs being trained and placed with physically disabled individuals to help these individuals with everyday tasks. In 1975, she founded Canine Companions for Independence (CCI), serving as executive director from 1975 to 1990. She developed this concept into an internationally acclaimed not-for-profit organization with five centers throughout the United States and an annual budget of $3 million. She presently serves as founder and director of research for CCI's newly created Research Center.

Philip S. Brain Jr., after thirty-eight years with a major organization serving youths and raising more than $38 million, formed Phil Brain Associates in Minneapolis, Minnesota, to help charitable organizations in planned giving. In 1979, he participated in the formation of the National Association of YMCA Development Officers and initiated formation of The Minnesota Planned Giving Council. In 1983, he was named the Fund Raising Executive of the Year by the Minnesota Chapter of the NSFRE; in 1984 he received the NSFRE honor of Professional Fund Raising Executive of the Year. He has been a member of The Fund Raising School's faculty since 1982.

Roger M. Craver is the founder of Craver, Mathews, Smith and Company (CMS) in Falls Church, Virginia, the largest public interest fund raising firm in the United States. CMS—whose clients include Greenpeace, Amnesty International, and Planned Parenthood—has pioneered the innovative use of new direct mail, telemarketing, and video technologies in both mass market and high-dollar fund raising.

Robert E. Fogal held positions of vice-president for development at Otterbein College in Ohio and chief development officer at Lancaster Theological Seminary in Pennsylvania. He taught for several years at the Protestant Institute for Advanced Theological Studies in Argentina before being named director of The Fund Raising School at the Indiana University Center on Philanthropy in Indianapolis in 1990.

Arthur C. Frantzreb is a native of Indianapolis, Indiana. He began his fund raising career with Marts and Lundy, Inc., of New York City in 1948. He has spent more than four decades counseling not-for-profits with a no-nonsense, candid approach to philanthropic results. In 1977, he became an independent consultant in philanthropy working out of McLean, Virginia. Among his many awards and honors are the honorary doctor of literature degree from Mt. Senario College in Ladysmith, Wisconsin, and honors from the

Council of Independent Colleges for outstanding service to small independent colleges.

Jane C. Geever is president of J.C. Geever, Inc., the first woman-led fund raising company to be admitted into membership in the American Association of Fund-Raising Counsel. Currently an AAFRC board member, she has been an NSFRE board member and an officer in both AAFRC and the NSFRE Institute. A member of the Philanthropic Advisory Council for the Better Business Bureau in New York, she is active in INDEPENDENT SECTOR's Give Five Program in New York and has been appointed to INDEPENDENT SECTOR's ad hoc Committee on Values and Ethics.

Kay Sprinkel Grace is Western Regional Director of The Fund Raising School and a San Francisco–based consultant who provides workshops and consultation to local, regional, and national organizations in campaign strategies, case and board development, and issues related to leadership of the fund raising process. Principal of her own firm since 1987, she has been a staff development officer for nearly a decade, serving several organizations. A graduate of Stanford University, she has been a volunteer leader in the university's $1.1 billion centennial campaign. In 1979, she received the Gold Spike, Stanford's highest volunteer award. She has served on NSFRE local and national boards.

Kim Klein currently is the endowment coordinator for the Funding Exchange in New York City, supervising a $15-million campaign. A full-time professional in the fund raising field for more than fifteen years, she was the founding director of the Appalachian Community Fund in Knoxville, Tennessee. With a background in theology and classics, she found her true calling in fund raising for social justice causes while studying for the ministry. Publisher of the *Grassroots Fundraising Journal* and author of *Fundraising for Social Change*, she is a contributing author to a wide variety of books and magazines related to not-for-profit organizations.

Sheree Parris Nudd is vice-president of Shady Grove Adventist Hospital in Rockville, Maryland. Formerly, she held positions as executive director of the Porter Memorial Hospital Foundation in Denver, Colorado, and director of development, public relations, and marketing at Huguley Memorial Hospital in Fort Worth, Texas. A charter trustee of the Milton Murray Foundation for Philanthropy, Nudd wishes to acknowledge Milton Murray as a mentor and friend, whose life and work personify philanthropy—the love of humankind. A graduate of Southwestern Adventist College in Keene, Texas, she is the youngest alumnus to establish a scholarship fund at that school.

Robert L. Payton is director of the Center on Philanthropy and professor of philanthropic studies at Indiana University. For ten years Payton served as president of Exxon Education Foundation. He has also served as president of C. W. Post College and Hofstra University, and as United States ambassador to the Republic of Cameroon. Among his many writings on philanthropy is his book, *Philanthropy: Voluntary Action for the Public Good*, published in 1988.

K. Scott Sheldon has been active in professional fund raising since 1977, working for educational institutions, first in New York City and then in Northern California. Active both as a member and a volunteer in the NSFRE, he was certified by that society in 1982. Specializing in corporate and foundation fund raising at the university level, he is now assistant director of development for the School of Law at Golden Gate University in San Francisco.

Eugene R. Tempel is vice-chancellor for external affairs at Indiana University, Indianapolis, and has been active in the fields of fund raising and administration management for higher education for many years. Before his current post, he spent six years with the Indiana University Foundation and has played a key role in establishing the university's Center on Philanthropy at its Indianapolis campus.

ACHIEVING EXCELLENCE IN FUND RAISING

A COMPREHENSIVE APPROACH
TO FUND RAISING

Fund raising has been an expression of the American spirit since the early colonial period. Major universities have been founded, hospital and medical centers have been built, and a wide range of cultural activities, human service programs, and social change agencies have come into being. Medical research has made awesome changes.

An expanding philanthropic experience that involves millions of people, foundations, corporations, associations, and even government in this country has made these advances possible. Ethical fund raising has been a proud servant to this achievement.

Fund raising has come of age in the past three decades. Workshops, seminars, training conferences, undergraduate studies, publication of books, and even a symposium entitled "Taking Fund Raising Seriously" (sponsored and conducted by the Indiana University Center on Philanthropy) are drawing attention to the practice that is encouraging, and challenging, the generosity of the American people. Yet the practice of fund raising continues to remain a mystery to a broad spectrum of our society despite the discourses and the expanding availability of academic courses and literature on the subject.

Part One endeavors to set aside some of the mystery of fund raising by reviewing the standards that give it a direction and by examining some aspects of its philosophical base.

A Philosophy
of Fund Raising

Fund raising is the servant of philanthropy and has been so since the seventeenth century, when Puritans brought the concept to the new continent. The early experience of fund raising was simple in form, obviously devoid of the multifaceted practices that characterize its nature in the contemporary United States. These practices now make fund raising more diversified and more complex than ever before.

The American spirit of giving is known and respected in other nations. American fund raising methods are equally known and admired abroad, as foreign citizens who have attended classes taught by The Fund Raising School will attest. Ironically, the practice of resource development that is so much a part of the culture, necessity, and tradition of not-for-profit organizations in the United States is not sufficiently understood, often misrepresented, and too often viewed with suspicion and apprehension by a broad section of our own population, particularly by regulatory bodies. Few will argue with the observation that fund raising has never been considered the most popular practice in this country.

Dean Schooler of Boulder, Colorado, a scholar and student of fund raising, takes the teleological view of a vitalist philosophy that phenomena not only are guided by mechanical forces but also move toward certain goals of self-realization. Indeed, fund raising is never an end in itself; it is purposive. It draws both its meaning and essence from the ends that are served: caring, helping, healing, nurturing, guiding, uplifting, teaching, creating, preventing, advancing a cause, preserving values, and so forth. Fund raising is values-based; values must guide the process. Fund raising should never be undertaken simply to raise funds; it must serve the larger cause.

Organizations and Their Reasons for Existing

Organizations of the independent sector come into existence for the purpose of responding to some facet of human or societal needs. The need or opportunity for service provides the organization with a reason for being, as well as a right to design and execute programs or strategies that respond to the need. This becomes the cause that is central to the concern of the organization. The cause provides justification for moral intervention, and this provides justification for fund raising.

The organization may *claim* a right to raise money by asking for the tax-deductible gift. It must *earn* the privilege to ask for gift support by its management's responsiveness to needs, by the worthiness of its programs, and by the stewardship of its governing board. An organization may assume the right to ask. The prospective donor is under no obligation to give. The prospect reserves the right to a "yes" or a "no" response to any request. Either response is valid and must be respected.

Each organization that uses the privilege of soliciting for gifts should be prepared to respond to many questions, perhaps unasked and yet implicit in the prospect's mind. These may be characterized as such: "Why do you exist?" "What is distinctive about you?" "Why do you feel that you merit this support?" "What is it that you want to accomplish and how do you intend to go about doing it?" and "How will you hold yourself accountable?"

The response to "Who are you and why do you exist?" is couched in the words of the organization's mission statement. This statement expresses more than justification for existence and more than just a definition of goals and objectives. It defines the value system that will guide program strategies. The mission is the magnet that will attract and hold the interests of trustees, volunteers, staff, and contributors.

The answer to "What is distinctive about us?" is apparent in the array of goals, objectives, and programs that have been devised to address the needs of the value system as well as serve as symbols of fidelity to it.

"How do we hold ourselves accountable?" is the primary question. It is a continuing call for allegiance to the mission. It acknowledges the sacredness of the trust that is inherent in the relationship with both the constituency and the larger community. The organization is the steward of the resources entrusted to its care.

It is axiomatic that change is a constant. Shifting forces within the environment quicken the pace of change, thus posing a new constant. Not-for-profit organizations must always be prepared to function in the center of whirling pressure.

Organizations cannot afford to be oblivious to the environment that surrounds, and indeed engulfs, them. Forces within the environment such as demographics, technology, economics, political and cultural values, and changing social patterns affect daily business performance, whether this performance pertains to governance, program administration, fiscal responsibility, or fund raising.

To Govern or Not to Govern

Governance is an exercise in authority and control. Trustees, directors, or regents—the interchangeable nomenclature that identifies the actors in governance—are the primary stewards of the spirit of philanthropy. As stewards, they are the legendary "keepers of the hall." They hold the not-for-profit organization in trust to ensure that it will continue to function according to the dictates of its mission.

The trustees must bear the responsibility to define and interpret the mission and ensure that the organization will remain faithful to its mission. Board members should accept the charge that trusteeship concerns itself with the proper deployment of resources and with the accompanying action, the securing of resources. Deploying resources is difficult if the required resources are not secured through effective fund raising practices. It stands to reason that trustees as advocates of and stewards to the mission must attend to the task of pressing the resources development program on to success.

Institutionalizing Fund Raising

Fund raising projects the values of the total organization into the community whenever it seeks gift support. All aspects of governance—administration, program, and resources development—are part of the whole. As such, these elements must be part of the representation when gifts are sought. Fund raising cannot function apart from the organization; apart from its mission, goals, objectives, and programs; apart from a willingness to be held accountable for all of its actions.

Fund raising is and must always be the lengthened shadow of the not-for-profit entity, reflecting the organization's dignity, its pride of accomplishment, and its commitment to service. Fund raising by itself and apart from the institution has no substance in the eyes and heart of the potential contributor.

Gift Making as Voluntary Exchange

Gift making is based on a voluntary exchange. Gifts secured through coercion, through any means other than persuasion, are not gifts freely given. They do not have the meaning of philanthropy. Rarely will gifts obtained under pressure or through any form of intimidation be repeated. These gifts lose their meaning.

In the process of giving, the contributor offers a value to the not-for-profit organization. This gift is made without any expectation of a material return, apart from the tax deductibility authorized by government. The reasons for making a gift are manifold.

In accepting the gift, it is incumbent upon the organization to return a value to the donor in a form other than material. Such a value may be social recognition, the satisfaction of supporting a worthy cause, a feeling of importance, a feeling of making a difference in resolving a problem, a sense of belonging, or a sense of "ownership" in a program dedicated to serving the public good.

Trustees, administrators, or fund raising practitioners so often misconstrue the true meaning of this exchange relationship, and they violate the acknowledgment process by offering a return of substantive value. This alters the exchange, reduces the meaning of philanthropy and diminishes the gift in its commitment to the mission. The transaction is one of a material exchange, a self-centered quid pro quo with none of the spirit of philanthropy in the exchange.

Substituting Pride for Apology

Giving is a privilege, not a nuisance or a burden. Stewardship nourishes the belief that people draw a creative energy, a sense of self-worth, a capacity to function productively from sources beyond themselves. This is a deep personal belief or a religious conviction. Thoughtful philanthropists see themselves as responsible stewards of life's gifts to them. What they have they hold in trust, in their belief, and they accept the responsibility to share their treasures effectively through their philanthropy. Giving is an expression of thankfulness for the blessings that they have received during their lifetime.

The person seeking the gift should never demean the asking by clothing it in apology. This robs it of its meaning. Apology seems to imply that we are ashamed because we are begging, that there is something indecent or embarrassing about the cause, or about the process of asking.

There is no reason to apologize for asking for a gift to a worthwhile cause. Solicitation gives the prospect the opportunity to respond with a "yes" or a "no." The solicitation should be so executed as to demonstrate to the prospective contributor that there can be a joy to giving, whether the gift measures up to the asking amount or not. Fund raising professionals must teach this joy by asking properly and in a manner that puts the potential contributor at ease.

The first task of the solicitor is to help the potential contributor understand the organization's case, especially its statement of mission. When a person commits to contribute to a cause and does so because of an acceptance of and a belief in the mission, then that person becomes a

"stakeholder" in the organization and that for which it stands. This emphasizes that philanthropy is moral action, and the contributor is an integral part
of that action.

Fund Raising as Servant to Philanthropy

Philanthropy is voluntary action for the public good through voluntary
action, voluntary association, and voluntary giving (Payton, 1988). Fund
raising has been servant to philanthropy across the millennia. Through the
procession of the centuries, the thesis has been established that people want
and have a need to give. People want to give to causes that serve the entire
gamut of human and societal needs. They will give when they can be assured
that these causes can demonstrate their worthiness and accountability in
using the gift funds that they receive.

Ethical fund raising is the prod, the enabler, the activator to gift
making. It must also be the conscience to the process. Fund raising is at its
best when it strives to match the needs of the not-for-profit organization with
the contributor's need and desire to give. The practice of gift seeking is
justified when it exalts the contributor, not the gift seeker. It is justified when
it is used as a responsible invitation, guiding contributors to make the kind of
gift that will meet their own special needs and add greater meaning to their
lives.

Understanding
the Fund Raising Cycle

A staff person sits dejectedly at a desk reading a memorandum that sets forth fund raising productivity expectations. The memorandum has been prepared by the chief executive officer of a not-for-profit agency as an introduction to an assignment for the new staff person: raising money for an agency that has never endeavored to do so in an organized, disciplined manner. The staff person's fund raising experience has been limited to minor special events, generally called "fund raisers," to the preparation of a simple application for foundation grants, and to mail appeals that produced little in the way of funds.

The questions coursing through the staff person's mind are many. Where does the new staff person begin? What is required in the planning for fund raising? When and how does the process begin to take form? What are the critical steps to intelligent planning? How can a determination be made about the amount of funds that can be raised for current program support, for special-purpose projects, for capital and endowment? How does one go about setting a goal? Should the beginning steps focus on planned giving? And what, by the way, is meant by "planned giving?" All of a sudden, fund raising becomes a confusing, complicated maze to the new staff person. Is it really complicated and does it have to be? Does it have to be so unnerving?

Fund Raising: A Complex Exercise

Fund raising in an environment that is ever-changing is a complex exercise. Harassed executives of not-for-profit organizations continue to search for the magic solution: an abundance of gifts to meet increasing budget require-ments for a minimum investment of time, talent, energy, and money.

Fund raising is not easy. No magic formula has ever been devised to transform a desperate wish into immediate gift funds to meet the not-for-profit organization's extensive financial needs. Yet, it does not have to be a frightening, unsettling experience to the fund raising practitioner. Much of fund raising's form is made of common sense.

The new staff person, the fund raising practitioner with limited or narrowly focused experience, must accept the reality that fund raising has a discipline that moves in orderly fashion from preparation to planning to program execution to control to evaluation and back to the renewal of the plan. This sequence can be depicted as a continuous loop, or, as it can be called, the "cycle" of fund raising. The loop or cycle can serve as an effective instrument to help executives or fund raising practitioners visualize the interrelationships of fund raising elements. It helps them to better under-stand the sequence to follow in moving from planning and preparation to the ultimate solicitation and then annual renewal of the gift. It emphasizes the basic truth that fund raising cannot and should not be a haphazard and impulsively devised undertaking in response to a crisis situation.

Fund Raising Checkpoint

The following checkpoints, or preparation phases, should be heeded by the practitioner in setting forth a plan for fund raising. The fund raising cycle itself will illustrate the sequence of these phases (see Figure 2.1).

The First Planning Checkpoint: Examine the Case. Fund raising planning must start with the definition of the gift seeker's case. Every not-for-profit organiza-tion has come into being to respond to a human or societal need. This need represents the cause that the organization serves. Its effectiveness in serving that cause becomes the organization's case, or a presentation of all of the arguments on why anyone should provide any level of gift support.

A clear and complete statement of case gives evidence of the organiza-tion's readiness to seek gift support from its constituencies. For this impor-tant reason, the organization should be prepared and willing to address specific questions about readiness that are essential to case determination:

1. What is the problem or societal need that is central to the organization's concern? Why does the organization exist?
2. What special service, or programs, does the organization offer to re-spond to the needs?
3. Who should support the program?
4. Why should any individual, corporation, or foundation contribute to a specific organization?
5. What benefits will accrue to the contributor who makes such gifts?

Figure 2.1. The Fund Raising Cycle.

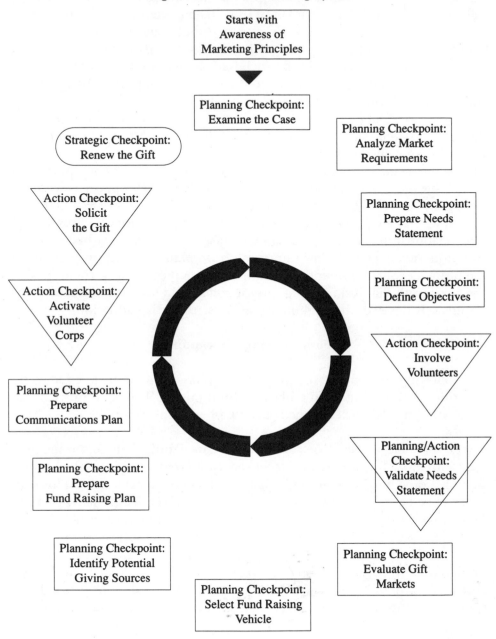

Planning Checkpoint: Analyze Market Requirements. A needs assessment is an important part of the planning process. What is the reality of the needs? Does the organization conduct periodic market assessments to determine the extent and continuing validity of the needs? Organizations that base their programs on valid needs justify their existence and therefore add currency to their case for continuing gift support. The case must be acknowledged by an informed constituency. If the market lacks knowledge of the organization and its case, if the constituency is ignorant of the needs or not supportive because it deems the needs to be insignificant, then the possibilities for effective fund raising become negligible.

When the organization has assessed the human and societal requirements and after it has examined community attitudes toward these requirements, it can offer positive responses to questions about case, goals, and needs. At that point, the organization can move to the next steps in preparation for fund raising.

Planning Checkpoint: Prepare Needs Statement. A needs statement, an essential instrument, provides testimony to the organization's right to exist. It is drawn from the findings of the needs assessment and prepared in draft form for review by individuals who are strategically involved with the organization, such as board members, major contributors, nonboard volunteer leaders — anyone who can affect the destiny of the organization and the outcome of its fund raising programs.

Once validated, a needs statement can be translated into program plans. The program plans can be defined to give substance to the financial needs. These needs, scrutinized and approved by key volunteers, will become the goals that highlight the fund raising plan.

Planning Checkpoint: Define Objectives. Before a program plan can be set to paper, it will be necessary to determine program goals and objectives. The objectives are specific explanations of how the goals will be accomplished.

For example, "elimination of hunger in the world" can be accepted as a philosophical goal. Tragically, it is more fantasy than reality. But providing hot meals to one, ten, or one hundred children every day for a week, a month, or a year can be a realistic objective. A donor would be hard put to evaluate the agency's ability to eliminate hunger in the world, but the donor can decide quite readily whether the agency can or cannot feed a prescribed number of children within a specified period of time.

Objectives move from the more general statement, or from global needs, "eliminate world hunger," to specific quantitative expressions, "feed one hundred children." This specificity establishes a natural link to program budgeting, program cost, and identification of program needs that provide the rationale for all fund raising.

Action Checkpoint: Involve Volunteers. Funds can be sought by mail, telephone, public media, and special events. The most effective solicitation method by far is the personal, face-to-face solicitation carried out by a potential contributor's peer. As a volunteer, the peer will agree to accept the solicitation assignment if he or she believes in the cause and all that it represents. Therefore, involving people to validate needs, approve plans, and help solicit potential givers is essential in the achievement of significant fund raising results.

Planning and Action Checkpoint: Validate Needs Statement. If the involvement of key volunteers is essential for fund raising to work, then it is logical to expect that these volunteers should be given opportunities to review, modify, accept, or reject needs-assessment reports. This is a needs-validation process. Through this involvement, volunteers tend to develop a sense of "ownership," a strong sense of belonging that strengthens the bond of the person to the organization.

Complacent or apathetic volunteers can be converted into supportive and dedicated givers and workers through such thoughtful involvement.

Planning Checkpoint: Evaluate Gift Markets. Once the needs statement has been prepared, and financial goals decided, it is important to determine which potential gift sources should be approached and the reasonable amounts that should be sought from each.

The conventional sources are individuals, foundations, corporations, associations, and government agencies. Historically, individuals have provided between 87 percent and 90 percent of the gift funds distributed annually in the United States.

The wise fund raising practitioner prepares a plan by analyzing the total community potential and by judging, after careful research, the gift ability of each major source identified above.

Broad-spectrum fund raising that seeks gifts from diverse sources promotes good health within the organization by making it more resilient, more aware of market requirements, more sensitive to changes within the environment, and more responsive to the service and support requirements of its constituencies.

Planning Checkpoint: Select Fund Raising Vehicles. The journey around the cycle continues. Selecting the appropriate fund raising method during the planning stages is as important as selecting the right gift sources. Fund raising methods include the annual fund, direct mail, phone-a-thons, telethons, special events or benefits known as fund raisers, special gifts, gift clubs, capital campaigns, grantsmanship, and planned giving. Each has its own function; each has its own impact.

The management process of "analyze, plan, execute and control" is an annual exercise that leads to the preparation of a new fund raising plan. Analysis must involve a review of the past. Study the current year's and the preceding two years' performance records by gift sources. Study the fund raising techniques that were used. Furthermore, study the effectiveness of each method as it was applied to different gift sources to identify strengths, weaknesses, and potential for greater gift production.

Planning Checkpoint: Identify Potential Gift Sources. Potential gift candidates can be found within every gift market. Prospect selection and evaluation is the process that is used to identify these resources. Each market segment and each gift source within that market segment must be identified and then evaluated in terms of gift ability, presumed interest in the work of the organization, and accessibility through either a staff member or volunteer leadership.

This "search-and-appraisal" procedure builds prospect files, which are an indispensable resource. Developing these files by continuing research is necessary for any organization that strives for greater fund raising effectiveness. This exercise pertains whether the prospect is a corporation, a foundation, or an individual or family.

A search-and-appraisal committee, or "prospect-development" committee as it is more commonly called, comprises knowledgeable individuals who are willing to assist with prospect research. Such a committee is extremely helpful in identifying valid prospect lists.

Planning Checkpoint: Prepare Fund Raising Plan. It must be stated and restated that fund raising is a management process and must follow the precepts of sound management: Gather the facts, study the facts, prepare the plan, execute the plan, evaluate, and modify wherever necessary.

All functions that lead to this position on the cycle have involved various degrees of fact gathering and analysis. Only after the hard questions of fund raising have been answered can the intention be transformed into reality of the plan. The hard questions, demanding taskmasters in themselves, require a review of the discipline of fund raising suggested in the first nine steps of the cycle.

Planning Checkpoint: Prepare Communication Plan. The case for financial support has no purpose or value until it is communicated in a compelling, inviting form to individuals who are in a position to commit their gifts or time and talent.

Effective communication is more than data dissemination, particularly in this era of the fertile word processor. It is more than the exaggerated production of paper, print, sound, and facts that confuses rather than convinces. Creative communication is a two-way instrument. It transmits what the market is both willing to receive and requires to help it understand the organization's mission goals and objectives. Such communication stands ready to receive feedback or questions to verify that the market is receiving and understanding the transmitted message.

Action Checkpoint: Activate Volunteer Corps. The practice of fund raising over the decades in this country has confirmed the truth that people give to people who believe so deeply in a cause that it motivates them to ask others to give. The most effective solicitor in any fund raising endeavor is the person who is committed to the cause, who is willing to contribute to its support, and who is willing to induce support of that commitment by contributing and by soliciting others. It is generally accepted that one effective volunteer is required for every five fund raising solicitations. If an organization is planning to solicit two hundred prospects in a fund raising plan, then it must be prepared to enlist forty volunteer solicitors to see the task through.

Expansion and activation of the volunteer corps, like prospect research, must be a continuing task in fund raising. Each willing volunteer who is enlisted represents a growing force of advocates for the organization and its mission and goals. Recruitment of dedicated, supportive volunteers must start early and end late.

Action Checkpoint: Solicit the Gift. All fund raising preparation, principles, techniques, and theories must focus on a single imperative: For fund raising to be effective, someone must ask someone for money. No other process, regardless of how cleverly devised, can match the effectiveness of a person-to-person, face-to-face, peer-to-peer solicitation of a gift. The wisest solicitation technique requires the solicitor to call on the prospect in person to explain the worth of the cause and its work in addressing human needs, to explain why the solicitor has given, and to ask the prospect to make a gift as an investment in the advancement of the organization and its mission. Give dignity to the asking and encourage the prospect to share in the joy of making possible the continuation of the work dedicated to the betterment of the human or social condition.

Receiving the gift is often considered the end to all action, which is quite contrary to the spirit of true fund raising. The receipt of the gift should mark the beginning of a continuing and important relationship with the contributor. A gift is received with the tacit promise that it will be used wisely. Proper stewardship requires periodic reports to the donor that the money indeed is so used. Sound business practice endorses the procedure of accountability and disclosure.

The Strategic Checkpoint: Renew the Gift. The annual renewal of the gift, and thus the annual renewal of the donor's association with the cause, does not complete the transaction. Instead, it returns the process back to the cycle's entry point of "Examine the Case." Just as the gift must be renewed, the case must be renewed by subjecting it to continuing scrutiny by the solicited constituency. Is the organization still responsive to changing needs? A gift cannot be taken for granted, and the case cannot remain static. Annual renewal is imperative if the case for support is to have meaning and if the gift level is to respond to the requirements imposed by the human and societal needs inherent in the organization's statement of mission as well as the internal needs imposed by the organization's budget.

Creating Advocacy in Fund Raising

Fund raising is not a simple process. It is a complex exercise that seeks to involve people in service to a cause that is responsive to human needs and that is worthy of support as a result of this service. By inviting a philanthropic response through gift making and voluntary service and association, the not-for-profit organization creates an advocacy force that becomes the core of its strength, thus ensuring its progress into the future.

The new staff person, the fund raising practitioner who seeks to expand fund raising horizons, the volunteer who aspires to greater meaning in service to philanthropy would do well to heed the discipline that is imposed on the planning and action course by each checkpoint in the fund raising cycle. This studied review of applicable principles provides an appropriate preamble to the main act that is fund raising.

PART TWO

PREPARING AN ORGANIZATION FOR FUND RAISING

Not-for-profit organizations exist in the environment of change and thus must be aware of the challenges and opportunities presented by the factors that influence change. Renewal is the ongoing process that keeps organizations alert to and ready for change.

Change is a constant. Yet, as John W. Gardner warns, as "[m]esmerized as we are by the idea of change, we must guard against the notion that continuity is a negligible—if not reprehensible—factor in human history. It is a vitally important ingredient in the life of individuals, organizations and societies. Particularly important to a society's continuity are its long-term purposes and values. . . . They do much to determine the direction of change. They insure that a society will not be buffeted in all directions by every wind that blows" (1981, pp. 6–7).

The challenges to not-for-profit leaders are complex. The not-for-profit corporation must be aware of those strengths that will help it cope with this changing environment. More important, it must be conscious of its vulnerabilities and their impact on its ability to adjust to or take advantage of the changes that are inevitable. It must remain true that an organization's enduring strength will be its long-term purpose and values.

Eugene R. Tempel   Chapter 3

Assessing
Organizational Strengths
and Vulnerabilities

Fund raising is an active management process that is built on organizational strengths. And fund raising fails because of organizational vulnerabilities. This chapter examines the various organizational factors that enable fund raising to succeed as well as sometimes cause it to fail.

Efforts to contribute to the public good; to initiate change; to preserve our heritage, culture, or environment; or to reduce human suffering may begin with individuals. However, if an effort is to be sustained, others must be drawn into supporting it. To one degree or another, voluntary, not-for-profit organizations are the means through which American philanthropy is effected. These organizations make up what many call the "independent sector," because it operates independently of or apart from the governmental and business sectors.

Volunteer time and voluntary giving are brought together through a wide variety of associations and organizations. The enlistment of volunteers on behalf of the organizations and the fund raising efforts that are necessary to stimulate philanthropic giving succeed and fail on the basis of these organizations' strengths and vulnerabilities. Therefore, it is essential that the fund raising programs of not-for-profit organizations not operate as separate, independent efforts. They should be integrated with the overall administration.

For an organization to be successful in fund raising, it must be connected to its external environment. It must understand the changing needs of that environment and its facility to respond to the organization's need for human and financial resources to remain functional. The organization must have management structures in place that interpret its mission in relation to changing external needs. An organizational tendency toward an "open system" or a "closed system" relative to the external environment has an impact on fund raising ability.

Organizations, both for-profit and not-for-profit, often operate on internal motivations and perceptions without paying much attention to the world in which they exist and how that world views them. Organizations that operate in this manner — as if they were independent of the external environment — are defined as "closed systems." Autonomy from the external environment is found especially in organizations with strong institutional value systems that they wish to perpetuate even in the face of unpopular public reactions. In the not-for-profit sector, this sense of autonomy may be especially strong in religious organizations in which the perpetuation of prescribed values and beliefs may be the major or sole reason for the organization to exist.

For some organizations, operating as closed systems is actually a strength. By perpetuating strong ideological or religious beliefs and values in the face of opposition, they draw in and sustain a membership that provides the necessary resources. This is true especially of most religious organizations and of many controversial organizations. For these groups, modification to a more open stance could leave them vulnerable to declining support.

Many organizations, however, seem to operate as closed systems through natural tendencies or by accident rather than through efforts to perpetuate strongly held beliefs or values. For these organizations, many of which search for broad-based support, operating as closed systems is a liability. They often become closed systems because of a natural tendency of their members to opt for stability and security instead of change. This tendency leads organizations to ignore an environment that might well call for change.

In addition, some groups take an arrogant attitude toward the external environment in the conviction that the organization can persuade the environment on its own terms. Examples of this occur in higher education, where the label "ivory tower" describes colleges and universities that are out of touch with the world beyond the institution.

When organizations desire or require a broad base of support or seek wider influence, they must be managed as "open systems." Open-system theory assumes that organizations are not independent of their external environments, that they have impact on and are affected by their environments. According to open-system theory, organizations depend upon a hospitable and supportive environment for supplies of human, fiscal, and material resources, as well as for consumption of goods and services.

To function successfully as open systems, organizations must continually monitor the environment and either adapt to changes or attempt to change inhospitable elements in the environment. Organizations that fail to adapt or fail to influence the environment eventually produce unwanted goods or unneeded services and lose their ability to attract vital resources.

Fund raising success depends on an organization's ability to adapt to surrounding conditions. A not-for-profit organization exists to provide services for which there is a public or societal need, often on a small or local level. If that need is otherwise met, then the organization's rationale for existence disappears. If it continues to provide staff and programs to fill the outdated need, then it will be viewed as wasteful, inefficient, and unresponsive. Its sources of support will diminish, and it will be forced to close. For example, the Young Men's Christian Association (YMCA) was established in the nineteenth century in response to the need for a healthful Christian environment for young men who moved from rural areas to the cities for jobs. Had the YMCA not adapted to a new environment by abandoning its "hotel" business when that migration ended and shifted to filling other needs in the urban environment, it might not exist today. Similarly, the March of Dimes was founded in 1938, as the National Foundation for Infantile Paralysis, largely through the efforts of President Franklin D. Roosevelt. When a vaccine for polio was developed and the disease eliminated, the organization lost its rationale for existence. In this case, the organization found another health problem, children's birth defects, that required solution and which allowed it to adapt to other social needs.

Responding to changes in the environment is not as simple as meeting current needs. Organizations that respond to changing needs by altering dramatically their own institutional value systems also risk their future. If traditional contributors fail to support an old institution in its newest efforts, then their contributions may be lost before a new support base is established. For example, consider a small Roman Catholic arts college built on the tradition of providing a well-rounded education based on Catholic values in a highly personal environment. The college might respond to declining enrollments by orienting itself toward meeting needs for continuing education in local workplaces. The college risks losing completely its traditional student base, however, as well as its existing alumni support. The college may gain an expanded new student body and obtain private dollars from the community, but it will be a different institution with different potentials for fund raising.

Many not-for-profit organizations cannot and should not become fully responsive to the market in order to enhance their fund raising. They must remain in harmony with the values and mission upon which they were founded. Organizations with strong internal value systems that give rise to their missions should become highly responsive by at least actively involving their clients and potential contributors in the organization's affairs. Fund raising success depends upon the sensitive inclusion of potential supporters in the life and spirit of the organization.

Open- and closed-system perspectives both have their limitations in helping to identify organizational strengths and vulnerabilities for fund raising. As stated early in this chapter, the independent sector exists to operate apart from business and government. It delivers needed services either not provided by or provided differently from the first two sectors, and it strives to solve problems that the other two sectors will not solve. Therefore, the value systems and beliefs that bring people together in voluntary action distinguish the independent sector from the other sectors' motivations— expected profits in the case of the business sector and public opinion and votes in the case of the public sector.

Although not-for-profit organizations do not exist to generate profits, their long-term survival depends to some extent on good business practices. Not-for-profits that develop surplus income protect themselves from fluctuations in client fees and fund raising levels. Surplus revenue also assures contributors that the organization has a future. Organizations that strive to provide the most effective services with the fewest resources are the most likely to generate surpluses. Organizations that are viewed as effective and efficient also have the best opportunity to attract philanthropic dollars. How well a not-for-profit organization is managed also has an impact on its ability to raise money.

Business techniques might be useful in managing not-for-profit fund raising. However, the values and beliefs that give rise to these organizations often lead them necessarily to defy good business marketing practices. New service initiatives that abandon mission to enhance revenue production can harm philanthropic efforts. And when unpopular causes must be pursued if the organization is to remain faithful to the requirements of its mission, then it must defy marketing information in favor of its mission.

Sometimes, fidelity to mission leads to conflict with sources of support. A conservative funding source might hesitate to support an organization that is serving a controversial cause because its employees, its customers, its stockholders might object. A for-profit industry that manufactures a product to reduce tooth decay might be eliminated by the successful efforts of a not-for-profit organization that seeks to eliminate tooth decay. Organizations that understand and manage this complexity put themselves in a position of strength when raising funds.

Fund raising is an effective test of organizational viability. As such, fund raising can become the catalyst for organization renewal and commitment. To be successful in fund raising, the organization must be viewed by potential supporters as responsive in its delivery of quality services. These services must be provided in an effective and efficient manner to constituents. Potential supporters must understand and accept the value systems that affect these services. An organization that lacks internal meaning has no basis for stimulating philanthropy.

The organizational strengths and vulnerabilities that must be addressed in preparation for fund raising can be discussed as follows: institutional readiness, human resources, markets, vehicles, and management.

Institutional Readiness

The premise of this chapter is that effective fund raising is built upon organizational strengths and that organizational weaknesses and vulnerabilities can undermine fund raising efforts. With this in mind, an organization preparing itself for fund raising must analyze its strengths and weaknesses and inventory those resources that are essential for successful fund raising.

Fund raising based on the strengths of the organization assumes a dignity that flows from those strengths, obviating any need on the part of staff or volunteers to apologize for the solicitation process. Fund raising based on values and mission is a meaningful part of philanthropy. To take its funding requirements to the public, the organization must have prepared itself internally to seek philanthropic funding.

An essential readiness element is the institutional plan. The plan attests to the stability and to the futurity of the organization based, as it should be, on an assessment of current and future social and human needs within the scope of the organization's mission. One of the greatest strengths that the plan can bring to the fund raising process is the affirmation that the organization is confident of its future and empowered by its vision of its own future.

An effective plan must go beyond a description of programs. Programs must be drafted in economic terms if they are to provide a suitable foundation for fund raising. The plan must project annual income and expense requirements for each program, both those in existence and those planned for the future. Equally, the plan should identify special purpose, capital, and endowment needs that are anticipated during the designated period. The organization is strongest when the prospective donor can accept the validity of the income and expense projections relative to past accomplishments and future program delivery. If financial accountability through the planning process can demonstrate efficient use of resources for effective programs, then good stewardship has begun.

The financial plan should go beyond ordinary income and expense projections. It should state the amounts that must be raised for current program support through the annual fund; the amounts required for special projects, some immediate and urgent, others deferrable; the amounts required for capital projects; and endowment and cash-reserve requirements of the organization. This comprehensive financial analysis with its realistic assessment of anticipated revenue and gift production forces careful evaluation of program proposals and responsible decisions when priorities are set.

Before the planning process can be initiated, the process itself should undergo scrutiny to determine the extent to which it has involved the organization's primary constituency. The sensitive and responsive plan involves the professional staff and volunteers from the board of trustees as the plan's architects. Both groups must commit themselves to implement the plan and to evaluate it on a continuing basis. Anything short of this will leave the organization vulnerable during the fund raising process. The organization can benefit by creating among the constituents "ownership" in the plan. This can be done by inviting leaders within the constituency to become part of the planning activity. The most affirmation there is of the organization's mission through planning, the better the chances to win the constituency's endorsement when the plan is finished. The plan will give substance to the various programs that have been devised to respond to the designated human and societal needs. From these program descriptions can be drawn the four, five, or more of the most salient and exciting expressions that will animate the case.

Human Resources

The most vulnerable element in the institutional readiness inventory is the governing board. A thoughtfully structured, involved, and dedicated board of trustees is a symbol of responsible governance and an asset to the fund raising process. Conversely, a passive, uninvolved, and disinterested board can be a major liability.

It is essential that board members be involved actively in the planning, from the beginning delineation of the planning format, through the periodic review, and as part of the final acceptance of the plan with its definitions of program and financial priorities. By accepting the plan, trustees accept the responsibility to give and to ask others to give in proper measure against the financial needs. This is trusteeship at its best. Finally, they must have integrity and credibility with the community, serving as they do at the organization's first point of accountability and as stewards of the public trust.

The board has a direct responsibility to press for the success of the organization's fund raising programs. To accomplish this, the board includes a fund raising or a development committee in its roll of standing committees. This committee should include in its membership those trustees who have the strongest interest in mission and who represent a certain degree of socioeconomic clout within the community. This group should meet regularly and actively develop, implement, and evaluate fund raising plans. Committee membership can be extended to those non-board members who would be willing to give, ask, and work as advocates of the organization.

The second point of strength is the professional staff: the chief executive officer, individuals responsible for managing programs and finances, and the fund raising staff. The not-for-profit entity's viability depends upon long-term delivery of quality services that the public perceives as needed. This focuses attention on the chief executive and the program staff. Filled with capable people, these positions provide an organizational strength.

For fund raising to be truly effective, it must require full-time attention by a professional who is competent to plan, organize, and manage the process. Fund raising management is a position that varies by organization as to the amount of time allotted to the task, and ranges from minimal part-time to full-time with a multiple-member professional staff. Fund raising's position is enhanced if it has full-time professional staffmembers at the helm who are dedicated to involving board members, other volunteers, and administrative, program, and support staffs so that they assist in the fund raising process.

The governing board must be prepared to become involved in fund raising. Board members must accept ownership of the organization and support it financially as a necessary first step in establishing institutional readiness. The final assessment of readiness is to determine the ability of board members, fund raising professionals, and key staffmembers to come together as a development team. There must be an understanding of and a commitment to the concept that successful fund raising depends upon the active participation of board members and key staffmembers on the team, both in the development and organization of fund raising programs and in asking for gifts.

Acceptance of this concept by all is essential to the fund raising process. Under the definition of this process, the professional staff will provide the management services for the fund raising program. The volunteers will provide the linkage and the leverage to the gift-making potential of the community.

Markets

Philanthropic funds originate in general areas of the economy referred to as "gift sources" or "markets." The five gift sources for fund raising activities are individuals, corporations, foundations, associations, and government. To some extent, each organization has potential supporters among these markets. Opportunities for fund raising come from recognizing the potential for support among specific subsectors of each market. Proper prospect-development practices will make it possible to effectively identify, cultivate, and solicit prospective donors within each subsector.

The organization must develop a program to understand what the gift source needs, what its preferences and perceptions are, and what it requires in the manner of a value exchange. What are the philanthropic interests and needs of the prospective contributor? This knowledge serves as the basis for a meaningful exchange of values between the asking organization and the potential gift source.

The organization must have sufficient information about the prospect's interests, ability, and willingness to give. By accepting this basic principle of fund raising, the practitioner can understand that the organization will approach fund raising markets from its strongest position when it involves its board members, non-board volunteers, and staffmembers in identifying, understanding, engaging, and soliciting potential contributors from any of the five gift sources.

Fund Raising Activities

The organization must have an appropriate array of fund raising activities or processes to carry out its resources development program. An organization that does not build flexibility into its plan with a variety of fund raising activities will be limiting its ability to raise funds. Different activities are used for different purposes and for different prospects to accomplish a variety of different results. If the solicitation plan is devoid of this variety of activities, or asking methods, then the plan is vulnerable and may be destined to fail.

Management

An organization that is not well managed, or is perceived to be poorly managed, will have difficulty raising funds. Sound management is an organizational strength. At one time, not-for-profit management was assumed to be less capable and less effective than for-profit management because of the different salaries paid in the two sectors. However, salaries in the independent sector have been increasing, thereby increasing the accountability of not-for-profit managers (Stehle, 1990; Greene, 1990). In addition, Drucker has noted that some of the best managers in the United States are in the not-for-profit world (Drucker, 1990).

The successful organization will have a management team of administrators, program managers, and fund raising managers who will operate the organization to some extent as an open system. This management team will involve its various constituents—clients, donors, trustees, volunteers, vendors, the community, and its own staff—in continued analysis and planning before executing programs and exercising management control over its programs. The successful organization will involve the same constituents in evaluating its programs as the management process of analysis, planning, execution, control, and evaluation begins another cycle.

In the strongest organizations, the fund raising manager has been successful in persuading the board of trustees and the chief executive to dedicate significant portions of their time and energies to the fund raising efforts.

Fund raising is a management process. It is based on the strength of the programs to fulfill the organization's mission. Therefore, the organization must be well managed. Managers of these entities increasingly are being called to account for themselves, illustrating to the public that they are good stewards of contributed funds. The successful organization must integrate the management of its fund raising program with the overall management of the organization.

Fund raising involves mobilizing commitments to organizational values and missions. It requires a comprehensive view of the client constituencies, the volunteers, the advocates, and those who are prospective contributors. It demands the mastery of professional technical skills that are required for fund raising and the ethical values that foster and protect philanthropy. It is the management of planning and other efforts that precedes many of society's voluntary actions for the public good.

Developing a Constituency: Where Fund Raising Begins

Whenever a fund raising staff sets out to plan a fund raising program, it begins by searching out from its constituency those individuals who will be willing to contribute, those who will be willing to serve on fund raising committees, and those who will be willing to act as solicitors. That is, the staff endeavors to identify "prospects," or prospective contributors, prospective volunteers, and prospective solicitors.

With this planning exercise, the fund raising staff measures its potential for productivity against whatever goal it is endeavoring to achieve. It does so by analyzing the capacity and the willingness of its constituency to contribute, to volunteer to serve on fund raising committees, and to participate in actual solicitation. These are the important qualities that will lead to fund raising success; these qualities are the substance of a dedicated, involved constituency.

Two terms in the vocabulary of fund raising practitioners confuse this process: *prospects* and *suspects*. Just what is a "suspect"? What is a "prospect"? And what separates one or the other from a contributor? Why are they so important to the fund raising process? Why should the fund raising practitioner be concerned about differentiating between the two? Too often, discussions about potential givers lock on the name of a well-known, influential person who is believed to have considerable assets. This is particularly true when the fund raising committee is seeking to solicit a very large gift. Staff and trustees agree that this person should be seen *immediately*. But neither anyone on the fund raising committee nor anyone on the management team knows or has access to this person. Considering these factors, this person cannot be accepted as a logical candidate for a gift at the level contemplated by staff and volunteers. The person is a suspect, not a prospect. Why? There is no access because there is no *link* to the person. Any time devoted to an effort to solicit suspects for a large gift can be time wasted. It may be wiser to invite this person to make a small gift as a beginning strategy to involve this person as a constituent.

A research concept known as the *L-A-I principle* of prospect identification will help fund raising planners separate suspects from prospects, thus enabling staffmembers to direct their solicitation or enlistment energies toward those individuals who are most likely to give or to volunteer their services.

What is the L-A-I principle and what is its function in both fund raising research and constituency development? The principle is timeworn. It is a heritage of the past, a piece of wisdom passed on from one clan of veteran fund raising practitioners to another, and it is as described below.

> *L—Linkage:* A linkage relates to a contact, a bridge, or an access through a peer to the potential donor. If there is access to the gift source, then this link to the prospect makes it possible to arrange an appointment to discuss the potential of a gift. If accessibility is not a reality, then it would be difficult or downright impossible to arrange for an appointment. Solicitation becomes a matter of a letter or telephone approach, and neither is effective in the production of large gifts.
>
> *A—Ability:* Through research, it can be determined that the potential gift source has sufficient discretionary holdings to justify a gift solicitation at the appropriate "asking" level. Two perceptions pertain: the asker's perception that the prospect has a gift capability at the level suggested, and the prospect's own perception that such a gift capability is a reality. Some wealthy but financially insecure individuals who are not brought up in the tradition of philanthropy are not sure that they have sufficient resources to give at the level requested. They may not be psychologically prepared to give.
>
> *I—Interest:* If the potential contributor has no interest in the organization or little knowledge about its work, then the person will be prone to make a small gift or none at all. Interest in the organization and an understanding of its mission and accomplishments are imperative in the identification of valid prospects.

The rules of fund raising, which have been authenticated across the decades, maintain that all three L-A-I principles must apply when separating prospects from suspects during the evaluation of gift potential within the constituency. The elimination of just one of the three principles will invalidate the process and reduce the gift candidate from prospect to suspect.

Constituents Are People, People Are Prospects

Fund raising is an interesting but quite complex art form. Its central force is people. The not-for-profit organization must involve itself with people on a constant and continuing basis if it is to justify its existence or, perhaps more important, ensure its future.

The central force in the structure of the not-for-profit organization is its constituency: a heterogeneity of people who give life, purpose, meaning, energy, and a reason for being to the organization. These include the people who need the services provided, those who support the issues espoused, those who sell the organization goods and services, those who are part of its staff or governing board, those who provide regulatory overview, and those who may constitute its philanthropic base as volunteers and as contributors.

The constituency also can be identified as including those who are currently involved with the organization, those who have been involved in the past, and those with the potential for some level of involvement in the future. These people hold a value for the fund raising process in that they can be identified as current and active contributors, past contributors who no longer give, or suspects and prospects who can be induced to give in the future.

Whether the organization is visiting a foundation, a corporation, an association, or a government office for the purpose of seeking a gift or a grant, it is negotiating with a person or a group of people to arrive at a decision that is responsive to the diverse needs of the nonprofit organization. It is asking for money, goods, services, or gifts of precious volunteer time. It is important, therefore, for key people within the organization, particularly fund raising staffmembers, to know the structure of the constituency and the interests, needs, wants, and requirements of the people who make up that constituency. It is these people who can affect the destiny of the organization in a positive or negative manner.

Since its genesis in the early colonial years of the seventeenth century, fund raising in this nation has preoccupied itself with the selective activation of people as contributors and working volunteers, as well as the advocacy core. Historically, the people who have been most willing to become involved in these activities have been those closest to the organization and most knowledgeable about its work. The rest can be cataloged into three groups: some active, many inactive; some supportive, others disinterested; and others distant and quite detached. All in all, this is the nature of a constituency.

The Concept of Ever-Widening Circles

An image of a constituency relationship with the organization can be formed by visualizing concentric or an ever-widening spread of circles (see Figure 4.1). The image can become sharper by envisioning these circles as a set of spreading waves set in motion by the impact of a rock thrown onto the still surface of a pond of water. A wave, a turbulence, a sequence of ever-

Figure 4.1.

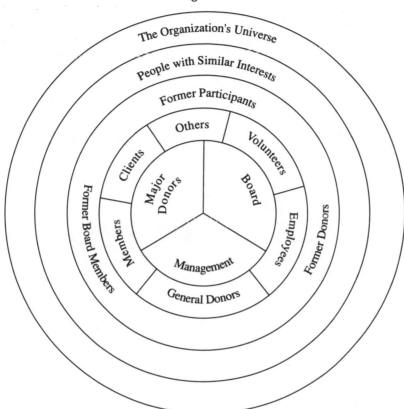

broadening circles are created on the pond's surface. This is the organization's power center and where the action begins. The waves gradually diminish in force as they move away from the impact point; so, too, does the power of the constituency diminish as it moves away from the center of the organization.

The central circle, where the rock makes violent contact with the still water, depicts the core circle or the energy center of the constituency (see Figure 4.2). The bonding to the organization is strongest and more lasting at this point. Its force is dissipated as it moves away from the energy center until it disappears altogether.

At least three primary components of the constituency are in the core circle: the board of trustees, the senior management team, and the major contributors. These constituency components are at the energy center of the organization because they exercise a strong influence on the affairs of the entity. They can significantly affect its progress as it reaches for the future in the following ways:

- The trustees as custodians of the trust in the public interest approve the mission and the vision and also set policy.

Figure 4.2.

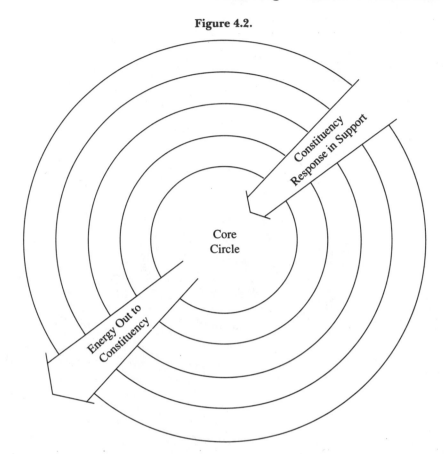

- The senior management team is the determining force for policy that will be reviewed and approved by the board. This team activates the programs that respond to specific needs.
- Major contributors are among the primary advocates. Their gifts are testimony to their commitment to the cause and its program of services.

   Larger organizations with more complex structures may be able to add more than three components to the core circle. Universities, for example, could well place their alumni boards and academic senates in the center circle. Hospitals might consider adding their joint conference committees of physicians and trustees. Organizations with separate foundations would do well to add the boards and executive staffs of each foundation to its core grouping, because foundation boards and executive staffs represent strategic forces in the constituency definition.

   The second circle, in an empathic proximity to the energy core, would include administrative and service volunteers, employees and other non-management employees, clients who are being served, and vendors. General contributors—those who make smaller gifts—are included in the second circle. They are important because they constitute the contributor base. Gifts in this base can and should be renewed and then upgraded because they represent the best potential for major gift development.

These constituency components are a necessary part of the organization. They are placed in the second circle only because they are not a part of the major policy-making procedure.

The core circle and the second circle of the constituency chart represent strategically important segments of the organization's market: the trustees and senior management staff, the clients who are being served, the people who are providing the services, non-board volunteers, employees, and funding sources (individuals, corporations, foundations, associations, and governments) who provide the funds to fuel the programs.

The third and fourth circles reflect significant drops in energy as each becomes more distant from the organization's vital core. These are the passive, uninvolved components. They hold a potential only to the degree that they can be activated through a creative outreach effort by the fund raising staff with proper support from the public relations staff, or marketing staff, or both.

Past participants, or individuals with previous involvement with the organization, reside in the third circle. These are former trustees, former staffmembers, former donors, and former members of a guild, an auxiliary, or an advisory council. Universities have a kindly, friendly title for past donors who are recorded in this quiet third zone. Alumni officers and resources development officers refer to this group as "LYBUNT" (*Last Year But Unfortunately Not This Year*) or as "PYBUNT" (*Previous Year But Unfortunately Not This Year*). Activating these constituents is an important assignment for the fund raising program.

The fourth circle presents an amorphous multitude. This is an unknown potential, a large number of people who can be invited to become constituents through the use of mail. When specialists reach out to this diffuse mass through bulk-rate mailings, they endeavor to particularize their lists by identifying people whose interests may parallel those of the organization. List brokers who work with national lists compile these names by demographic and psychographic indicators: that is, by geographic or census distribution or by behavior patterns. Behavior patterns, or psychographic indicators, are useful in identifying "people with similar interests." These interests may signal a possible kinship with the values reflected in the organization's mission. These people may qualify as suspects. The task now is to convert them into prospects and then contributors by exciting their interests through an intelligently conceived and properly directed mail solicitation.

Beyond the fourth circle, there may be a constituency of unknown potential. This fifth and most distant circle is identified as the "universe" of the organization. Its presence should remind anyone who endeavors to evaluate a constituency's giving potential that such potential may be considerably more than any organization dare think. It never achieves final definition.

When judiciously employed, patience, persistence, and creative energy can help to capture this potential. There is quiet, undisturbed potential within the constituency universe of every organization. The size of the gifts may be small during the prospecting stages, but they will increase in value as interest deepens and strengthens through proper cultivation.

Characteristics of a Constituency

The Transiency Factor. A constituency is an ever-changing thing. It is as fluid and as transient as the environment in which it functions. Organizations can expect as much as a 20 to 35 percent annual change in the base of its constituency, judging from the comments of development office managers who are charged with the continuing management of data. As the pattern of transiency changes through the 1990s, the character and personality of each organization's constituency will change, thus adding to the complexities of fund raising.

The transitory quality of the constituency may be reflected in a change in residency from an intemperate to a more temperate zone, a conversion in political philosophy, a change in religious affiliations, a financial setback, or a sudden disinterest resulting from lack of attention. Continuing cultivation of a constituency is an imperative for the not-for-profit agency.

Constituents Can Be Nongivers

It is a fallacy to believe that all members of a constituency will contribute to the organization. Not all can qualify as contributors; not all have an interest in giving.

For example, an agency set up for the purpose of providing shelter for the homeless will have the homeless as its clients. Clients are part of the constituency. Yet this component of the constituency cannot be expected to give simply because the homeless do not have the resources to do so. If they did, they would not be homeless.

Building a Constituency

Some aspect of the constituency comes into being automatically. For instance, the client base becomes an immediate adjunct of the constituency because it acts in response to the services offered. Trustees, management staff, and beginning program staff become an early part of an organization because they must make available the services that are needed by their clients. Contributors, volunteers, and advocates take longer to develop. They must be sought out and invited to become the philanthropic base that will augment and celebrate the organization's work.

The fund raising person must be sensitive to the fact that there is constant interaction within and between the constituency circles and among the elements that make up each circle. Individuals gravitate toward the core circle as their interest is touched and then deepened; they drift away if their interest slackens, if they are ignored, or if their interests change or are neglected. A studied program of constituency involvement and thoughtful cultivation is necessary to maintain the vitality of the constituency base.

A responsible fund raising staff should assert itself continuously to develop an *awareness* within the constituency of the organization's mission, goals, and objectives; to foster an *understanding* of the service to that mission; and to invite constituency *commitment* to the organization through the process of making a gift. This gift-making process forges a strong bond of the constituency to the not-for-profit organization and its mission.

An effective, outreaching communication program is the first necessity. In developing any human relationship it is necessary to get the attention of the subject, the person whom the organization wants to involve. The person must be made aware that the organization exists, and that it exists for a purpose that may hold an interest to him or her. Awareness must be converted into understanding, first of the guiding mission that delineates the human or societal needs that must be addressed, and second of the programs that will respond to these needs. From awareness to understanding to acceptance is the direct path to people involvement and the process that is so necessary for constituency development.

People will identify with an organization if they understand and can accept its reason for being, if they accept that the programs are valid and responsive, and if they strongly believe that the people associated with the organization are competent and trustworthy in their service to the mission.

Various techniques are applicable to this process of identifying and involving a constituency, particularly that element that can be induced to contribute funds and to volunteer time.

One of the first and most effective instruments for constituency development is fund raising. The fund raising process is based on intelligent, purposeful communications with the amorphous and unidentified market, including suspects, prospects, and donors. A sensitively managed communication will invite interest in the organization, its mission, its goals, and its programs. The outreach or public relations effort should include quarterly newsletters that contain information of interest to the reader. These publications too often are self-serving informational instruments that extol the accomplishments of staffmembers while neglecting the concerns, questions, and curiosity of the constituency. Periodic surveys of readers' interests and reactions to the value of the newsletter might well evoke the kind of response that will heal the myopia of an overly abundant self-interest.

Special events offer an opportunity to attract the attention of potential constituents. A special event may be defined as an activity that is designed to accomplish a variety of objectives, one of which is to invite possible constituents to become involved and to learn more about the organization. Events may include open houses, come-and-see tours, 10-K runs, leadership dinners, fashion shows, discussions, seminars, workshops, annual meetings, and book sales.

Properly staged events can serve purposes other than just raising money. They can induce people to become part of the organization's expanding constituency base.

Wheel of Roles and Responsibilities

Some individuals are much involved in community life; others live a relatively quiet existence. Some individuals are linked in interest and influence with many people in the community; others by nature of their work, family interests, or other preoccupations limit their contacts to a few. Some individuals are busy with their work but sufficiently disciplined in time management to be able to accept voluntary leadership assignments; others are so preoccupied that they cannot manage the time to volunteer productively.

The wheel of roles and responsibilities depicts the various roles and responsibilities that are assumed by individuals within the local, regional, national, or international community (see Figure 4.3). These roles and responsibilities represent positive and negative influences that may affect the behavior and ability of constituents to perform productively for the organization. Fund raising practitioners would do well to study these criteria when evaluating prospects for major gifts or candidates for top volunteer leadership positions within the organization. This thesis was postulated in 1974 by Joseph R. Mixer, one of the founders of The Fund Raising School, in his classroom teachings.

The various roles and responsibilities that may demand an undue

Figure 4.3. Wheel of Roles and Responsibilities.

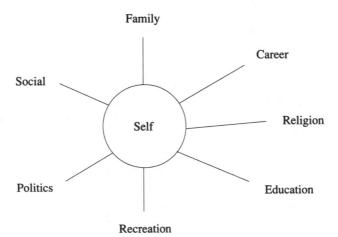

portion of an individual's time, energy, and inclination to perform at the level desired by the fund raising program are shown in Figure 4.3. The individual who is a prospect for a major gift or a prospect for top leadership is in the center of the wheel. Each spoke represents an element that affects the person's ability to perform in one manner or another. These elements include family, career, religion, education, recreation, politics, and sociability.

Family. In most lives, family is of central concern. The family's interests can be a positive resource, exerting a major influence on a person, and very often affecting decisions on gift making. But family relationships also can bring disharmony or severe opposition to a major gift. Intrusion by the wrong family member in the solicitation process can be disastrous. What pertains in each case? It is the responsibility of the fund raising practitioner to find out.

Career. A business or professional career opens up opportunities for a constituent to use power linkages with prospective donors, top-level leadership candidates, and people in positions that can affect the final approval of large gifts. Indeed, a constituent's business association can provide the leverage that is necessary to secure that strategically important gift. But business obligations also can be so demanding that they limit or eliminate that constituent's available time for volunteer work. And at other times, the not-for-profit organization's values may be in conflict with those of the business corporation.

Religion. Philanthropy is rich in the tradition of religion. Individuals who are strong in their faith give generously and thoughtfully of their financial resources, time, and energy as advocates of the cause in which they believe so strongly. To them, giving is a privilege. Their gifts are philanthropic and made thoughtfully and without reluctance. However, their commitment to their church or temple can reduce their available finances and energy to such a degree that they have little of both left to give to other causes.

Education. Education offers a distinct advantage to the fund raising process. The full development process practiced at many large universities in this country has done an excellent job in schooling their constituents to give and to volunteer their time. The practices learned under the aegis of such colleges and universities are transferable to other institutions. In addition, university alumni have developed many bonds with other alumni, many of whom are influential and linked to potential giving sources. This linkage can be used to advance the fund raising programs of other organizations. But as with religious commitments, loyalty to the university may deter generous giving and enthusiastic service to other not-for-profits.

Recreation. Gifts have been sought during an afternoon of golf, after tennis matches, and during bowling meets. Spectacular successes with solicitations during these activities may be more apocryphal than real. Recreational preoccupation offers both benefits and drawbacks to the fund raising process—as a distraction or as a possible inducement to become involved. As such, recreation must be evaluated as an important facet of a constituent's life.

Politics. Each person is a political animal to a major or minor degree. This facet of a constituent's public demeanor does not necessarily refer to involvement in any formal political activity. It does relate to the person's ability to interact with others and to practice his or her citizenship. This is a benefit because it promotes a constituency linkage with a quality leadership that, once developed, could well serve the needs of the organization. In other cases, however, this may involve candidacy for public office. Under these circumstances, politics becomes a distraction. Political candidates face the continuing need to cultivate their own constituencies and to raise their own money to support their own activities.

Sociability. Social acceptance is important to each person. To many people, social interaction comes easily; it is a normal part of their daily lives, and they accept it graciously and easily. Social ease is an attribute that enables a person, or a couple, to cultivate a wide circle of acquaintances. Such individuals are an asset to a not-for-profit organization, because they can attract others to the constituency and to the support base through the strength of their personalities. To others, however, social acceptance becomes an addictive quantity, one that almost completely preoccupies and consumes their energies and sometimes their financial resources. Ironically, these searchers for social acceptance use the organization as a mechanism for social advancement. Their actual contributions are minimal.

Conclusion

In summary, the constituency gives meaning to the not-for-profit organization. It is a composite of all individuals who are currently associated with the organization in some manner, those who have been associated in the past, and those who might become involved in the future.

Some organizations protest that they do not have a constituency because they are not universities with alumni, churches with congregations, or symphony orchestras with season subscribers. Let it be established here that every organization that has been qualified as a 501(c)(3) tax-exempt, not-for-profit entity has a constituency. If it does not, then it simply does not exist. These organizations should spend little time in bemoaning their imagined deficiencies and a maximum of time in identifying, cultivating, and bonding constituencies to their missions. Such a constituency holds the potential for service as volunteers, contributors, and advocates. The mission is the message that will provide the bonding influence.

Preparing a Case
That Empowers Fund Raising

Not-for-profit organizations do not come into being for the purpose of conducting fund raising programs. They seek a presence in the community of agencies, institutions, and organizations for the purpose of responding to some human or societal need. This need serves as their imperative, the cause to which they dedicate themselves.

The *case* is an expression of the cause, or a clear, compelling statement of all of the reasons why anyone should consider making a contribution in support of or to advance the cause (Seymour, 1966, p. 43).

It is true that fund raising is not the reason why not-for-profits come into existence. But once they do form, fund raising becomes a central concern because it has the capacity to provide the funds that the organization requires for current program support. The case justifies that concern, orders it in a form that can be presented to the community, and expresses it in clear and exciting terms to invite the gift.

This chapter will address two dimensions of case: the *internal case*, or the compilation and the centralization of the knowledge base essential to the definition of the case statement, and the *external case*, which distills the data base into a statement that will justify the fund raising effort.

The Internal Case

The internal case is not a brochure, a fund raising letter, or printed promotional materials. The internal case is a "data base," a compilation of information that will support the preparation of various documents and publications that will explain the organization's work.

39

What are the most compelling questions that challenge the existence of each not-for-profit and demand responsible attention in the case definition? The questions have been propounded by veteran fund raising consultant and practitioner Dan Conway and they are stated as follows: Who are you? Why do you exist? What is distinctive about you? What is it that you want to accomplish? How do you intend to accomplish it? How will you hold yourself accountable?

Twelve elements of the case make up the knowledge base that will enable the practitioner to respond to these questions. Information about these elements should be gathered and stored in such a manner that it is easily retrieved when promotional materials are being prepared. The twelve elements of the internal case are mission, goals, objectives, programs and services, staffing, governance, facilities, finances, planning, statement of needs, evaluation methods, and history.

Mission. The mission is a statement of values, a philosophical statement of the organization's reason for being. The mission statement identifies the human or societal needs that are central to the concern of the organization and explains *why* these needs should be addressed.

Too often, mission and goals are confused. Development officers are prone to claim "The mission of our agency is to feed the children of our community" or "Our mission is to eliminate or at least reduce the devastating force of violence in our nation." Whenever the infinitive form of the verb is used as in these phrases, the statement becomes a statement of a goal, not a statement of mission. Mission answers the questions "Who are you?" and "Why do you exist?" The interrogative that challenges the mission is the "Why?" *Why* is the organization committing itself to the needs that have been identified? Or simply, *why* is it doing what it is doing? Goals are not responsive to these questions.

Classroom exercises devoted to writing mission statements have brought forth excellent samples. The two examples below are used here with the permission of The Fund Raising School, a program of the Indiana University Center on Philanthropy. Such exercises emphasize the thesis that a case statement must respond to the six compelling questions noted above. Answers to these questions will provide a foundation for the organization's case position.

> There is no greater gift to the future than a generation of young people who are empowered with leadership skills and deeply committed to employing those skills in their local, state, national and global communities. The challenges to our society require leadership that is ethical, sensitive and aware of the needs of people and the environment. Without this leadership, our future as a nation and as a world is in peril.

Hunger hurts. It denies dignity, lessens human energy, erodes community stability and impairs the potential of people and societies to achieve. Long the land of plenty, America now faces a crisis of hunger. An increasing number of its citizens are without food for the first time in their lives. For those of all ages who now confront hunger, sustenance must be provided and solutions must be sought.

Both mission statements identify a need. The first advocates for an organization that teaches leadership skills to young people, and the second statement supports a food bank that provides meals to the poor and the homeless. Both are expressive in explaining why the needs merit attention. Both invite a constituency to share in and dedicate itself in service to the values inherent in their reasoning.

Goals. Goals concern themselves with the question "What is it that you want to accomplish?" In other words, now that you know what your mission is, what do you plan to do about it?

Goals reach into the future. They seek to inscribe a road map, to set a direction. Goals do not define. They prod and push.

Exhibit 5.1 is another example of mission language. The statement "That mission is carried out in four ways" expresses the purpose of the Iowa Humanities Board and serves as a prelude to the four goals that are listed in the statement's text.

Objectives. Goals are expressed in generalities. Objectives, however, are expressed in specifics. "How do you intend to accomplish your goals by achieving *what* measurable objectives?" Each goal should have at least three and no more than four specific objectives. For example:

Goal: To provide meals for impoverished school children who are suffering from malnutrition, which affects their ability to learn and advance in school.

Objectives: We will serve a nourishing breakfast to one hundred school children each day of the school week. We will continue this program through the school year. We will involve twelve volunteers to gather, prepare, and serve the breakfasts at each of the four primary schools in our city.

Each objective quantifies. Each is stated in measurable terms. Each is realistic and achievable.

Programs and Services. Mission, goals, and objectives must take shape as activities within a plan of action. Specifics about programs and service must

Exhibit 5.1. The Humanities.

Humanities are the scholarly fields of study that explore what it means to be human: history, philosophy, language, literature, ethics, art history and criticism, and jurisprudence, to name a few. We may not consciously recognize the humanities as readily as we do art, but we rely upon the humanities daily to make sense of the world, to find our place in it, and to change it when that is our desire. They help us to understand, communicate, analyze, refine, and interpret. Our languages, our writing, and our ability to organize thought in meaningful patterns are all part of what we call the humanities.

Our purpose is simple, yet comprehensive: to serve all by fostering greater public awareness and appreciation of the humanities. That mission is carried out in four ways:—

- By providing grants to not-for-profit organizations
- By creating our own humanities programs
- By providing support services, technical assistance, and referrals
- By advocating a greater role for the humanities

Source: Adapted from Iowa Humanities Board, *Meeting the Challenge of Change, 1971–1986.* Used with permission of the Iowa Humanities Board.

be entered in the knowledge base—that is, the internal case—that is being maintained by the central fund raising office.

Staffing. Identification and description of each staff and volunteer position within the organization should constitute a major entry in the knowledge bank. In larger organizations, the maintenance of such an informational file might be cumbersome and perhaps difficult. In this case, the development staff should have access to such information in other offices whenever it might be needed.

At the very least, the development office should maintain an easily accessible file of key names of people who hold administrative and program positions.

Governance. The governing board is a central element in the structure of the not-for-profit organization. Information about each board member and about board activity salient to the development operation should be stored and periodically updated for use by the development staff.

Facilities. Much work is done to raise special gifts, major gifts, and the periodic big gift through capital campaigns. Information about the physical plant—buildings, land, furnishings, technical equipment, and so forth—represents critical information that can support both the more sophisticated major gifts and capital fund raising plans.

Finances. Development practitioners must be accountable. A high level of responsibility should be shown in all of the information that is maintained: Budgets, current financial statements, annual reports, gift-income progress reports, budgets, fund raising cost analyses, and other financial data.

Statement of Needs. A current, regularly updated statement of current program support, special purpose, capital, and endowment needs is an essential component in the fund raiser's tool kit. The statement of needs is a constant prod to the thoughtful planning that is so necessary to productive fund raising.

Evaluation Methods. Again the question "How will you hold yourself accountable?" comes to mind. Trustworthy, accurate, and honest evaluation of the organization and its development program on a continuing basis is a key to accountability.

History. The history of the organization is often misused by case writers (unless, of course, the asking agency is a historical society). History substantiates. It is testimony to the organization's durability, but it should not be the central appeal. If history is to be included, then it should be expressed in the warm tones of human experience, of heroic accomplishments, of the people who made things happen. The case files should stockpile stories of accomplishments, mistakes, renewal experiences, and heroes.

With the compilation and storage of this information, the internal case is in place and readily available. This compendium of information should enable the development officer to respond to any questions posed by the organization's constituency, including those asked by prospects, contributors, and representatives of regulatory agencies.

The External Case

The internal case orders the documentation. The *external case* tells the story of the organization to its constituencies.

It must be accepted that asking for money because the organization needs money is not the most creative or most inviting presentation of the case. Only in rare situations does the contributor give because the organization needs funds to balance its budget, avoid a deficit, or retire a debt.

A primary purpose for giving is the strong belief in the organization and its mission, goals, and accomplishments. People give to resolve problems, to capture opportunities, to serve a purpose much larger than themselves. Dire financial needs hold no excitement for the potential contributor, no enticement to give. Financial problems should not command a central position in the organization's case expression.

In contrast to the internal case, which is a vast data base of knowledge, the external case is an expression of the cause in the form of a brochure, a letter, an annual report, a speech before a service club, a presentation to a foundation or corporation. It is the case at work.

A working sequence for stating the external case might well take the following course.

1. *Identify and validate the needs.* These are *not* the organization's operating budget requirements. Rather, these are the human or societal needs reflected by the organization's mission. They constitute the primary reason for fund raising.

2. *Document the needs.* Testimony as to the validity of the needs should be expressed by some source other than the organization, such as an accrediting body, planning agency, or other authoritative source.

3. *Identify programs and strategies designed to address the needs.* Provide the prospective contributor with enough information to show that programs can properly respond to problems or capture potential opportunities.

4. *Establish the competence of the organization and its staff.* Assert that staff members, board members, and volunteers have the appropriate skills to respond efficiently and effectively to the demands of the organization's programs. In other words, proper stewardship of contributed funds must be demonstrable.

5. *Explain who will benefit from the services that will be made possible by philanthropic support.* To identify the person who is on the receiving end of services is not enough. People beyond the immediate client will benefit. Project beyond the individual to the family, the neighborhood, the community—to society at large. A touch of imagination will help whoever is preparing the case text think and write about benefits in global terms.

6. *Identify the resources that are required to fund the programs.* The previous five items help to make the case. Now the organization must explain and identify the cost of funding current programs, underwriting special projects, financing capital expansion, or building endowment holdings. Make the case first, and then ask for gift support.

7. *Explain why the prospect should give.* Too often, the solicitor comes too quickly to a judgment that the prospect knows enough about the cause and has the resources to give, and therefore no time should be devoted to any further explanation of the case. This is a mistake. The case should help the prospect understand the validity of the need, the importance of the gift, and the justification for the solicitation.

8. *How can the prospective contributor give?* The ways are many. The external case should list the variety of gift opportunities that are available. This will encourage prospects to select the giving method that best fits their interests and financial situations. When personal and organizational needs blend, the potential for generous gift making increases.

9. *Respond to the unasked question in the prospect's mind: What's in it for me?* This often is perceived to be a selfish question, but it is not. It is a human question, and it merits a response. Tax deductibility is not the prime motivation. Deductibility empowers giving, but it does not necessarily cause the gift to be made. It has been said that the prime return value in giving can be some form of a "psychic paycheck," some spiritual return to the contributor. Ensure that the case definition offers a richness, perhaps

spiritual in nature, as a response to the asked or unasked question of return value.

Underlying all of these considerations is the need for planning, both short- and long-term. Planning is the continuing evaluation that keeps current the organization's responses to the community and its client constituencies.

The organization's messages will be communicated to a community of diverse interests. It will be important for the person writing the case to understand the need for different interpretations for different segments of the gift market. Corporations will seek case information that meets their requirements, foundations will have other requirements, and individuals yet others.

These varying interpretations of the information and program support data should not cause concern within the organization. Gift markets are interested in different aspects of the case. A flexible fund raising staff should be able to respond to each request with relative ease and confidence if the initial compilation of internal case data has been done with careful attention to detail and completeness. The integrity of the mission is not at stake.

Who Prepares the Case Statement?

The myth is perpetuated that the task of writing the organization's mission statement and case position should be assigned to the chief executive officer and the members of the governing board as one of their primary responsibilities. This myth is heard more often in the understaffed busyness of smaller agencies where board members are more apt to be involved in the day-to-day administration of the agency's affairs and in program activity, and where there is no fund raising staff.

Chief executive officers and board members have the distinct right to accept, modify, or reject case and mission language. However, it is rare that executives or board members of either small or large organizations have the energy, time, or inclination to do the creative writing that is required to articulate a mission or to write the complete case statement. Because the case statement will provide the rationale for all fund raising, it should be written by the staffperson who bears responsibility for fund raising. In the organization that has no fund raising staffperson, the case will have to be prepared by the executive working with a committee of the governing board.

There is a good reason to assign this task to the fund raising practitioner. This person serves in a dual role as an "inside" person with a commitment to the organization's values and as an "outside" person with a sensitive view of the community and its needs. This requires the fund raising person to ask the hard questions, and also requires candor and honesty from board members, the executive, and the program staff when presenting and representing the organization to its various constituencies.

The case statement's initial text is always prepared in draft form so that it can be reviewed by appropriate staffmembers and board members. The purpose of this process is to give both groups a sense of participation, which is crucial to their involvement as part of the team. This can make a difference in the way that strategically important people will come to accept the case and the mission statement, and how they will devote themselves to making the fund raising program work. Their commitment will be either intellectual or emotional. Intellectual involvement is passive, quiescent, and frequently unproductive: "You're doing fine. Everything looks just great, but don't count on me to give or to solicit. I just can't do it." Emotional involvement is active, supportive, and responsive: "This program means a great deal to me. Count me in. I'll not only give one of the top gifts that are required, I'll be responsible for bringing in at least three more gifts." Fund raising needs emotional involvement from an organization's top leaders.

Written Case Versus Oral Case

Fund raising practitioners have the ability to express themselves well enough through the spoken and written word. A fund raising executive is quite capable of writing text that sparkles. Words are thoughtfully selected, and each has polish. The words assume a special luster when they are printed on high-quality paper stock and use the most attractive typefaces, the best ink, and the most modern printing methods.

There is one problem with this process. The words will belong to the author, the graphics will belong to the artist, and the printing to the printer. How can all of this glory be brought to life for that special volunteer who will use the printed words to encourage a major prospect to give?

Words on a printed page have a special value. They offer moral support to the volunteer, and yet too often they are used with minimal impact during face-to-face discussion with a potential contributor.

Time-tempered veterans of fund raising urge their colleagues everywhere to help their volunteers lift the words from the paper and translate them into the idiom of the solicitation. Ask the volunteer solicitors—and sometimes the staff solicitors—to talk about the reasons they give, volunteer their time, and accept so willingly assignments to solicit their friends and associates for gifts. What does the organization mean to them? Why do they give? This is the oral case, the expression of dedication, the testimony to the worth of the organization and its work. So many times, it is far more expressive than the written word.

Draw excitement from the "living history" of the organization. Dig deep into the soil that gives sustenance to the roots. Extract the excitement of past accomplishments, tales of mistakes and misadventures, stories of heroic efforts. Color these stories with the passion of the mission and the power of the organization's vision for the future. This will bring the case to life.

If the volunteer can be made to feel comfortable with this storytelling, conversational style of case expression, then solicitation might even turn out to be fun. More often than not, the prospect will be moved to invite the solicitor to return for a second or even third visit to continue the negotiation until the solicitation is completed.

The beautiful brochure with its compelling case printed in four colors should be made available to the prospect for casual reading during the interim between solicitation calls. During this period, it will have the power to quietly sell the reader. The brochure will serve as an effective tool in meeting the volunteer solicitor's need for moral support. It should be used strategically and should never substitute for the solicitor's testimony about the worth of the organization and its work.

Conclusion

In summary, the internal case is preparation: the gathering, sorting, verifying, ordering, and storing process of the salients that give substance to the case.

The external case tells the story. It reaches beyond the organization to where present and future constituents live. Its purpose is to inform, inspire, excite, uplift and motivate the reader of the written case and the hearer of the oral case to become involved with the cause as advocates, contributors, volunteers, and informed constituents.

The spark of creative energy is the core of the case. The mission is that philosophical statement of concern that justifies the organization's existence and invites constituency interest, support, and dedication.

PART THREE

KEY METHODS
FOR RAISING MONEY

Fund raising has many parts, each an essential element of the whole. Packaged together tightly, these elements project the total organization into the marketplace, where it can be judged for its relevance on the basis of the appropriateness of its case, the urgency of its needs, the effectiveness of the programs that will respond to these needs, and the quality of its governance and management.

Basic to all of this are the fund raising methods, or the "vehicles" as they are referred to in professional jargon. The basic methods are:

> The *annual fund*, which seeks gifts from income to meet the not-for-profit organization's income needs;
> *Direct mail*, which is concerned with acquiring contributors;
> The *special gift*, or the solicitation of special-purpose gifts;
> The *capital campaign*, which raises funds to help meet the capital or asset-building needs of the organization;
> The *planned gift*, or gifts from the prospective contributor's investment holdings or estate; and
> *Grantsmanship*, or the organized solicitation of every type of foundation.

All six methods are interrelated. All must be fully developed to realize the productive capacity of the entire process.

The Annual Fund:
A Building Block
for Fund Raising

The annual fund is the building block for all fund raising. It serves to establish a base of donors that can serve as an effective device to involve, inform, and bond a constituency to the organization. It can further serve as an instrument that compels accountability to the market the organization is serving.

In formulating and executing programs in service to their missions, not-for-profit organizations incur a variety of financial needs. Fund raising, or what is currently known as resources development, has the functional responsibility to secure money, gifts-in-kind, or noncash gifts, volunteer services, and a range of additional services from the community.

The annual fund is the cornerstone and the key to success for all aspects of the resources development program.

The objectives of this chapter are to identify the principles and techniques that pertain to the annual fund, to explain the "arithmetic of fund raising" that can facilitate the preparation of a plan, to describe a planning tool called the "ladder of effectiveness," and to offer methods to apply these principles and techniques.

The focus of the discussion will be on individuals as primary contributors to the annual fund rather than corporations, foundations, associations, or government. The bulk of the money that is given away annually in the United States comes from individuals. It stands to reason then that they represent the most reliable source of givers to the annual fund. Other chapters in this book will discuss the giving patterns of corporations and foundations.

Reasons for Giving

People give away money for many different reasons. Veteran fund raising professionals recall an old axiom to emphasize one of the "carved in stone" principles of fund raising: "People do not give to causes. They give to people with causes." To this piece of wisdom can be added another: "People will not give simply because the organization needs money." Both offer important guidelines to fund raisers. Contributors will not give simply to help an entity balance its operating budget. They are moved to give by the urgency of the community's needs. In addition, they will give because they respect the organization's commitment to carry out programs that are responsive to the needs that are central to its concern.

Individuals tend to give from three sources: discretionary or disposable money, capital holdings, and estates. This statement does not seek to belittle the practice of sacrificial giving. People with strong religious beliefs, or those who share a tradition of philanthropy, will tend to give sacrificially. For the most part, however, the bulk of contributors will not make any gift that will compel them to give up something important to them or cause them to change their standards of living. Nevertheless, they continue to give generously to various causes.

Contributors will give for current program support, to meet a special purpose need, for capital purposes, or to help build the organization's endowment holdings. This sympathetic broad-based giving pattern is not haphazard. The interests of the contributor must be nurtured. Involvement is invited through the annual solicitation of gifts to the annual fund. The very process of solicitation can induce the contributor to become more knowledgeable about the organization, more understanding, and therefore more supportive.

For this important reason, the annual fund is much more than an unrelated series of special events, direct mail, phone-a-thons, and other activities. It is a thoughtfully devised and executed plan that creates a strong force of advocates who will dedicate themselves to the organization's advancement through their philanthropy and volunteer services.

The primary objectives of an annual fund should be the following:

- to get the gift, to get it repeated, and to get it upgraded;
- to build and develop a base of donors, and through this process to establish habits and patterns of giving;
- to raise annual unrestricted and restricted money;
- to inform, involve, and bond the constituency to the organization;
- to use the donor base as a vital source of information to identify potential large donors;

- to promote giving habits that encourage the contributor to make capital and planned gifts; and
- to remain fully accountable to the constituency through annual reports.

Exhibit 6.1 offers a summary of these points.

Exhibit 6.1. The Development Process.

The Objective	The Process	What Is Required?
Identify suspects	List development	Build lists of, identify, and research constituents
Convert suspects into prospects	Test list effectiveness, identify linkages	Refine prospect development
Convert prospects into donors	Build on linkages, test interest, ask, acknowledge	Solicit by personal visit, telephone, direct mail, and special event
Convert initial giver into donor of record	Build on interests and linkages, ask, acknowledge	Report use of gift, invite to renew
Increase the gift	Research, build on interests, linkages, inform, ask, acknowledge	Report, involve, invite to renew and increase gift, use gift-club concept
Secure special gift ($1,000 +)	Continue research through linkages, involve, build on interests, ask, acknowledge	Describe special needs, how money is used; solicit personally, invite to gift-club membership
Secure major gift ($10,000 +)	Use all linkages to validate as major prospect, ask, acknowledge, reward	Involve in institution: planning, case evaluation, needs determination, cultivation events, personal letters
Secure big gift	Continue involvement through linkages, add to interests, foster desire to give, ask, acknowledge, reward	Report: Involve constituent as important advocate, involve through cultivation events, personal reports, personal contacts
Secure planned gift	Continue involvement, create feelings of belonging to and identifying with institution, foster mutuality of interests	Strengthen linkage, strengthen involvement

Source: Adapted from instructional materials prepared for use in The Fund Raising School's classroom. The Fund Raising School is a program of the Indiana University Center on Philanthropy, Indianapolis, Indiana.

The Arithmetic of Fund Raising

Larger nonprofit organizations with experienced staffs carrying out sophisticated and successful fund raising programs may not be subject to the faults
that so often plague smaller organizations with less experienced staffs. In the
case of less experienced staffmembers, planning for the annual fund tends to
concentrate more on scheduling events than on applying time-tested working principles. Perhaps the most time-honored principle of all is the one that
pertains to the "arithmetic of fund raising."

The arithmetic of fund raising concept in planning for an annual fund
directs the fund raising practitioner to determine the quality and number of
gifts that are required to achieve the organization's goal. Decisions about the
plan's strategies should be delayed until the following determinations have
been made:

What quality of gifts are required, and how many are needed in each
   gift category?
What should be the ratio of prospects to donors?
Does the donor base have that number of prospects?
Is it realistic to expect that these prospects can be identified?
If these questions cannot be answered clearly and factually, then is the
   goal for the annual fund realistic?

The use of such arithmetic to determine the number of quality gifts
that are required to ensure the achievement of a fund raising goal had its
genesis in the planning for capital campaigns. Only recently has this planning device been employed as a method to determine the course of an annual
fund. Such terms as *gift-range charts* or the synonymous *standard of gift charts*
are common in the vocabulary of the capital campaign. The terms are used
infrequently in any discussion about the annual fund, although they do have
their application to the annual fund.

The information that follows is from experienced and veteran fund
raising practitioners who have successfully used gift-range charts in planning
for both capital and annual fund raising campaigns. It is logical to think that
the chances for success will be made stronger during planning if a determination can be made about the numbers and quality of gifts that must be
produced to ensure that a goal is reached.

The arithmetic concept as it pertains to the annual fund means that a
large amount of the money to be raised will come from a small number of
contributors who are encouraged to provide what will necessarily be larger
gifts. The arithmetic is this: Ten percent of the gifts received during the
annual fund have the potential to produce 60 percent of the money required
to meet the goal. The formula can be elaborated as:

$$\underline{\text{Gifts } (\%)} = \underline{\text{Money Raised } (\%)}$$

Gifts (%)	Money Raised (%)
10	60
20	15–25
70	Remainder required

It is generally accepted among professional fund raisers that 3 percent to 5 percent of contributors enrolled in an organization's donor base have the ability to make major gifts. When this supposition is applied to the gifts that are needed to properly achieve a goal, it follows that 10 percent of the gifts generated for an annual fund indeed have the potential to produce 60 percent of the funds received through gifts.

To make this principle work, the top two gifts that should be sought in the annual fund must each equal 5 percent of the goal. For example, if the goal is $100,000, then each of the top two gifts should be $5,000 for a cumulative value of $10,000. All other gifts in the arithmetical computations should scale down from the $5,000 level.

The gift distribution can be evaluated in a form called the *gift-range chart*. This planning tool aids the fund raiser in determining the optimal gift distribution. Tables 6.1 and 6.2 illustrate how the computations can be made.

In Table 6.2, the goal of $20,000 is more typical of the amount of money that would be sought by a smaller organization with limited current program support requirements. A slightly different ratio is used than in Table 6.1. The ratios are changed to provide for 70 percent of the funds to come from larger gifts, 20 percent from midsized gifts, and only 10 percent from smaller gifts.

The purpose of the revised chart for the smaller goal is to avoid the necessity of asking for $5, $10, and $15 gifts that are costly to raise through direct mail and other impersonal fund raising methods. Such gifts should be

Table 6.1. Gift-Range Chart: Annual Fund Goal: $100,000.

Range of Gifts ($)	No. of Gifts	No. of Prospects	Subtotals ($)	Totals ($)
5,000	2	8	10,000	—
2,500	4	16	10,000	—
1,000	10	30	10,000	—
500	20	60	10,000	—
250	(116)* 80	(274)* 160	20,000	60,000
100	250	500	25,000	25,000
Less than 100	Many	Many	15,000	15,000
				100,000

*Indicates that 116 gifts can be successfully solicited from 274 prospects for $60,000, or 60 percent of the goal.

Table 6.2. Gift-Range Chart: Annual Fund Goal: $20,000.

Range of Gifts ($)	No. of Gifts	No. of Prospects	Subtotals ($)	Totals ($)
1,000	2	8	2,000	—
500	5	20	2,500	—
250	16	48	4,000	—
100	(78) 55	(196) 130	5,500	14,000
50	80	160	4,000	4,000
Less than 50	Many	Many	2,000	2,000
				20,000

acknowledged properly when received, but they should not be actively solicited.

Certain principles become apparent quite readily. The gift-range chart gives form to the planning. The initial planning focus is not on a range of activity, but on the more practical aspects of fund raising, the acquisition of large-dollar gifts that will make the critical difference in achieving the goal.

From the two gift-range charts, several concerns can be addressed. First, how many gifts and at what amount must the fund raising team produce to make the goal? Are the prospects available? If not, what can be done about it?

The chart is a flexible instrument. The ratio of prospects from the top of the chart to the bottom of the chart may be changed to coincide with the reality of the donor base and the availability of prospects. Flexibility pertains also to the numbers of donors and prospects that are required at each gift level. In some situations, it may be possible to secure more than the required two gifts at the top of each chart. Do not deny the reality of the figures, but be assertive when prospecting. Only through continual research will prospects be found.

It is easy to submit to the easy rationale that many small gifts will be easier to secure than the two largest gifts. But think about it. This will require that one hundred $100 gifts substitute for two $5,000 gifts in Table 6.1; this means that four hundred prospects must be solicited to secure the substituted one hundred gifts.

In Table 6.1, it is truly possible to secure 116 gifts from 274 prospects to reach the 60 percent mark, particularly if these prospects are part of the donor base that has a history of giving to the organization. Included in the prospect listing are individuals, associations, foundations, and corporations that give to annual funds, small businesses, and so forth. The only relevant criterion here is, do they give to current program support?

In Table 6.2, 78 gifts are required from 196 prospects to achieve 70 percent of the goal. This can be easier than scheduling a host of special events or filing a host of grant applications with foundations and corporations, most of which will not give for annual support purposes.

The range of gifts dictated by the gift-range charts gives eloquent testimony to the need for a properly assembled and properly conditioned donor base. Within that base are individuals with the capability of making an extraordinary gift to the organization. And yet in many cases, the gift will not be made simply because the organization has not asked for it. It is axiomatic that the contributor will give only at the level of his or her perception of what the organization requires. If the gift is not actively sought, the larger gift in most cases will not be made. Rightfully or wrongfully, the potential contributor will assume that the larger gift is not needed.

One of the many realizations that surface through the gift-scaling technique imposed by the gift-range chart is that the potential for the large gift lies within the base.

Effective Fund Raising Plays by the Rules

Fund raising is relatively simple in form, but do not be fooled by its simplicity. Fund raising is a demanding taskmaster. Attention must be given to the simple common sense rules that can make a difference. One of the simplest of these rules is to scrutinize and analyze the gift potential in the donor base before making any effort to put the fund raising plan on paper. Ask and seek answers to the hard question: Are there sufficient prospects within the base who have the capability to give at the level that is required?

Profiling the base annually or semiannually provides the organization with a wealth of information about the potential giving patterns of its constituency. An understanding of this pattern can be a major benefit to the fund raising program. The following questions should be asked about the base:

1. How many donors give annually?
2. What is the frequency of the gift? Once a year, twice a year, or more often? How many donors give on a monthly basis? What is the date of the most recent gift?
3. What is the level of giving? How many give $1,000 or more a year; $500 to $1,000; $250 to $500; $100 to $250; $50 to $100; less than $50?
4. Do the records indicate the names of donors who give consistently to the annual fund as well as make special-purpose, capital, or endowment gifts during the course of the year?
5. What is the pattern of giving by staffmembers, trustees, and members of advisory councils or non-board-related support committees?

This is prospecting, the eternal search for vital information that is so important to fund raising. It is an essential part of the fund raising office's intelligence bank. The information in this bank will enable the person planning the fund raising program to identify the potential gifts required by the gift-range chart.

As the chart below shows, the data retrieved from the donor base as a result of this search can be organized easily to analyze the base's potential. These data should reflect the number and dominance of gift ranges during the current year, last year, and previous two years.

Gift Ranges($)	Total $			
	Current Year	Last Year	2 Years Ago	3 Years Ago
1,000–5,000				
500– 999				
250– 499				
100– 249				
50– 99				

By replacing numbers with names, these data can be converted to a workable form. In Chapter 7, Craver refers to the strategic qualification of donors by finding and recording donor information about longevity, frequency, recency, and amount. This measurement could be applied to all gifts of $100 or more. Gifts at this level show the greater tendency to repeat and to be upgraded, thus creating the opportunity for the solicitation of the special gift, the major gift, or the planned gift.

To define these terms, *longevity* refers to the number of years that the person has been giving, *frequency* to the number of gifts during the year, *recency* to the most recent date, and *amount*, of course, relates to the dollar value of the annual gift or the cumulative value of multiple gifts made that year. This information becomes the determining factor in evaluating whether the donor of record might respond positively to a request for one of the larger gifts designated on the gift-range chart.

Reckless guessing has no place in fund raising planning. Hard questions require hard responses. If a goal is to be justified, then the justification must come in the form of hard information that the numbers of prospects required are indeed available and that the prospects do have the ability to give at the level indicated by the gift-range chart.

In Table 6.1, 274 prospects are potentially required to produce 116 gifts. Are the prospects available? If the response is *yes*, then the plan should be activated to solicit each prospect with the hope that the designated gifts can be secured. If the precise number of prospects at the top level ($1,000 to $5,000) cannot be identified, then the fund raising planners must make some serious decisions. Is the $100,000 goal feasible? The answer may well be *yes* if the prospects listed against the numbers required at the top of the chart are quality prospects. There is a better than average chance that they will make the gift if properly approached by the right soliciting team.

The prospect-to-donor relationship depicted on the two gift-range charts in Tables 6.1 and 6.2 may seem imposing and perhaps somewhat disconcerting to both the fund raising professional and the fund raising volunteer with little experience. The question asked may reflect such despair:

"How is it possible to effectively solicit 196 prospects? That will require an army of volunteers. How can they possibly be recruited to the task?"

This is a reasonable reaction. The questions are logical and appropriate. If money is to be raised, then prospects must be solicited. And, unfortunately, fund raising has never been voted as the most popular indoor or outdoor sport in this, or any other, nation. The volume of volunteers required may not be available.

The Ladder of Effectiveness

The ladder of effectiveness may serve to allay some of the fears that naturally surface when the reality of solicitation must be confronted.

In descending order, the ladder portrays the relative effectiveness of the various methods used to solicit gifts. Each step down the ladder indicates diminishing effectiveness in the soliciting procedure. Face-to-face solicitation by a peer of the prospect is the most effective method; solicitation through media or by direct mail is the least effective, as attested to by the ladder:

1. *Personal visit by a team.* This is the most effective method. Two people can make up the team: a peer of the prospect accompanied by the organization's chief executive, the fund raising officer, or a program person. The peer is a volunteer and the advocate for the organization; the staff-person is the expert witness.
2. *Personal visit by one person.* This can be an effective approach if the person is committed to the organization's mission, and if he or she feels comfortable about soliciting. If the person is uncomfortable or reluctant to solicit, do not risk the danger of an ineffective solicitation — that is, one that is painful to both the solicitor and prospect.
3. *Solicitation by personal letter with a follow-up telephone call.* In this method, a peer communicates with a personal friend through personal stationery. If appropriate, the solicitor encloses a self-addressed, stamped envelope in the carrier envelope to encourage a response directly back to the solicitor. If there is no response to the request within seven to ten days, then the solicitor calls the prospect to follow up on the solicitation. In this process, however, the peer uses up a certain number of social "credits."
4. *Solicitation by personal letter without the follow-up telephone call.* If the prospect fails to respond to the letter appeal, and the solicitor declines or fails to place a follow-up call to request the gift, then usually a gift will not be made.
5. *Personal telephone call by a peer with a letter follow-up.* If the prospect agrees to give, the calling peer will immediately dispatch a brief letter expressing gratitude for the gift commitment; the letter will include a stamped

envelope to provide for the return of the gift. This is a gentle, subtle technique that discourages procrastination.

6. *Personal telephone call without letter follow-up.* This method places too heavy a responsibility on the telephone. The donor certainly should be thanked for making the oral commitment to give. To neglect to do so is not proper. If the prospect promises to give, then a letter with an enclosed self-addressed return envelope should be mailed immediately after the call to express thanks and to invite the gift. Even in the event of a *no*, the solicitor should express thanks to the prospect for receiving the call.

Each of the procedures above requires some form of personal contact with the potential donor. In Table 6.1, each of the 54 prospects listed against the $1,000 and more gift level represents a major opportunity to secure a gift. Each prospect must be approached on a personal basis by visit or telephone call.

If at all possible, the personal approach should even be extended to the prospects in the $250 to $999 categories. These prospects are too valuable to the program to be relegated to the impersonal approaches that are listed below. An impersonal approach to the potentially major contributor is a grievous error of strategy.

The descent down the ladder continues:

7. *The "house list."* This is the nonprofit organization's own list. It comprises donors in the donor base, particularly those who cannot make the largest gift in the upper ranges of the chart. The list generally includes current donors, lapsed donors, clients currently being served, staff-members, governing board members, individuals who receive newsletters, and any constituent with an active tie to the organization. Upgrading and renewal mailings are sent to appropriate segments of these lists.

8. *Grantsmanship.* This form of fund raising is directed more specifically at winning grants for special program or project support. Only rarely is grantsmanship effective in securing annually renewed funds for budget support.

9. *Phone-a-thons.* These are solicitations made by telephone, sometimes by volunteers, and other times by regular staffmembers or by staffmembers hired specifically to conduct the telephone campaign.

10. *Special events.* These are activities that are staged for a variety of reasons, one of which is to raise money for current program support. Other reasons include calling attention to the work of the organization, strengthening its image in the community, and recruiting and involving volunteers.

11. *Door-to-door.* This method also is known as "door knocks" in other nations. Only more established organizations—notably the American

Red Cross and the American Heart Association — experience any real success in the use of this arduous method of fund raising.

12. *Media use.* The use of newspaper advertising space and radio and television spots requires a strong emotional appeal such as that evoked by earthquake, hurricane, or accident of major proportions. Such events encourage what are essentially impulse givers to respond.

13. *Direct mail.* This interesting fund raising tool has a primary purpose: to achieve donors. It neither pretends to nor is it effective in raising the quality money that is needed for program support. Only the process of renewal and upgrading of gifts, an extension of the direct mail strategy, will produce money for the operating budget that funds the program. Yes, there are rare instances when direct mail does produce a modicum of money for the budget, but this requires the extraordinary combination of perfect lists, perfect timing, and perfect packaging.

The Annual Fund Calendar

When should an organization raise money? Whenever it needs money. When is the money most urgently needed? Every day of the year. So when should the organization raise money? Every day of the year.

This ancient wisdom applies today as much as in decades past. But variations in the interpretation may be necessary. Fund raising every day of the year may be difficult and somewhat tiring. Taking advantage of the entire year, all twelve months, is a wise use of time. This permits sufficient time for planning, research, volunteer recruitment, cultivation, and solicitation of the critically important major donors.

The quiet days of July and August offer manifold opportunities for retrospection. The pace of fund raising drops off somewhat. Time becomes available to study what has been accomplished and to compare current production with the previous year's production. What inferences for planning purposes can be drawn from these accumulated data? A planning draft can be prepared for revision, updating, and expansion during the final months of the year.

Planning includes analysis — that is, a prodding curiosity about the diversity of financial needs that will affect fund raising plans in the fiscal year ahead. In addition to current program support, will there be a need to raise special-purpose, capital, and endowment money? How will this affect the annual fund plans?

The solicitation of gifts in person, by mail, by telephone, through special events, and through grant applications is a year-round activity. A wisely developed plan will provide for multiple mail solicitations during the course of the entire year. Some of these involve acquisition mailings. Others will involve upgrading mailings and appeals for special-purpose gifts.

The year's fund raising calendar will include scheduled dates for special events, some designed to raise operating funds, others planned for the purposes of attracting attention to the organization or contributing to the luster of its image, and still others as fun-filled activities to recruit, involve, or recognize volunteers.

Perhaps one of the greatest results that can accrue through the use of a year-long annual fund calendar is flexibility. This enables work to be done with major-gift prospects in accordance with their requirements and without the artificial constraints of an unrealistic and too tight time line imposed by the organization. The volunteers' time throughout all of this must be used judiciously. A flexible timetable also will permit that. Sensitivity to the importance of building and maintaining a relationship with major contributors demands it.

Building the Annual Fund Team

Team building is important in the annual fund raising process. The volunteer as a member of the team becomes a strategic force: an advocate, a peer, a link to the larger community, and an asker without a vested interest. It is essential to involve key volunteer leaders, preferably from the governing board, in the membership of an annual fund committee.

The fund raising officer, either a development officer or an annual fund director, serves in a staff-support relationship to the annual fund committee. The staff person in this support position assumes responsibility for preparing the annual fund plan in draft form for review, study, modification, acceptance, or rejection by the annual fund committee. To enhance the workability of this plan, early in the planning stage the fund raising person must involve the chairperson and other strategic members of the committee. This takes delicate handling. At no time should the fund raising practitioner lose control of the preparation process. Ownership of an idea can be negotiated. The committee should harbor the feeling that its wisdom and involvement have been needed from the beginning. Certainly, its wisdom and involvement are needed during the implementation period.

After accepting the annual plan, the primary function of this committee is to execute it. In accepting the plan, the committee as a whole attests to the validity of the financial needs that justify the goal. It acknowledges that the goal is reasonable and achievable. It gives evidence of the committee members' willingness to make their own gifts at the level of their capabilities at the beginning of the program, as well as to join in the soliciting process by asking other prospects to do the same.

As stewards of the organization, committee members can perform yeoman service to the cause by assisting staffmembers in identifying potential contributors within the constituency. Prospect research is a staff responsibility. This research can be expanded and enriched significantly through a working partnership of staff and informed volunteers who have a knowledge of the financial structure of the community in which the fund raising is to be accomplished.

The annual fund should be the province of a subcommittee of the development committee. As a management force for the annual fund, this subcommittee should invite to its membership those individuals within the community who are willing to give the time, energy, and talent needed to ensure a successful, productive undertaking.

In summary, the annual fund is the following:

- the annual definition and validation of program and special needs;
- a sensitive outreach effort to identify existing and potential constituents and to invite their continuing liaison with the organization;
- the inquisitive and continual prospect research that identifies every potential gift source;
- the enrollment of capable volunteers to provide leadership and to give and to urge others to give;
- the building of linkages between the volunteer leadership and potential large-gift donors;
- the solicitation process that seeks to build a strong donor base by getting the gift and getting it repeated and upgraded;
- the productive solicitation of that critical 10 percent of donors who have the capacity to give 60 percent of funds;
- the efficient records that constitute the information bank used in planning all fund raising programs;
- the acceptance of the principle that people tend not to give to causes, they give to people with causes;
- the acceptance of the principle that the right time to ask for the gift is when the organization needs the money;
- the annual gift, the special gift, the big gift, and the planned gift, each made as a statement of conviction and commitment to the cause that the organization serves;
- the strategic procedure of asking the right person to solicit the right prospect for the right amount of money at the right time;
- a coordinated plan of fund raising that uses each fund raising vehicle in a disciplined, interrelated fashion to ensure maximum income to meet the nonprofit organization's annual program and special needs; and
- the ongoing process of seeking and receiving supportive testimony to the fact that the organization is responding to human and social needs through valid programs that merit community support.

The annual fund is all of the above and so much more. It is the fund raising event, the acquisition, the renewal and upgrading letter, the special gift letter, and the personal letter soliciting a major gift. It is also the phone-a-thon, telemarketing, grantsmanship, door-to-door solicitation, collection boxes on store counters, car washes, and bake sales. These are the impersonal, mechanical ways to ask for money used by persons who are uncomfortable with, or inexperienced in, the face-to-face, personal solicitation that represents the more dynamic, more effective form of fund raising.

In the words of fund raising consultant Dan Conway, the annual fund is in essence the process by which a not-for-profit reaches out to and invites its constituency to share in the fulfillment of its mission. The time-honored phrase "get the gift, renew the gift, upgrade the gift" is the basic truth of the annual fund. It is the most effective strategy to invite, involve, and bond the constituency to the organization, making it the organization's primary strength. This strength will enhance the organization's ability to raise funds for current program support, for special purposes, and for capital and endowment development because the organization will be asking a constituency that has been properly informed and conditioned by an effective annual fund to provide that support.

The Power of Mail
to Acquire, Renew,
and Upgrade the Gift

Old myths that minimized the importance of direct mail as a fund raising tool in the past are fast disappearing. By the estimates of some practicing specialists, direct mail is the medium that accounts for between $20 billion and $25 billion of the charitable educational and social change dollars contributed by Americans each year. The numbers are increasing as more fund raising practitioners become proficient in the use of the medium to acquire, renew, and upgrade contributions in support of not-for-profit organizations. Experience and technology coupled with the increasing difficulty of mobilizing volunteers to solicit annual program support money makes direct mail the fund raising medium of choice for increasing numbers of organizations and institutions.

Direct mail has been deprecated as a fund raising tool because the gifts it produces are relatively small, costs are relatively high, and, as a rule, the technical and professional skills required to manage a professional mail program are not available on many fund raising staffs. However, the organization that asserts itself in learning the real purpose and proper use of the medium will reap significant rewards, discover new special-gift and major-gift prospects, educate its constituency, and reach its peripheral constituencies, thus making them more active contributors.

Direct mail is first and foremost a process of financial management. Although the creative and technical functions are important (these will be explored in detail later in this chapter), they must take place within the context of an overall financial strategy. Just as a film or a television commercial is not created without first determining goals and strategies, neither is a direct mail program begun by rolling a sheet of paper into the typewriter. Successful direct mail fund raising begins with a plan, and all direct mail fund raising begins with a series of basic, yet challenging, financial questions that go to the essence of investment, risk, and return. How much money is to be raised and by what date? How much can be spent to match the task? Can the organization afford to lose all or most of this money?

Prospecting

The initial effort in any new direct mail fund raising program is that of finding and enlisting new contributors, the process known as *prospecting*. Prospecting is the most costly and riskiest part of the direct mail effort because it entails mailing materials to thousands of people who have not demonstrated any interest in the organization through financial commitments. These are the suspects who reside in the fourth and fifth regions shown in Figures 4.1 and 4.2 (pages 31 and 32). The percentage of response from these individuals will be considerably lower than that enjoyed by organizations that send their mail appeals or annual support renewal notices to people who have been part of their contributing base.

In short, prospects are people who are likely to be interested in but who have never given to a particular organization. Sometimes they are constituents, alumni, former patients, friends, neighbors, clients, volunteers, and those who agree with the organization's value system but who are not acquainted with the organization itself.

Generally, a response of 1 percent to 2 percent with an average gift of $18 to $22 is considered successful for a direct mail prospecting effort to a "cold" list of individuals who have never made a gift to the organization. For example, a cold mailing dispatched to 50,000 homes returns 500 gifts, or 1 percent of the mailing with gifts averaging $18 to produce $9,000. This will not cover the cost of the mailing, but it does produce 500 new contributors for the organization. Remember: The goal of prospect solicitation is to acquire contributors, not dollars.

More than any other phase of the direct mail cycle, prospecting calls for the most sensitive and intensive investment management skills. Because the purpose of prospecting by mail is to bring in new contributors rather than make a profit, the goal is to acquire new contributors at either low or some break-even cost. By continually engaging in this break-even transaction, organizations can ensure a steady flow of contributors who then can be induced to increase their gifts and to replenish the supply of contributors who are lost through attrition.

A certain irony manifests itself in considering the various aspects of direct mail prospecting, and one of the more profound ironies is that if the organization is making a profit from its prospecting mailings, then it may be doing an inferior job of fund raising. In all likelihood, it is not maximizing the number of first gifts from a prospect group; it is not prospecting. Remember again: The goal of prospecting by mail is the acquisition of *donors*, not dollars.

Donor Development

The key to effective direct mail lies in the second step of this distinctive fund raising method: the resolicitation and upgrading phase called *donor development*. This process is also referred to as "house file mailings" and "resolicitations." A "house file" is made up of active contributors, past contributors, friends of the organization, clients, and so forth. Active strategies are used to encourage current contributors to both continue and increase their gifts to add to the strength of the contributing base.

It is in the development phase that the true productive capacity of a direct mail program is realized. In this phase, the response rates increase from 6 percent to 15 percent and the average gift falls in the range of from $20 to $2,000, or possibly more, depending on which segments of the base are being contacted and what size contributions are being requested.

The dynamics of direct mail fund raising may be better understood through an analogy of insurance sales. Insurance companies pay the bulk of the first year's premiums in sales commissions (prospecting) and make their profits in the second and subsequent years when those premiums are renewed at very little cost (donor development). Unlike an insurance company, however, the fund raising program of a not-for-profit organization does not have to wait for the premium to come due. In fact, the key to successful direct mail is the continual and assertive resolicitation of an organization's contributors.

Successful direct mail is aggressive direct mail. Individuals contribute because they are interested in and care about an organization that is performing a worthwhile service that they feel they cannot perform themselves. The organization is their advocate in service, and each individual wants to be involved in some way, thus the gift. The better the contributor, the larger the gift, and the more likely that the contributor will want to hear from the organization more frequently. Fund raising staffs are counseled to structure the scheduling and creative approaches to both prospecting and contributor development mailings to cover a wide range of subjects and needs to ensure that those who read the mailing will find something that appeals to them.

Market Segments and Mailing Lists

Direct mail distinguishes itself by the fact that it is the most selective of the mass media. Unlike television, newspaper, or magazine advertising, direct mail can focus on individuals and individual characteristics just as do

telephone and person-to-person solicitations. It is the collective characteristics of any select group of individuals that constitute a market or a market
segment. The best market for fund raising purposes is the organization's own
contributors. Obviously, the best segments within the particular fund raising
market are those who give frequently and those who make large-dollar gifts.

For planning purposes, markets are divided into two broad categories:
(1) prospective contributors or prospects and (2) known contributors or the
organization's own house list.

The first question asked by organizations that are endeavoring to build
their own giving base is "How are lists found?" The answer is not always
simple, but the following set of criteria should be applied when a mailing list
is being compiled: responsiveness, analogous interests, demography, special
factors, and natural constituencies.

Responsiveness. Is the list responsive to direct mail appeals? In such fund
raising, the past is often the best predictor of the future. List of donors of
similar organizations or of causes that reflect like-minded ideologies hold the
greatest potential for positive responses to a direct mail appeal.

Mailing lists can be rented for one-time use, or they can be exchanged.
Organizations often trade names as a way to build their own lists. However,
the counsel of list brokers should be sought when selecting a proper list.
Names of mailing list brokers who specialize in particular areas of interest are
available from the Direct Marketing Association.

Analogous Interests. Many lists are available that may not be donor lists, but
which may carry the names of individuals that the organization wants to
reach. Chief among these are lists of periodical subscribers who stand for the
same issues and concerns that reflect the mission of the organization. Examples include *The New Republic, Conservative Digest, The Nation,* and *National
Review,* as well as other specialty publications such as farming and gardening
magazines, health publications, and city or regional magazines. The reading
and buying habits of people often reflect their charitable behavior and social
action interests. This is the realm that marketeers refer to as "psycho-
graphics," or the identification of a constituency as more than the demographic characteristics of age, income, home ownership, and so forth.

For a fascinating look at most of the lists that are organized by interest
categories, the fund raising practitioner would do well to review a library
copy of *Standard Rate and Data,* which identifies and describes more than
20,000 markets and lists.

Demography. Demographic lists are less effective for fund raising purposes
than those previously reviewed. Beyond individuals' known giving, reading,
and buying habits is a world of inference and deduction. Demographic lists
are compiled from census data and other sources and reflect an effort to
identify specific groups of people by income, age, education, home

ownership, automobile ownership, and so forth. Unfortunately, although these lists may be helpful in deducing a group's financial capability, they do little in determining what might motivate these people to give.

Special Factors. Increasingly, efforts are being made by direct mail data suppliers to take massive demographic lists and construct what are called "overlays" or "screens" to extract the names of people who will most likely qualify for inclusion on a mailing list. Thus, a list can be compiled by ethnic criteria, income and buying patterns, or income and reading habits. For most organizations, this highly sophisticated compilation of mailing lists may not be warranted. It would be wiser for the organization to limit its options to the proven, more efficient lists of known donors or suspected donor types rather than risk its resources on the more esoteric enticement of screened lists.

Natural Constituencies. Those who make a gift to a not-for-profit organization become part of that organization's house list, a major element in the constituency structure; as such, they merit special attention. How these names and the information connected with them are used will determine the effectiveness of the direct mail fund raising program.

The first task in the successful use of house lists is to segment the mail list or to select special names from the general data base. In this respect, the computer becomes an indispensable tool. Unlike lists generally used for prospecting purposes, the house list has established itself as a depository of names of individuals who are interested in the organization. The strategy used in working with house lists is to encourage each contributor to give on a continuing basis, to increase the gift, and to make a large gift.

Developing Contributor Interest

The following criteria are central to the strategy of developing contributors' interest and willingness to give at their levels of capability. This strategy should be reflected in the way that information on contributors and their gifts is recorded and the ready accessibility of these data. The criteria are recency, frequency, and amount.

Recency. Contributors are most responsive to an additional request for money the closer that response comes to their last gifts. This is why it is best to ask for a gift when the previous gift is acknowledged. That is also why selecting *active* contributors who have given in the past year or six months is better than soliciting those who have not given in more than a year.

Frequency. Any group of contributors has individuals who will give virtually every time they are solicited. They are called "multiple" contributors. They help to make direct mail fund raising far more efficient and effective than it would be without them.

Adequate records should be maintained to identify multiple contributors, those who have given more than twice a year or perhaps more than twice in the last six months. These individuals should be asked to give again. It is not rude or impolite. Frequent contact keeps contributors involved and active in the manner that they first chose to be active: by contributing.

Amount. Within any contributing group, there are individuals who will give more than others. Each individual seems to follow a preordained pattern of giving, based not only on the organization's needs, but also on the pattern of the person's giving to other organizations. Direct mail specialists study giving habits because they want to ask on the basis of what the contributor is most likely to give. What is "likely" is determined in large part by past giving. When it comes to direct mail fund raising, it is unwise to ask the individual who has given $25 to consider a $1,000 gift unless it is personally known that the contributor can do so. Conversely, a $500 contributor should not be asked to give $15. This greatly reduced gift would tend to confuse — and even possibly offend — the contributor and most likely would affect the next gift.

Through the proper use and study of gift records, the organization equips itself to relate in a sensitive way to the interests, wants, and giving habits of the contributor and asks for an amount that reflects the person's past range of giving.

Combining Economics and Market Segments

At the start of each year, the experienced direct mail fund raising professional will establish a detailed plan of action for carrying the program forward for the next twelve months. This assertive plan has two basic elements: a renewal series and a series of special appeals. The first priority of that plan will be to make certain that current contributors stay with the organization. Unless the plan succeeds in its efforts to maintain the loyalty of current contributors, the giving base will be in a never-winning, downward spiral of attrition.

The best assurance for maintaining the currency and the involvement of existing contributors is through an annual renewal program. Fund raising staff should be ever mindful that the psychology of giving works in the organization's favor when it seeks to renew its annual gift support. Consequently, a four-, five- or even seven-part renewal series should be made an integral part of every direct mail program. This series should be mailed on a monthly basis beginning three months before the anniversary of the contributor's initial gift or, if an annual renewal program is preferred, in November and December of each year.

The key components of every mailing acknowledge that the recipient of the letter is an important part of the organization's support and what that support has meant to the organization in the year now ending. Set forth the challenges and the needs the organization faces in the year ahead and seek a level of support 15 percent to 25 percent higher than the contributor's previous level of support.

Once the renewal gift has been received, the organization should then move to pursue the special needs through a series of special appeal mailings to contributors who have received their first renewal notices. Those who give frequently should receive more mailings. Those who give less frequently should receive fewer mailings. The ideal mixture of renewals and special appeals for most organizations is a four-to-six–part renewal series that is interspersed with at least four special appeals each year. Every organization that is worthy of public support has a valid reason to communicate with its supporters and to seek their support at least once a month.

Special appeal, or special project, mailings are the direct mail package that offers a unique opportunity to communicate very specific needs and "inside" information to contributors. If annual renewal mailings provide an overview of the organization, then special appeals mailings are a way to present specific aspects of the program and to ask for support to address these very special needs.

Once the economics and programs for the coming year are in place, the detailed task of preparing a direct mail program that works begins.

Competing in a Crowded Environment

Direct mail packages do not arrive as lone messengers to be welcomed and cherished by their recipients. They arrive in an unceremonious heap along with catalogs, magazines, and appeals from other charitable organizations and public-interest causes.

Will a particular direct mail package even be opened? If so, will it be read and acted upon? These are key questions that must be considered actively at the beginning of the direct mail creative process. Before delineating the specific parts of a direct mail package — the envelope, the letter, inserts, response forms, and so forth — we must understand certain fundamental rules that guide every successful direct mail effort.

Next to a personal visit or a telephone call, direct mail is the most intimate of all media. It is an "I-to-you" communication, and its success rests on the fundamental bond that is established when one human being communicates with another in personal and conversational terms. The trick in this mystery is creating that credible, personal "feel" of a direct mail letter. It is a far simpler task than generally believed, provided that the organization is willing to suspend certain rules about writing that have prevailed over the decades. Creators of a direct mail package must be willing to violate the rigid rules that might be described as "the barriers of artificial good taste and dignity." The rules pose a variety of "don'ts" that stand in the way of effective, believable personal communication. These are some of the proscriptive don'ts:

- *Don't* end a sentence with a preposition.
- *Don't* break up sentences. Have all sentences that form a complete thought included in the same paragraph.
- *Don't* use so many "I"s.
- *Don't* be repetitive.
- *Don't* write long letters. Be brief, concise.

When it comes to fund raising by direct mail, the list of taboos grows even longer:

- *Don't* be aggressive; that is, *don't* ask for money.
- *Don't* overstep the bounds of propriety; having once received a gift, *don't* ask for money again.

To create successful direct mail, the writer of the copy that will go in to the direct mail envelope must be willing to set aside the ingrained admonitions of teachers, parents, secretaries, friends, and others. No more sentences with the "I" deleted and the royal "we" inserted. No more lofty and well-balanced objective prose. In its place, write the kind of simple, straightforward language that a friend would want to read—personal and conversational. Good direct mail language describes the needs of the organization, the merits of the program, the beauty of the campus, or the evils of the disease that must be eliminated.

The techniques that are being reviewed in this chapter should not be used carelessly or casually. The writer or the designer of the direct mail package should endeavor to anticipate what the reader will follow. How will this person think? What will this person want? What might induce the eventual receiver of this package to open the envelope, read this letter, and respond with a gift?

When writing to someone who is a current contributor, care must be taken to give the envelope the appearance of a personal communication. The envelope must clearly display the name of the organization sending the letter. This may prevent the receiver from discarding the mail because the envelope indicates just "another one of those direct mail appeals."

Current contributors should be drawn into the spirit of the organization through the choice of a proper message, and through the choice of a proper envelope to deliver the message: A thank-you letter should be personal; an emergency appeal for funds should be packaged to achieve an urgent effect; and a campaign update or full report might be mailed in an oversized envelope. Care must be taken to package each piece of communication properly.

Furthermore, if there is a flood of competitive direct mailings to the organization's constituency, then care must be taken to use envelopes that are so different from the others that they draw the reader to the material inside.

Main Components of a Direct Mail Package

The carrier is the device that carries the contents of the direct mail package. In most cases, it is an envelope, but it may also be a tube or anything else that meets postal regulations. The carrier is an important part of the direct mail package. It is the first element seen by the prospective reader, and if it cannot compete effectively with other carriers that arrive at the reader's mailbox on a particular day, then it has not done its job.

Messages. Successful direct mail practitioners devote considerable time to creating the carrier. After all, it does not matter what goes inside if the carrier is never opened. The carrier forms the reader's first impression. It sets the tone and signals whether the message inside is urgent, personal, informational, or official.

- *Urgency.* Many successful formats can be used to convey urgency. The Western Union mailgram is one, and many other gramlike formats can be designed to do the same thing. Envelopes with a red stamped effect that screams "URGENT," "DATED MATTER," or "EMERGENCY DISPATCH" indicate that the material inside the envelope demands immediate attention.
- *Personal message.* The effect, the look of a personal message is first conveyed by the carrier envelope. In designing or purchasing an envelope for a communication, size is the key. Generally, the most successful "personal" direct mail packages are those in monarch-sized envelopes using ivory, grey, or light blue stock.

    The ultimate personal letter is handwritten and hand-addressed by the signer. Organizations that seek only a few larger gifts may be able to use this technique effectively. Others will have to compromise by using techniques that simulate handwritten personal appeals.
- *Official message.* Many times the organization will want to convey the importance of the enclosed message. To convey the "official" or serious nature of a communication, most copywriters use a legal-sized carrier with the upper left-hand corner of the envelope indicating some official sender such as "Office of the President" or "Office of the Executive Director."

The Envelope. The physical appearance of the carrier envelope can set an official tone. Large manila 9×12-inch envelopes have a certain official, business-like aura about them that attracts interest and curiosity. A slightly oversized manila envelope, or brown kraft envelope, such as those used by banks and lawyers, have an attractive quality about them that draws the interest of the reader to the material inside.

The envelope's physical appearance—size, shape, and color—and contents are important considerations in the preparation and development of an effective package. Two items also contribute to the carrier's appearance.

- *Teaser copy*. This is the text or headline that is printed on the face of an envelope to "tease" the reader into opening the package and reading the inside material. Examples of such copy are "Amazing Offer," "Are you prepared for the coming recession?," and "10,000 homeless sleep on our streets with no protection every night!"

   The conventional wisdom among seasoned direct mail practitioners is that these teaser devices are generally ineffective, particularly when they are designed by inexperienced copywriters. If teaser copy is to be used, seek the assistance of a highly experienced, creative copywriter to prepare text that is appropriate to the solicitation. Otherwise, consider that a plain envelope is often the best teaser.

- *Postage*. Beyond paying for the delivery of the mail, postage itself sends a message. The effect of a message can be diminished or ruined by the third class indicia that shows the package to be part of a bulk mailing. The importance of a larger envelope can be magnified with an attention-getting string of postage stamps marching across the top of the envelope.

   The reddish stamp of a postage meter imprint can project the image of an official letter, and perhaps would be appropriate in certain cases to hold the attention of potential readers. Utility companies, banks, credit card companies, law offices, and many other business entities use metered mail. Although such an imprint does not convey that the envelope contains a personal letter, it remains superior to the printed indicia.

The Letter. There is no one magic formula for writing a direct mail letter, but there are some proven rules. Most letters follow the traditional problem-solution form of advertising: "Acid indigestion: Take Rolaids"; "Our values are being eroded: Let's work together to strengthen our value systems"; "Children of poverty-stricken families are nearing starvation: Help us to gather surplus food to feed them."

Thus, the outline for a direct mail fund raising letter should follow a set of guidelines that will enable the reader to understand why the organization is writing (the problem), what it intends to do about it (the solution), and what the reader can do about it (again, the solution). Whether the style of the message is personal, urgent, or official, this approach applies. Within this general framework, the following suggested process will lead to an effective fund raising letter.

- *Get right to the point*. After writing the first draft of a letter, read the third or fourth paragraph. That is probably where the letter should have started. Do not fall victim to warm-up copy.
- *Recognize the reader*. Early in the letter, bring the reader into the message.

When writing to a person who has already given money, recognize his or her involvement and generosity; for example, "You have been such a good and generous friend that I thought I must write you immediately. . . ."

- State what the organization wants. Early in the letter—perhaps by the end of the first page—let the reader know what he or she can do to help solve the problem.

- *State the problem by using specific examples.* To obtain the reader's involvement or money, convincing copy that uses plenty of detail is required. No one outside the immediate family is going to contribute unless a detailed case is made as to why the money is needed, how it will be used, and how the individual's contribution will make a difference.

- *Restate the problem and its solutions.* The belief that recipients "never read those long letters" must be suspended when it comes to building an effective direct mail letter. Redundancy, to put an unkind word to the technique of reinforcing sales messages, is an essential quality of persuasion in the fund raising letter. That is one of the major reasons why the fund raising letter is long. People do not read everything word by word. They scan; their eyes move around the page. It is the writer's responsibility to make sure that the essential points appear often enough to make an impression on the reader's mind.

- *Ask for the money.* Be frank and direct in the writing. The letter is a fund raising letter. The writer should be precise in setting forth this concept. Tell the reader how much money is wanted, what it is wanted for, and the time by which it is wanted. Confusion is the enemy of good fund raising, and nothing is more confusing than an otherwise excellent letter that does not give the reader any guidance about what the reader can do to help the cause. "Please give what you can afford" is an empty statement. Equally as futile is the plea "I hope that you will help by giving today" without any suggestion about the amount that truly will help. Far better is a specific request: "Your $35, if received by March 5, will help to pay for this critically important study."

- *Ask again.* Just as the problem must be restated several times, so must the writer ask in a variety of ways.

- *Be timely.* It is normal for well-intentioned people to procrastinate. The writer should give some urgency to the appeal by stating that contributions are needed by a certain date. After all, if the individual's contribution does make a difference, then there must be some urgency, reason, and deadline for seeking it.

Other Components

Beyond these components, three others are critical in persuading the prospect to donate: inserts, response forms, and return envelopes.

Inserts. As with any communication, a direct mail package depends on credibility for success. The message must be believable. Sufficient information must be provided to encourage acceptance of the message in the reader's mind. That is why the package frequently includes more than a letter and a return envelope. The purpose of the insert is to reinforce and to add credibility to the entire package. Examples of inserts include newspaper clippings, draft budgets, photographs, testimonial letters, birthday cards, charts, graphs, and maps.

An effective insert *adds* to the effect of the mailing and is real and believable. Avoid the incantations of graphic designers who insist that your mailing will work so much better if an award-winning four-color brochure is enclosed. In direct mail, four-color brochures do not touch any responsive chord in the reader's heart. A valid narrative detailing of a real need will do this far better.

Response Forms. Direct mail campaigns that fail do so not because people will not give, but because they have not been directly asked to give. As simple as it may seem, the basic reason so many direct mail fund raising appeals fail is that they never ask for the gift. The objective of a direct mail package is to ask for and to receive a contribution, or to prompt the reader's support and participation, or to achieve whatever end the organization is seeking to achieve with its mailing. The envelope invites the reader's interest; the letter informs, motivates, and asks for the gift; the insert adds credibility; and the response form urges immediate action. Too often, too little attention is given to this key device.

The following are basic rules for creating an effective response device.

- *Rule 1: Resell the reader.* The response device must be a miniature direct mail package in itself. It retells the story contained in the letter and endeavors to motivate the reader to give. Much as a good lead paragraph in a news story does, the text on the response form summarizes the contents of the message and then impels action.
- *Rule 2: Involve the reader if possible.* People give or act not only because they know that an organization needs help, but also because they want to be involved. Wherever appropriate, seek the participation of the reader. Some mailings use surveys as part of the response form, others use petitions, and still others use a simple question-and-answer device. Consider adding exhibits. Response forms that use participation devices such as surveys, petitions, and referenda have the second goal of seeking money. As a consequence, *two* objectives must be emphasized, and the enclosed devices thus should dramatize the duality of the appeal.
- *Rule 3: Ask for action and be specific.* Whether seeking a gift of money or some other form of participation, a good response form will be direct in stating the action that is being requested. If the purpose of the letter is to ask for a contribution, then the message in the letter should be clear: Ask for the money and ask for it in specific amounts. It is critically important to help the reader to relate to a goal in a tangible, specific way. That is why,

whenever possible, requests for gifts should be related to a specific time period or to a specific need for the money as it pertains to programs.

- *Rule 4: Make sure that the reader knows what to do with the response form.* When people read their mail, they tend to separate the mail enclosures by retaining the response form and the return envelope, perhaps planning to use the return envelope to send in a check the next time they pay their bills. For this reason, it is important to be sure that the response form contains the required instructions for making a gift: to whom to make their checks payable, and where to mail the response form and the gift check.

There are myriad formats for the response form. When designing one, let imagination and common sense guide the process. Remember, however, that the response device must be created as part of the entire mailing piece. It carries the central theme and if it asks for the gift in a specific way, it will have done its job. If not, it will fail.

Beware of cost savings when it comes to response forms. Expenses are often a critical issue when the fund raising office is endeavoring to accomplish its task within a limited budget. The planner of the package is apt to fall prey to "inexpensive buys," such as the wallet flap envelopes that "we'll be able to use in every mailing from here to eternity—just think what we'll be saving by buying in quantity." If the desire to save money is stronger than the desire to create the most effective mailing, then the optimal package will not result.

As discussed before, the amount being requested is a strategic element, and one that is clearly stated in a well-crafted response form. Do not ask a person who has given $100 for $25; such "downgrading" should be avoided. By the same token, do not ask the regular $10 contributor for a $250 contribution unless it is known that this person can afford and has made a gift at that level before. The response form also should reflect a range of giving options from which the reader can choose. Once the contribution is obtained, response forms in subsequent mailings should acknowledge the initial gift amount and offer additional opportunities for upgrading subsequent contributions.

A final thought: Having labored over the carrier envelope, the letter, the insert, and the response form, the fund raiser's natural inclination is to include a business-reply envelope in the package and to be done with it. It would be wiser at this juncture to pause and consider what else can be included in the mail package that would enhance or reinforce the message and ensure the highest possible response rate. Return envelopes play a major role in this respect.

Return Envelopes. The return envelope conveys as much of a message to the reader as the carrier envelope, the letter, the insert, and the response form. It is a significant device with the facility to urge the reader to take some action.

When designing the return or reply envelope, consideration should be given to the overall effect of the mailing. If the message in the mailing is an urgent one, the planner should use a return envelope that creates a sense of urgency. A rubber-stamped message on the front of the envelope reading "OPEN AT ONCE—EMERGENCY RELIEF FUND" or some similar message conveys such urgency. A small calendar in the upper left-hand corner of the envelope with the appropriate deadline date circled in red also creates specificity and heightens the recipient's awareness.

A return envelope with the contributor's name and address typed in the upper left-hand corner, the name of the organization's executive typed in the center of the envelope, and a first-class stamp all lend a personal effect to the mailing. A brown kraft envelope or grey financial-style envelope with a return address to the organization's treasurer will convey a fiduciary effect.

The use of first-class stamps on return envelopes when seeking an upgraded gift solicitation should be tested. The results could be pleasantly surprising. However, the use of first-class postage on "cold" prospect mailings could be costly and unproductive.

Conclusion

Hanging on his office wall is a typed letter appeal signed by Helen Keller and sent to this writer's father in 1943. It is there as a reminder that the more things change, the more they remain the same. The basic precepts of sound and successful direct mail are constant: One human being communicates with another despite the advent of faster and more sophisticated technology.

The arrival of relatively inexpensive technology in the fund raising office has created the temptation to exaggerate the personal element in fund raising appeals. Transparent examples are in mailboxes every day. Witness the fictitious Ever-Blooming Tulip Company that sends computerized letters touting the benefits of its bulbs in the "Jones family garden at 123 Main Street." Other solicitors repeat the recipient's name thoughtlessly in a vain and frequently annoying effort to convince the reader that the writer is communicating on a personal basis.

Fortunately, other direct mail packages show thoughtful and proper use of technology. The most suitable application of technology is that which enables the user to (1) appropriately target segments of the mailing list with (2) messages that reflect the known interest of contributors by (3) asking for amounts that reflect past patterns of giving.

Resources

For both experienced professionals and newcomers to direct mail fund raising, two periodicals—*Fundraising Management Magazine* and *Direct Marketing Magazine*—that cover direct mail fund raising as well as the closely allied field of commercial mail are recommended. Both are published by Hoke Communications.

Two recent books on the subject of direct mail fund raising also belong in the practitioner's library. They are *Dear Friend. Mastering the Art of Direct Mail Fundraising* by Kay Lautman (1984), and *Revolution in the Mailbox: How Direct Mail Fundraising Is Changing the Face of American Society and How Your Organization Can Benefit* by Mal Warwick (1990). For a "hands-on" education, carefully study the mail in the mailbox each day and ask friends and associates to share their direct mail fund raising appeals.

Asset Building
Through Capital Fund Raising

One of the most important fund raising activities of the not-for-profit organization is the capital campaign. This intensive function is designed to raise a specified sum of money within a defined time period to meet the varied asset-building needs of the organization. These needs can include the construction of a new building, the renovation or enlargement of an existing building, the purchase or improvement of land, the acquisition of furnishings or sophisticated technical equipment, and additions to the endowment holdings. All of these are asset-building items. All can have a place in developing a goal for capital fund raising.

This intensive form of fund raising has passed through some interesting evolutions in past decades to take on different definitions and structures. The best known form of capital fund raising is the traditional, or classical, intensive campaign that has a specific goal related to building construction, renovation, or expansion. This is generally referred to as "bricks and mortar" fund raising because it pertains to the construction of a facility. In its early years, it also earned the interesting sobriquet of the "once in a lifetime" campaign because of the size of the goals and the size of the gifts that had to be solicited to meet those goals. That reference faded quickly. It is not unusual for organizations to schedule capital campaigns every five to seven years. Thus, "once in a lifetime" becomes a misnomer.

The comprehensive or integrated development program is reviewed in the final chapter of this book. This fund raising concept is based on long-term comprehensive analysis of the organization's diverse needs: current program support, special purposes, capital, and endowment. Once identified, all of the needs are incorporated into a single goal—generally, a megagoal—and addressed through a fund raising program spread over five, six, or seven years. The integrated development program is slower-paced and lacks the frantic intensity of the traditional campaign. It uses all of the techniques of fund raising in a coordinated fashion to meet its goal, whether annual fund, special gifts, capital fund raising, planned giving, or, particularly, big-gift fund raising. Its primary focus is on the very large gifts.

Endowment programs use many of the techniques of capital fund raising. A variation of this form is the extensive use of estate planning through planned gifts and big-gift solicitation. Endowment fund raising may at times follow the various designs of an intensive capital campaign to reach a specific goal. More often, it is slow-paced to permit more time for proper cultivation of planned gifts and big-gift prospects.

Another variation of the capital is the major-gift effort. This device does not require the discipline, the timetable, the complex volunteer-committee structure that is identified with the intensive capital effort. The focus is on an array of special-purpose needs that may require major gifts or big gifts. The development's strategy is to identify potential large contributors (individuals, corporations, or foundations) whose interests might justify a solicitation in the hope that it will produce a significant gift or grant to meet a special need. Essentially, this is a large-gift program that is designed and executed to raise the special-purpose money that is required from a limited number of major-gift prospects, thus avoiding the necessity of mounting an intensive campaign.

This chapter's primary focus will be on the traditional form of the capital campaign. The capital campaign has a number of characteristics that set it apart from other fund raising activities. Its strategy requires the solicitation of gifts that are much larger than those generally sought during an annual fund. Gifts to the capital campaign can be made in cash, as a pledged amount that is payable over a number of years convenient to the donor, or through the transfer of appreciated real or personal property.

Another characteristic of the traditional capital campaign is the involvement of strategically important volunteers who are capable and willing to commit their gifts and to provide access to or solicit from other potential donors. This "human capital" in the form of dedicated volunteers is a precious resource. Its availability—or its lack of availability—can affect the outcome of the fund raising effort.

Discipline is the nature of this intensive campaign. It requires unremitting attention to campaign details starting with responsible preplanning analysis, continuing through goal setting and leadership enlistment, to program execution and conclusion.

The analysis process starts with the determination of the various asset-building needs that will make up the goal. Too often in too many not-for-profit organizations, too little attention is given to this most important aspect of campaign preparation. The project cost statement is incomplete, carelessly contrived, or unrealistic in identifying and estimating the costs of these needs. Lack of realism and objectivity at this stage will cause serious problems later when potential donors will test their intent to give against their acceptance of the validity of the needs statement.

During the precampaign period when the size of the campaign goal is being considered, the management team and trustees of the organization must examine the eligibility of each capital need suggested for inclusion in the goal: Which needs should be included? Are they all valid? Are they all urgent? Are they all high priority?

Costs relating to construction, such as architecture, engineering, land acquisition, site preparation, furnishings, equipment, start-up, and endowment are essential parts of a needs statement for fund raising purposes.

Other costs also should be included as part of the total project. These are the hidden costs that, if forgotten, will complicate the financing process during or after the construction period. These include:

- *Fund raising costs.* All expenses that will be incurred as part of the capital campaign are a logical part of project costs.
- *Attrition costs.* This type of fund raising will attract large gifts that will be paid over some number of years. These are pledges or commitments to pay. Some of the value of these gifts will be lost through nonpayment. In a properly conducted campaign, however, this nonpayment should not exceed 10 percent of the goal. In most campaigns, attrition costs are considerably less than 10 percent. These losses should be anticipated and entered into the project's cost projections.
- *Inflation.* What impact will inflation have on project costs? What will actual costs be when the building is finished and ready for occupancy and use? It is difficult to estimate what the actual costs will be when the project has been completed, but during planning, a contingency factor for inflation should be added to computations of cost.

The Feasibility Study

Equal in importance to compiling and verifying needs is the precampaign planning study, which should examine the feasibility of the fund raising program to address the organization's needs.

What happens before capital fund raising starts is the most important part of the work. Questioning, measuring, qualifying, verifying, listening to hard answers to hard questions, weighing judgments expressed by potential key volunteer leaders and potential key contributors are all parts of strategic market testing. This process is called the *feasibility study*, the *fund raising planning study*, or *precampaign analysis*. In straightforward terms, it is a thorough examination of the institution's readiness to ask and the community's preparedness and willingness to give.

The questions most often asked are: Can the organization conduct its own feasibility study? Should the staff fund raising person undertake the task of interviewing key people in the community? Is it necessary to retain professional counsel to conduct this study?

It is quite difficult for an inexperienced fund raising staffmember or the executive staffmember without experience in fund raising to undertake this sensitive assignment. A staffperson often does not know what questions to ask, how to evaluate the answers, or how to judge the campaign's feasibility from the answers that have been provided. Objectivity is important to the process. The staffperson who is committed to the cause finds it difficult to remain objective. A certain tendency to convince the respondent seems to insinuate itself into the discussion when an enthusiastic staffperson conducts the interview.

A staff-directed study may not be wise economy for the organization that is seeking to save money while at the same time securing wise and objective input from community leaders.

How are the names of intended interview respondents selected? To gain the insights required to determine the campaign's feasibility, a list of key interview candidates is developed. This list can range from as few as thirty names to as many as one hundred fifty. It may include senior managers, program staffmembers, board members, current major-gift donors, potential big-gift donors, and campaign-leadership candidates.

All interviews are in-depth, generally lasting an hour or more. All information gathered during the interview is held in confidence; if it is divulged, it is with the promise that its source will not be attributed. Only in this manner can sensitive information critical to the progress of the campaign be elicited from interview respondents.

Hard, straightforward answers are required to the hard questions that will make a difference in the course the campaign will take. The following questions are indicative of the type that usually are asked during the feasibility study. They seek information about the eight most important components of the capital campaign.

1. *The appeal (case).* Is the case or argument for a capital campaign well defined? Does it reflect the institution's mission, goals, and objectives? Does it have a strong appeal? Will it be understood by the organization's constituencies? Will it motivate potential donors to give?
2. *The needs.* Have the needs been studied and accepted by the governing board? Are they valid? Do they reflect a sense of urgency? Are they understood and accepted as valid by the constituency that will be asked to give?
3. *The goal.* Is the proposed goal realistic for this community? This region? If not realistic, why not? What are the problems?
4. *The prospects.* How many gifts will be required and at what level? Do potential sources for these gifts exist? Are they expected to come from

Exhibit 8.1. Capital Gift-Range Chart: $3,000,000 Goal.

Gift Type	Gift Range ($)	No. Gifts Required	No. Prospects Required	Subtotal ($)	Total ($)
Strategic	300,000	1	4–5	300,000	—
	150,000	2	8–10	300,000	—
	100,000	3	12–15	300,000	—
	75,000	4	12–16	300,000	—
		10	36–46	1,200,000	—
Major	50,000	8	32	400,000	—
	25,000	20	60	500,000	—
	10,000	40	120	400,000	—
		68	212	1,300,000	—
General	5,000	50	100	250,000	—
	2,500	60	120	150,000	—
		110	220	400,000	—
	Less than 2,500	Many	Many	100,000	
					3,000,000

Note: It must be remembered that these charts are flexible instruments. The relationships in each phase—strategic, major, and general—can be altered. However, if the top gifts cannot be secured, then the campaign is weakened. For example, if the top gift of $300,000 cannot be raised, and the emphasis shifts to getting six more gifts at $50,000, then the number of gifts required at the $50,000 level would increase to fourteen, which requires the identification and solicitation of forty-two rather than thirty-two prospects. Can these prospects be properly qualified and solicited?

individuals, corporations, foundations, or associations? How many from each category and in what range? Is it possible to secure one gift worth 10 percent of the goal? Two gifts each worth 5 percent of the goal? What solicitation strategies will be required to meet the goal?

5. *The leadership potential.* If the campaign is to succeed, leaders must be able to give and to solicit at the upper levels depicted by the gift-range chart used (see Exhibits 8.1 and 8.2). Can this quality leadership be enlisted first from the membership of the governing board and second from the larger constituency? Who is a possible candidate to be the general chairperson for the campaign? What is the proper strategy to enlist this person?

6. *The timing.* Is this the proper time for a major campaign? Are there conflicting campaigns in progress or contemplated in the near future? What impact will they have on the one being discussed? What amount of time is required to ensure the success of this campaign: nine, twelve, eighteen, or more months?

7. *The public relations requirements.* Are there public relations problems that will have to be resolved before any campaign can start? What public relations or promotional activity is required to motivate the community to support this program?

Exhibit 8.2. Capital Gift-Range Chart: $1,000,000 Goal.

Gift Type	Gift Range ($)	No. Gifts Required	No. Prospects Required	Subtotal ($)	Total ($)
Strategic	100,000	1	4–5	100,000	—
	75,000	1	4–5	75,000	—
	50,000	2	8–10	100,000	—
	25,000	8	24	200,000	—
		12	40–44	475,000	—
Major	10,000	10	40	100,000	—
	5,000	20	60	100,000	—
	2,500	80	160	200,000	—
		110	260	400,000	—
General	Less than 2,500	Many	Many	125,000	—
					1,000,000

Capital Gift-Range Chart: $500,000 Goal.

Gift Type	Gift Range ($)	No. Gifts Required	No. Prospects Required	Subtotal ($)	Total ($)
Strategic	50,000	1	4–5	—	—
	25,000	3	12–15	—	—
	10,000	7	21–28	—	—
		11	43–48	200,000*	—
Major	5,000	10	40	50,000	—
	2,500	20	60	50,000	—
	1,000	70	210	70,000	—
		100	310	170,000	—
General	Less than 1,000	Many	Many	130,000	—
					500,000

*This is not an error. Gifts of appreciated property will increase the value. The table represents a *range* of gifts.

8. *The budget.* What is the budget that will be required to finance the campaign? Will this be adequate? Will the community accept this as a reasonable budget? Will the executive and the board make these funds available? What budget-control and reporting methods will be required for proper accountability?

This is the feasibility study: An in-depth evaluation of those factors that will make a difference as to whether or not the proposed campaign will succeed. Other factors that can easily affect the outcome of the program will be reviewed later in this chapter as well as in other chapters in this book.

The Capital Campaign Starts at the Beginning

Validating the needs that justify the capital fund raising and placing them in a priority order is a logical first step. Testing the validity of the needs and the reality of a goal is a reasonable second step. Building the plan around leadership enlistment, identification of major-gifts prospects, the development of time lines and designs for essential activities and the solicitation strategies that will flow from all of this must follow. The first and second steps have been cataloged in previous pages. This section of the chapter will address the essentials of planning and preparing for capital fund raising, drawing on the findings, conclusions, and recommendations stated in the feasibility study.

Articulation of the case for a capital campaign merits priority consideration at the beginning of the planning and preparing period. Staff-members, trustees, and volunteers who are not experienced in this specialized form of fund raising would tend to express the case for the campaign in simple terms: "We need a new building. We're trying to raise one million dollars to build the building. We're asking you to give so that we can start with construction." This is not a convincing case expression.

People give because they believe in the organization. They can identify with its mission and goals. They know the people who are part of the organization and they share their values. People will not give because the organization feels that it should have a new building. The case must be stronger, more compelling, more exciting, and more inviting to persuade prospects to give at the level required by capital fund raising.

The definition of the overall case for the organization (see Chapter 5) with its statement of mission and goals precedes the preparation of a case for the capital campaign. The rationale for this level of fund raising must come from the mission statement. It is the mission that identifies the human or societal needs that are at the center of the organization's concern. The programs or strategies that serve the mission, goals, and objectives give evidence to the needs that will justify the capital fund raising goals. Simply put, new building construction, purchase of land, acquisition of technical equipment, additions to endowment holdings — all capital needs — must contribute directly to program advancement, program improvement, or enhancement of services. "This will help us to teach better." "This will help us to serve more people." "This will provide us with the most advanced technology to help us respond more effectively to your health care needs."

As stated before, one of the oldest maxims of fund raising is, "People do not give to causes. They give to people with causes." Indeed they do. In contemporary fund raising, this maxim might be modified a bit. People give to people with causes, but they give to the cause that they know, understand, and believe in strongly.

It has been stated previously that the capital campaign is a demanding taskmaster. The most demanding of its disciplines is the unremitting focus on large gifts and the requirement that these gifts must be secured at the very beginning of the campaign.

What is meant by "large gifts"? For decades, planners of capital fund raising have been guided by the age-old rule that the first ten gifts in a capital campaign should provide funds that equal one-third of its goal, the next one hundred gifts should equal the next third, and all of the remaining gifts should provide the rest of the funds required.

Contemporary fund raising uses a different standard of gift production. The rule of thirds has been set aside, except in cases where it may apply to the very small campaign within a confined constituency. Capital campaigns seek to secure 90 percent or more of the required funds from 10 percent or fewer of the contributions that are received. To ensure this quality production, at least one gift at 10 percent and two gifts each worth 5 percent of the goal are sought at the beginning of the campaign.

This standard of giving can be portrayed in a form called, variously, a gift-range or a standard-of-gifts chart (see Exhibits 8.1 and 8.2). This instrument provides a method to determine the quality of gifts, the quantity of gifts, and the number of prospects that will be required to ensure achievement of the goal. A similar chart can be used to compute gift requirements for an annual fund. However, the arithmetic for an annual fund differs from the arithmetic that applies to the capital campaign.

The gift-range chart illustrates a method for computing the arithmetic of capital fund raising. It must be remembered that the chart does not represent a rigid formula. It is a flexible instrument that can be adjusted to the market, the environment, or the fund raising experience of the organization. The chart is valid only to the extent that the planning team can identify the prospects required in each gift range.

The ratio of prospects to donors at the top of the chart is four or five to each gift that is required. Fund raisers endeavor to identify prospects at this top range. Some of these prospects will *not* make a gift at the suggested level; they will make a smaller gift. Thus, a two to one ratio of prospects at the bottom level is acceptable, because a number of prospects at the top of the range will give at the $100 or $500 or $1,000 level rather than make the $100,000 requested gift. Thus, if the selection, qualification, and assignment of prospects has been properly attended to, then the chances for successful solicitation of gifts at each level are excellent.

Leadership and Campaign Management

The leadership team is second only to the appeal or case in its importance in capital fund raising. People who have the fire of leadership burning within their souls, and who have that deep commitment to the organization's mission, will drive any program through to success. Seymour (1966, p. ix) is expressive in describing their importance: "Every cause...needs people more than money. For when people are with you and are giving your cause their attention, interest, confidence, advocacy and service, financial support should just about take care of itself. Whereas without them — in the right quality and quantity, in the right places, and the right state of mind and spirit — you might just as well go and get lost."

The four components of the leadership team are the board of trustees, board or non-board campaign chairpersons, executive and key program staffmembers, and fund raising staffmembers. Each serves in a different functional relationship to the campaign.

The Board of Trustees. The governing board must be the activating force for the capital campaign. As the primary stewards of the not-for-profit organization, trustees hold the power to approve or disapprove capital projects and the fund raising activity that will support them. It stands to reason that if the trustees exercise their authority as stewards to approve the expenditure of funds for capital development, then they must accept the parallel responsibility of helping to raise the funds.

Non-Board Volunteers. Ideally, the general chairperson of the campaign should come from the board of trustees. But under certain circumstances, this may not be possible, practical, or wise. Board membership may be geographically dispersed, coalitional, lacking in leadership capabilities, or constituted of program experts who lack the socioeconomic clout that is so precious to fund raising. This is not a rare condition today, nor will it be in the decade that lies ahead. In these situations, campaign planners must be prepared to look elsewhere for those capable people who can provide the spark of energy that makes a campaign succeed. A properly developed constituency holds unexpected potential. There are times when this potential must be tested and invited into the leadership ranks of the campaign.

Executive and Program Staff. The executive and key program staffmembers can exert considerable influence to help prod the campaign to success. The executive as the visionary and program staffmembers as expert witnesses who are able to speak eloquently about the mission and program strategies can serve as information resources and as gift cultivators and askers. This is a precious resource to support the management team.

Fund Raising Staff. At times, in-house fund raising staffmembers can function as managers of the campaign, providing they have the experience and can afford to meet the time demands of the campaign. Experienced staffmembers with larger organizations can handle the assignment; overburdened staffmembers with a smaller organization will find it difficult, if not impossible, to cope with the assignment. Most of the time, more experienced outside professional counsel is retained to direct the campaign on a full-time resident-management basis.

If internal fund raising staffmembers decide to assume full responsibility for directing the campaign, then they should take advantage of the objective counsel that an outside consultant can offer. In either case, internal or external professional staffmembers must assume full responsibility for planning, organizing, and managing the program.

Fund raising staffmembers who have survived the battles of this kind of fund raising make doubly sure that key leaders are involved in the more important campaign decision-making process; they help to make those vital decisions that will affect the course of the program. Staffmembers' primary roles as activators and managers of the process are in seeing that the top leadership is provided with the information required for wise decision making.

Certain components should be noted on an organizational chart that depicts the campaign's working elements (see Figure 8.1 for an example). The primary element on the chart is the "campaign cabinet," "management cabinet," "second centennial fund," or whatever the management committee calls itself. This cabinet, council, or committee comprises the most capable campaign leaders who can be enlisted. It is headed by a general chairperson and staffed by the campaign director.

This managing group is made up of seven to nine thoughtfully selected individuals who possess the willingness, creative energy, and socioeconomic clout to stir the constituency to action, to enlist other leaders of equal caliber, and to solicit the quality gifts that will make a difference in achieving the organization's goal. This cabinet's responsibility will be to approve and to execute the plan, to identify strategic prospects with the ability to make the big gifts, and to accept the charge to solicit these prospects.

Any final delineation of the organizational chart will depend on the requirements of the campaign plan and whether it is complex in structure or neat, clean, and tight enough to discharge the task in the most efficient and effective manner possible. The caliber of the leadership; the availability of qualified prospects; the willingness of the trustees to give, to ask, and to work; and the organization's fund raising experience will prescribe the hierarchy of the chart and the campaign's timetable.

Establishing Goals

Generally, the senior management team consults with appropriate program staffmembers to make certain judgments about a possible campaign goal. These judgments are reviewed with the appropriate board committee and then perhaps with the entire board. A tentative goal will emerge from these discussions, one that will be tested during the feasibility study. The study's findings, particularly those pertaining to the goal, are discussed by the fund raising staff, by the trustees, and possibly by other influential volunteers who may be involved. Acceptance of the main and subsidiary goals should not be considered final until they have been cleared and accepted by the campaign

Figure 8.1. Capital Campaign Organizational Chart

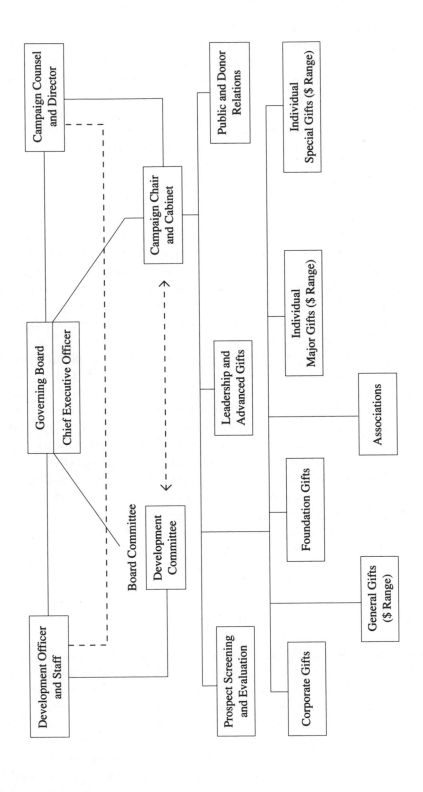

management committee. This is common sense. Those who have to assume responsibility for raising the money should be given the opportunity to accept the goal or to suggest any modifications they feel are necessary. Emotional and intellectual acceptance by those people who are key to the completion of the program is essential at this point.

The overall goal is the primary goal. Subsidiary goals reflect the obligation of various campaign divisions: personal gifts, staff and trustees, employees, corporations, foundations, associations, and others. In addition, there are divisions necessitated by the soliciting strategies, such as strategic or "pacesetter" gifts, major gifts, and general gifts. All are subgoals. All must be properly recorded and reported.

Assignments of goals to subordinate units must be based on realistic expectations of what these divisions are capable of producing. Are valid prospects available to each unit? Have these prospects been properly evaluated with suggested giving amounts appended? Are judgments about giving potential based on accurate information secured from authentic sources? Has the proper person been identified to solicit the right prospect for the right gift at each level?

Are Support Services Available and Adequate?

Support services can make a difference in a capital campaign. Sufficient to the purpose, they will help to advance the program. If they are inadequate, they will inhibit its progress. Before any serious activity can be set in motion, arrangements must be made to provide a competent staff, adequate campaign headquarters space, clerical staff trained in data management, proper use of telephones in working with volunteers, use of word processors, computer banks, calculators, and other equipment so important to efficient office management.

The office staff will have as its daily concern such routine but sensitive details as master records, alphabetical and divisional volunteer worker records, gift-recording-and-acknowledgment procedures, and campaign promotional materials.

The Budget

The budget is the description of the program in dollar terms. It should provide for sufficient funds to meet the expenditure requirements of an active, forward-moving campaign. Too tight a budget can be inhibiting; too generous a budget can invite questions and criticism from the campaign management committee and possibly from prospective donors.

The budget must be approved in advance by the chief executive and by the governing board. Regular monthly reports are mandatory and should be submitted to the chief executive, the campaign committee, and the governing board.

When setting up the campaign structure, it would be wise to include a position for an auditor, generally the treasurer of the board or a financial person who is supportive of the campaign. The auditor, especially a sensitive one, can be of considerable help to the campaign director by assisting in the overview of campaign financial activity and by submitting budget reports and campaign progress reports to the campaign committee and the board.

The Art and Purpose of Sequential Solicitation

Out of the accumulated wisdom of legions of capital campaigners emerges an imperative that will taunt all fund raising practitioners: To be effective, all fund raising must be "top down and inside out."

This dictum is translatable into sage counsel for the less experienced fund raising professional, for staffmembers and volunteers taking part in fund raising that requires the solicitation of the larger gift. The "top down" part of the equation pertains to a strategy known as *sequential solicitation*. The sequence starts with the largest gift that is required, which is listed at the top of the gift-range chart. This is essential because this gift will set a pattern for the remainder of the gifts to be solicited.

If the top gift is at the level required by the gift range, then all other gifts will relate to it. The top gift will set the standard for all of the remaining gifts: If it is too low, other gifts will drop accordingly and the outcome of the campaign will be in doubt. Sequential solicitation is a necessity to the goal attainment in capital campaigns. It forces a focus on the larger gifts and discourages a preoccupation with the smaller gifts at the bottom of the gift-range chart. Small gifts are graciously received, but they do not contribute as much to the desired outcome as do the larger gifts.

"Inside out" means that all fund raising should start with the "family" inside the organization. This is the internal phase of the campaign. With the completion of this phase, the program reaches out to the external constituency, reports what the family has been able to accomplish, and invites others to join in support. The family is the senior management and program staff, the governing board, employees, and then the broader constituency. An inviolable rule dictates that every member of the board should be considered a prospect and solicited as such. Each solicitation should be based on a specific asking amount determined by a committee of peers.

It stands to reason that if a board of trustees approves a program that will involve significant capital expenditures and the money to cover these expenditures will have to be raised through a capital campaign, trustees must commit themselves to contribute and to help raise the rest of the required funds. That is the primary meaning of the charge "top down." That is also the working meaning of the word *stewardship*.

The Words, Ideas, and Meaning of Fund Raising

All of fund raising has its supply of jargon, favorite words with special meanings to those who labor in Seymour's "vineyards" of philanthropy. The capital campaign has its own storehouse of jargon, some of it distinctly militaristic in expression. There is the *campaign* that is headed by a *general* chairperson. The campaign itself is divided into *divisions*. The divisions and the teams in the division are directed by *majors* or *captains*. The plan is comprised of the overall *strategy* and the operational *tactics*. The line of command is *hierarchical*. The command operates out of a command post that is campaign *headquarters*. In headquarters is a management staff that manages the *intelligence bank* and provides *logistical support*.

This is the form of the classical campaign, an intensive activity with a specific goal measured against the not-for-profit organization's specific asset-building needs. By the definition of the plan, the goal is to be achieved within a determined time frame, perhaps eighteen months or less.

There are other types of campaigns. These are generally referred to as "programs" rather than "campaigns." They are described in Chapter 23, "Integrated Development Plan as a Strategy."

Critical to the success of any capital fund raising program is the readiness of the institution to take on this complex, intensive, energy-demanding exercise. It is demanding because it focuses on command and attention to details, requires control, and insists on quality of leadership throughout. The "Test for Readiness for a Capital Campaign" that follows offers fund raising practitioners, managers, and trustees of not-for-profit organizations an opportunity to assess their preparedness for this level of fund raising.

Testing Readiness for a Capital Campaign

The test for readiness that follows is an adaptation of a comparable test prepared by two fund raising consultants, Arthur Frantzreb and his former associate, the late Francis Pray. The test will help senior managers measure an organization's preparedness to undertake a major capital campaign. As in all instruments of this type, the test score is not the final word in measuring readiness. Other, more definitive tests should be applied. If anything, the test for readiness will prove of value by alerting staffmembers and trustees to any weaknesses that may deter productive capital fund raising.

The twelve test components are explained in detail below. Scores for each component follow the test.

1. *Institutional plans.* Has a three-to-five year plan been prepared by senior staffmembers and approved by the board? Does the plan identify capital as well as current support needs for the planning period? Have staff and board members committed themselves to meet these financial needs through fund raising?
2. *Written statement of case, needs, and goals.* Does a written statement of the case exist? Does it identify the mission as an expression of the organization's values? Can a strong case be made for capital fund raising?
3. *Constituency.* Has the organization identified its constituency beyond

those who are closely involved with its programs? Has it analyzed the constituency for fund raising purposes by asking, Who are the potential contributors? Has a constituency cultivation program been devised to involve the constituency?

4. *Market involvement.* Do staffmembers and trustees know the makeup of the market? Are they knowledgeable about market needs, interests, and inclinations? Does the organization have a history of interacting with its markets and their various segments? Is fund raising structured so that it appeals to the specific interests and requirements of different market segments?

5. *Gift support history.* Has the fund raising program historically sought gifts for current program support, special gifts, capital, and endowment? Has this gift experience been cataloged in a way that enables staffmembers to analyze the potential for a capital campaign? Has the fund raising program been active in its approach to larger donors: individuals, corporations, foundations, and others? Does the fund raising staff spend time periodically evaluating the potential of its donor base?

6. *Prospect development plan.* Is there an active prospect-development plan in place? Does this plan include the presence of a prospect-development committee? Is time devoted periodically by staffmembers and volunteers to discuss large-gift prospects? Has this prospect-research information been recorded in a manner that will make it available to staffmembers and volunteers for use in their fund raising assignments?

7. *Efficient record-keeping system.* Is a proper record-keeping system in place? Does it provide for responsible storage and retrieval of confidential information? Are gift-receiving, gift-recording, and gift-reporting procedures set in place? Will these procedures permit the appropriate acknowledgement of gifts within forty-eight hours?

8. *Communications.* Is the communications program a two-way system of informing and receiving feedback from the constituency? Is the feedback heeded at the time that the communications program is designed and the materials are prepared? Does communications go beyond simple data dissemination—printed words on paper—to a more sensitive program that seeks to inform and to involve people?

9. *Fund raising staff.* Is competent, qualified staff available to plan and direct the capital campaign and to provide the level of support that volunteer leadership will require? Is this staff able and in a position to devote its full energy and time to this fund raising assignment? Will the rest of the staff, management, and program and support staff give their full support to the fund raising team during the period of the campaign?

10. *Involved board of trustees.* Have the trustees asserted themselves as primary stewards of the organization? Have they been active in planning,

approving and clarifying policy, supervising management of resources, and generating resources through fund raising? Has the board been responsibly involved in the planning process for the capital program? Are the trustees willing to give according to their abilities and to ask others to give to the capital campaign?

11. *Potential large gifts.* These are the top eight or ten gifts that are required to produce from 35 percent to 50 percent of the campaign goal. The top gift should be a minimum of 10 percent of the goal and the next two gifts each should equal 5 percent of that goal. Have valid prospects for these gifts been identified?

12. *Fund raising leadership.* Does the organization have as part of its actively involved constituency that quality of volunteer leadership—creative leadership—that will give the energy, enthusiasm, and drive that is necessary to press the campaign on to success? Will this leadership be willing to give and ask at the level required, and will it commit itself to do so?

Scoring the Test

Each item should be evaluated by those responsible for authorizing a capital campaign. Scoring will be subjective based on each person's interpretation of the factors represented in the questions. Scores should be recorded within the indicated ranges, from high to low according to the degree of readiness in each case.

Items	*Scoring Ranges*
Items 1 to 8	Score from a high of 5 points to a low of 0 for each item
Item 9	Score 10 high down to 0
Items 10 and 11	Score 15 high down to 0
Item 12	Score 20 high down to 0

The maximum score is 100. Very few not-for-profits can score this high. A score of 75 to 100 indicates a reasonable chance for success. A score of 50 to 75 means there are problems that may have to be addressed before any decision can be made to move forward with a campaign. A score below 50 serves as a warning that the organization is not ready and that there may be problems that will have to be addressed before any efforts can be made to start a campaign. Remember, the score for the last four items—fund raising staff, involved board of trustees, potential large gifts, and fund raising leadership—*total 60 points.* If there is a serious readiness weakness in this area, any plans for a campaign should be held in abeyance until these weaknesses can be corrected or eliminated.

Establishing
a Planned Giving Program

In recent decades, more and more organizations have come to accept the importance of endowment funds to provide increased annual income from investment earnings. Along with this awareness comes the realization that such funds are generally not acquired as quickly as those acquired through the annual support effort or through a campaign for capital funds. The gathering of assets in sufficient quantities to undergird a not-for-profit organization's operation and programs is an ongoing exercise because needs of the organization traditionally exceed available resources.

Planned giving programs provide a way for an organization to develop the financial resources that are needed to ensure its future. Planned giving also serves an organization's constituency by providing important benefits for personal and family financial planning, particularly in the preservation and use of accumulated assets.

This method of fund raising, with its orientation to the larger gift that comes primarily from the estate of the contributor, can and should be part of the total development program of all 501(c)(3) organizations, both large and small. It has its place in the small fund raising office with a more limited action by encouraging constituents to develop their own charitable gift plan through bequests, transfers of insurance, trusts, and contracts. And it definitely has a place in the diverse fund raising strategies of larger development programs.

The term *planned giving* is commonly used to describe a form of gift legally provided for by a contributor during his or her own lifetime. Cash or assets in the form of stock certificates or other real or personal property are relinquished by the contributor to make a gift as a trust, contract, or gift annuity. The principal benefit of the gift is not available to the organization until some future date when the gift matures—with the death of the contributor or possibly the death of a surviving beneficiary, or at the end of a specified term.

This charitable gift is generally made from a contributor's accumulated assets and is part of the contributor's overall estate plan—hence the term *planned giving*. In contrast, most annual-program support gifts are made from current income. Gifts from assets that make up the estate are made as revocable or irrevocable trusts, gift annuities, contracts, bequests from wills, testamentary trusts, or insurance policies.

Types of Gifts

The Deferred Giving Program created by Congress in the 1969 federal tax act defines the giving methods generally referred to as planned giving. (The terms *planned giving* and *deferred giving* are used interchangeably, although *planned giving* has greater acceptance within the fund raising profession. The term *deferred giving* has been set aside because, in reality, the making of the gift is not deferred. The gift is made by the contributor. It is the receiving by the not-for-profit organization that is deferred until the gift's maturity date. In addition, some planned gifts are immediate gifts, assets transferred from the estate holdings during a lifetime to satisfy a desire on the part of the contributor to make a large gift.)

These programs provide income as well as tax advantages to the contributor. The income can be for a lifetime or for a stated period of years, and the income can also be directed to other persons designated by the contributor. At the maturity of the gift—at the contributor's or surviving beneficiary's death or at the end of a defined term—the not-for-profit organization receives the gift's charitable remainder. These methods include the charitable remainder unitrust, charitable remainder annuity trust, charitable lead trust, pooled income fund, charitable gift annuity, and bequest.

Charitable Remainder Unitrust. With a charitable remainder unitrust, a contributor irrevocably transfers money, stock certificates, personal or real property to a trustee who pays the contributor and possibly others income for life or for a period of years as determined by the donor at the time the assets are transferred. The income recipients receive annual payments from the trust based on a fixed percentage selected by the donor and applied to the market value of the assets as determined each year. This means that the income will vary from year to year. (Note: The nation's laws set the minimum rate or the percentage that the trust can offer at 5 percent.) If the organization is named trustee of the trust, it determines the maximum interest rate that it will be willing to pay out to protect the integrity of the gift.

Charitable Remainder Annuity Trust. The charitable remainder annuity trust is similar to the charitable remainder unitrust in many respects, but with two important differences. The annual income that the recipient receives as a result of the gift will always be the same regardless of the changing annual value of the assets. The percentage selected by the contributor applies to the *original* fair market value of the assets at the time the gift is made, and that amount will pertain for the lifetime-income period. Once assets are placed in a charitable remainder annuity trust, the contributor cannot add to the trust capital to provide for a greater charitable deduction. In this situation, the contributor seeks financial security by expecting that a *fixed* amount of income will be paid annually regardless of market conditions.

Charitable Lead Trust. The income from the trust property is directed to the charitable organization for some period of years—often ten or more. At the end of the stated number of years, the trust becomes the property of the individuals named by the donor, such as children or others, or it can revert to the donor. The lead trust differs from the unitrust or annuity trust in that the charitable organization receives the income from the trust during the trust period rather than receiving the trust corpus at the end of the trust period.

Pooled Income Fund. Also known as a life income contract, a pooled income fund is the organization's trust fund. It operates very much like a mutual fund. A contributor makes a gift of cash or property to the not-for-profit organization with a request that the gift amount be invested in the organization's pooled income fund. The contributor receives income from the fund each year based on his or her share of the net earnings of the fund, or in the same manner that an investor in a mutual fund would receive income.

Charitable Gift Annuity. The charitable gift annuity is a contract between the contributor and the not-for-profit organization whereby the organization promises to pay a certain amount of money each year in exchange for the gift property.

Bequests. The simplest and perhaps most common of all planned giving methods is the bequest or devise. This is not a complicated instrument by any means, and yet too few organizations promote their use. A bequest is an instrument of a person's will that sets aside a sum of money or a portion of the estate or a portion of the estate's residuary for distribution to a charitable organization to which the testator is committed. The bequest can be small or large. It can be assigned without any qualifications by the contributor, or it can be designated or restricted for use to a program of interest to the contributor. Any bequests, particularly restricted ones that violate the values of the organization in any manner, can be rejected by the board of trustees.

Each of these income-providing planned giving methods has significant other benefits for contributors who are interested in the work of not-for-profit organizations. There is, of course, the psychic satisfaction of contributing to the support of a worthy organization. There are the more pragmatic rewards of tax benefits, all legal and all sanctioned under the nation's tax laws. A valid gift will offer savings in four areas: income tax, capital gains tax, gift tax, and estate tax. In addition, the recipient organization assumes the full duty of providing responsible management of the assets during the lifetime of the gift at no cost to the contributor.

The tax benefits and the benefits of avoiding management costs do not pertain to revocable gifts for the simple reason that under this arrangement, the contributor does not give up ownership of the assets. Thus, there is no immediate gift, and there are no tax advantages to the contributor.

Ten Characteristics of a Planned Giving Program

Although planned giving is a component of the complete or total development program, it has its own particular characteristics that differ from the annual and capital components in significant but complementary ways.

The contributors' objectives come first. In both annual giving and capital fund raising, the needs of the organization come first. The governing board and administrative officers have determined the program objectives to be accomplished and the related costs to be met before they ask constituents to provide the funds required.

In planned giving, the opposite is true. The contributor's needs must always come first. The contributor's needs may be to preserve accumulated assets in a manner that will provide for a spouse and other heirs, as well as to secure his or her own financial future through sound estate planning. In the potential contributor's mind these are priority needs. They come before those of the not-for-profit organization. Planned giving can help the donor achieve those objectives. One important caveat must be noted, however: The gift must be activated by a charitable intent. To justify income tax deductibility, the contributor has to want to make a charitable gift with the assets given away irrevocably. If there is no charitable intent, there is no valid gift; and if there is no gift, there are no tax benefits under the law.

The contributor has to *want* to make a charitable gift. If the individual is interested only in using the assets for investment purposes, then other investment opportunities apart from the charitable gift might prove to be more profitable and at the same time ensure continuing control of the assets.

The planned giving program does not start with a kickoff and end with a victory celebration. Once started, the planned giving program continues year after year with much of the current year's effort reaching a conclusion in succeeding years. This requires patience and understanding on the part of staffmembers, board members, and volunteers.

The contributor's largest gift will often come through planned giving.

Some individuals who have been providing support year after year will use this form of giving to make the biggest gift that they have ever made. There are also individuals who, because of their circumstances, can only make a large gift by using one of the methods that provides them a source of income.

A case in point: An elderly couple purchased a piece of real estate many years ago—perhaps a farm—at a time when the cost was very low. Because of inflation, the land has increased in value over the years from $25,000 to $400,000. Income from the property annually is minimal at the level of 1 percent of the property's value, which is insufficient to meet the needs of the elderly couple. If the property were to be sold to permit an investment with a higher income yield, the required capital gains tax would reduce the value of the assets significantly.

A gift of the property at full market value in some form of a charitable remainder trust or contract to a not-for-profit organization that the couple wants to support would enable them to avoid the capital gains tax, would provide an income at a minimum of 5 percent and possibly much more, would offer them an immediate income tax deduction based on the value of the charitable remainder as permitted by the tax laws, and would return a satisfaction to them for supporting a charitable program of their choice. The charitable organization would receive the assets at the maturity of the trust, or when the last income beneficiary died. The transaction would be legal, ethical, and morally proper in every respect.

To secure planned gifts, the organization must educate its constituency. It is mistaken to assume that a one-time mailing about this gift method or an attractive brochure that describes planned giving will fully inform everyone who needs to know about this type of giving. Repetition of information is necessary. Individuals who develop an interest in planned giving tend to accumulate information and become more and more interested in planning their estate assignments and distributions as each year goes by.

Among the questions asked so often by administrators and board members are these: What level of budget is required for a program of this type? What kind of a return can we expect on our investment? Can't we accomplish all of this through mass mailings? There are many others as well. Responses are guided by a number of institutional variables: Experience of staffmembers, the organization's fund raising history, the size and sophistication of the fund raising program, responsiveness of the constituency, and so forth.

Measuring the progress of the program is difficult. The dollar goal, the organizational steps, and the time schedule of an annual fund or a capital campaign provide definable goals. Because it is more apt to be spread over a period of time, planned giving requires a different set of values to measure the effectiveness of activities and relationships that lead to results. For example, it is quite unusual to complete a transaction during the initial visit with the planned gifts prospect. It is not unusual to devote as much as three months to as long as twelve or twenty-four months to the cultivation and solicitation of a potential contributor. The size of the gift might well justify this investment of time. The truth is basic that in the initial years of a planned giving program accomplishments must be measured more in the number of calls made, in the number of prospects that have been identified and developed, and in the effectiveness of the overall marketing activity than in the numbers of gift dollars produced. Gift dollars during the beginning years will be few.

Planned giving will impose a number of new responsibilities on the organization. Serving as trustees of charitable trust funds, charitable gift annuities, or pooled income funds makes it necessary for many charitable organizations to take on new investment, fiduciary, and administrative duties with which they may not be familiar. Board members and staffmembers must be briefed on their new responsibilities.

Staffmembers must be trained or retrained. Planned giving is a specialized activity that requires technical knowledge about the various gift methods associated with the form. An understanding and acceptance of these technical features can be developed through training. Such training must be repeated at least biannually because of constantly changing tax laws and regulations that pertain to this aspect of fund raising.

Planned giving contributors require as much time as do the prospects. This aspect of fund raising is seldom accorded the attention that it deserves and requires. The not-for-profit organization must provide continuing service to individuals who have made planned gifts. These contributors tend to become loyal advocates of the organization and especially of this form of financial support and often encourage others to consider making this type of gift. If satisfied with the results of the initial planned gift, these contributors become interested in making a second gift.

The initial and repeat contributions are quite often made because of the trust that develops between the individual and the staffmember or volunteer. Any failure to nurture this relationship is unfair to both the individual and the organization.

Prospecting for planned gifts carries many surprises. In spite of all the efforts to correctly identify and cultivate potential contributors, individuals who are not listed or identified as viable prospects will nonetheless make quite substantial gifts. This attests to the value and the attractiveness of this important fund raising instrument.

Testing Feasibility

An organization that contemplates adding planned giving to its fund raising program must attend to the planning and preparation in a proper and thoughtful manner to ensure itself the success it warrants. There are some probing questions that will have to be answered by the organization's chief executive officer, the governing board, and the fund raising staff should there be one. (Note: If there is no fund raising staff managing at least an annual giving fund, then the organization will have to think long and carefully about the wisdom of starting this type of program. The lack of basic annual giving activity would indicate that the organization has done little to condition its constituency to give. Planned giving can never serve as a substitute for annual giving.) These questions include the following.

How eager is the organization to embark on a full-fledged planned giving plan? Will the chief executive officer accord the program the time that it will require? Does the governing board understand its role and responsibilities? Will board members give active support to the best of their abilities? Is there a trained planned giving officer presently on staff? If not, will arrangements be made to employ such a person, or will a member of the fund raising staff be trained to assume the responsibilities of that position? Will a budget sufficient to the requirements of the program be authorized by the chief executive and the board?

Serious answers to these serious questions will prod the organization's leaders to examine all aspects of planned giving. This thoughtful approach holds a number of values for staff and board members. Perhaps the greatest value will be their heightened awareness of the benefits that can accrue equally to contributors and the organization through responsible management of this fund raising activity.

The not-for-profit entity that considers embarking on a planned giving program should examine its readiness to undertake such an endeavor. Procedures to carry out this evaluation vary according to the sophistication of the overall fund raising program.

Generally, the task of evaluating such readiness should be assigned to the fund raising staff. Although rare, sometimes when a governing board activates a program it will appoint a task force to conduct a study. In such a case, the board should authorize the retainment of a qualified planned giving consultant to assist the task force with the evaluation, or what may be called a planning or feasibility study.

It is important to make sure that each step in the preliminary process provides ample opportunity for as many people as possible to become informed about planned giving and the many benefits that it has to offer. This is particularly true during the study period. Board members, key staff members and key contributors should be involved to the extent that they can be. This nurturing process imposes a price in terms of time and energy on the part of the staffmembers and board members to give it meaning. The end results justify this effort.

The study should examine the organization's record of annual support. This should include an analysis of the organization's gift history: numbers of contributions, ranges of gift amounts by contributors from smallest to largest, the frequency of gifts, and the multiplicity of gifts from individual contributors during each of the years examined. The numbers of bequests and planned gifts received in past years, even though the organization does not have a planned giving program, should hold great interest for the study team. Has the organization conducted capital campaigns, and have these campaigns succeeded? What has been the organization's history in attracting large gifts, particularly gifts of assets in the form of real or personal property?

Other factors that should be of concern to the fund raising staff or the board's task force include the age of the organization; the age of its constituency; its history of accomplishments; its predictable future, which is based on whether the needs expressed in its mission are short-term or long-term; and the commitment of its board members to both the organization and the concept of a planned giving program. What start-up and continuing costs can be anticipated, and what are possible sources of funds for the "phasing-in" period of two or possibly three years?

Ideally, the governing board should be involved with this study in an active way through membership on the task force and through expressions and action of support. However, not all not-for-profits can enjoy the privilege and joy of a concerned and involved board. In this case, the staff—especially the fund raising staff—should bear the responsibility for finding out what will be required to move forth with a planned giving program. The study report prepared by staff should include the following:

- Specifications for staff and logistical requirements
- Policies and guidelines for managing a program
- Budget projections for the first three years
- Goals and objectives for the first year
- Training recommendations for staff and volunteers
- Plans for identifying and cultivating prospects
- Marketing plans
- Plans for recognizing and thanking contributors.

In accepting the planning study's or staff's recommendations to proceed with a planned giving program, the governing board must understand that it is committing itself and the organization's resources to the continuation and long-term implementation of the program. This is a necessity if the effort is to be more than perfunctory.

The Planned Giving Staff Position

The selection and assignment of the staffperson responsible for program execution is crucial to the success of the activity. The staff position is pivotal to the entire program. Whoever serves in that capacity becomes an energy center who actuates all activities that give life and meaning to the program. Rarely is the volunteer group self-activating when it comes to the formulation and execution of a program of this scope and complexity. This is not to demean any volunteer group, it is just a simple truth. The governing board or a committee of volunteers needs and welcomes the guidance that can be provided by a professional who is practiced in planned giving.

An organization starting a planned giving program has several options. First, it can assign the responsibility to a fund raising officer who is already carrying a full load but who is interested in learning about this form of fund raising. This person can be relieved of other development duties and assigned to this office on a part- or full-time basis. It is essential for this person to receive adequate training in the policies, procedures, and strategies of planned giving. This, of course, will activate the program, but it will do so at a pace slower than would occur if the organization were to employ a full-time, experienced practitioner to dedicate the time and talent to immediate program development.

A second option, of course, would be to employ an experienced professional to this position on the fund raising staff. In considering the wisdom of this step, the executive and the governing board must be willing to commit the required resources to make the program operative, and they must be ready to assure this new staff member that he or she will receive their full cooperation for the duration of the program.

A third option that is often considered by organizations is to delegate this responsibility to the chief executive officer. Usually, these organizations are not cognizant of the strict demands imposed by this fund raising activity. As a rule, the chief executive's daily calendar is too full to permit proper allocation of creative energy to this task.

A report issued by the Northwest Area Foundation of St. Paul, Minnesota (1980) described a training program undertaken by the foundation to help private colleges develop effective planned giving officers. The report followed the completion of comprehensive training for planned gifts officers of private colleges in the foundation's service area. The report attested to a significant difference in results over a ten-year period between planned giving officers who devoted their energies full-time to the function and practitioners who had to dilute their energies with job assignments unrelated to the planned giving responsibilities.

What are the attributes of a competent planned giving person? The following characteristics merit attention:

> *Good interpersonal relationship skills.* The ideal staffperson has the ability to relate effectively to other people and the capacity to develop a long-term relationship of mutual trust.
>
> *An apt student.* The ideal planned giving staffmember is capable of learning and coping with a technical body of knowledge that constantly changes, is able to adapt to the changes in the promotion of planned giving, is able to empathize with the needs and concerns of contributors, and is able to guide contributors to the consideration of these alternate methods of giving.

A motivator. The ideal staffperson is able to motivate and inspire volunteers as well as prospective contributors.

Experience in training others. The staffperson is able to train staff and volunteers to work with this complex form of fund raising and to accomplish their diverse assignments efficiently and effectively.

Self-motivated. The ideal person is able to maintain a drive and an enthusiasm for the work even though the results and the benefits to the organization may not be apparent for a number of years.

Experienced in making presentations. The staffperson is able to be coherent, sincere, and convincing in explaining planned gift instruments and their values to a variety of community groups; to board members, staffmembers, and volunteers; and at estate-planning seminars.

Public relations skills. The ideal staffperson is creative in devising and using methods that inform the constituency about the benefits that can be derived through planned giving.

Confidence in own skills and knowledge. Being properly schooled in the law and procedures of planned giving, the professional is confident about his or her ability to discuss the complexities of the instruments with the contributor's financial and legal advisers, including attorneys, estate planners, trust officers, and insurance counselors.

The Role of the Volunteer

The volunteer has an important role to play in the planned giving program as the bridge between the prospect and the organization. This person, who quite often is a member of the board of trustees, establishes and nurtures a relationship with the prospect that centers on mutual interest. In the process, the volunteer attempts to qualify the other person's level of interest in considering some form of planned gift and, at the appropriate time, brings together the prospect and the organization representative who can help this person carry out his or her objectives.

Volunteers need an orientation to the planned giving concept, but not for the purpose of making them experts on planned giving. The primary purpose of orientation is to help volunteers acquire a basic knowledge of this fund raising instrument and an understanding of the resulting benefits to both the contributor and the organization. In reality, the volunteer should require little knowledge about the technicalities of planned giving methods. A personal interest in and a commitment to the organization combined with a general knowledge of giving methods will suffice.

A strategic force in the design of a program is the planned giving committee. This is where the planning and the implementation begin. Working in conjunction with the planned giving officer, the committee can ensure continuity and results. Therefore, the selection of a volunteer to chair the committee and individuals (preferably volunteers) to serve on the committee requires serious thought and attention.

The committee chairperson should be a person who is respected within the community and has the respect of the organization. This person can be a current or former board member or an individual who has a strong presence in the community. He or she should be capable of recruiting the individuals needed to make up an effective committee. Among the attributes that might characterize the worth of this candidate are knowledge about and belief in the organization, an understanding of the mission and its values, and advocacy of the organization's overall fund raising program, especially planned giving.

This group is a committee of the development or fund raising council, which in turn is an official committee reporting to the governing board. The planned giving committee works in harmony with the planned giving officer in planning and executing the plan. The committee and the program's staff manager cooperate in preparing the plan. It is important for this committee to have a strong sense of participation in and responsibility for the formulation of the program. Certainly, this should lead to their direct involvement through the gift-making procedure. Committee members as active participants and givers generally are advocates for the program.

Committee membership should be open to but not limited to members of the governing board. Size will vary, but a committee of ten to twelve individuals would be a good starting point. Guidelines for selecting members should point to individuals who are familiar with the organization, who have a history of providing financial support, and who believe that the organization should offer planned giving opportunities to its constituency.

Some of these individuals should be older, or at that stage in life when endowing one's charitable interests has some appeal. The group also should include young and middle-aged persons who have influence among their peers and who can see the wisdom of long-range financial planning.

The question is often asked, Should the committee consist of or include professional advisers such as attorneys, financial planners, trust officers, and life-insurance representatives simply because these individuals are familiar with some technical aspects of this particular fund raising instrument? These persons can and do play an important role in the development and execution of the program. However, some organizations have found through experience when these professionals are on such committees that other members who are not knowledgeable about various aspects of estate planning tend to withdraw. They leave much of the committee's most sensitive work entirely in the hands of those members who seem to be most familiar with the forms of planned giving.

In some cases, this thesis is true. Board members may be quite sophisticated about these planned giving instruments. In many other cases, however, this is not true, because this form of fund raising is highly specialized and, as stated before, is subject to different interpretations in the changing legal environment. The professional adviser does not have the time and in many cases does not have the inclination to keep abreast of the more complex aspects of taxation and the law as they pertain to this charitable gift. The committee needs the talent that can be provided by the professional adviser, whether attorney, accountant, or estate planner, and so forth. However, committee members who are not professionals still have important roles to play in this program: They can serve as links or "door openers" to potential major prospects for the planned gift.

Some organizations have found one possible solution to this dilemma: Include one or two professional advisers on the planned giving committee while at the same time establishing an advisory committee made up exclusively of professional financial and legal advisers.

An advisory committee can be a productive adjunct of the planned gifts committee, involving as it does professionals with both working familiarity with some techniques of estate planning and a knowledge of the community and its potential for support. This committee should include attorneys, trust officers, estate planners, certified financial planners, realtors, and chartered life underwriters—individuals who serve as legal, financial, and business advisers to their clients.

In forming this committee, program planners should look within the organization's constituency for these professional advisers. Some of them probably are or have been members of the governing board or actually involved with the organization in some way.

The primary purpose of this committee is to advise the staff, the board, and the planned giving committee about the technical facets of the plan that relate to their area of proficiency. This committee can help provide training for staff members, volunteers, and board members as well as participate in clinics and seminars on wills and estate planning. It can serve by disseminating information about planned giving opportunities to other advisers in the community. Individual members of the advisory committee should not be asked to provide professional services on a volunteer basis. For example, an attorney who is asked to prepare a charitable trust agreement or to review a trust agreement should not be asked to volunteer this service. Valid professional services should be reimbursed at the standard rate.

The planned giving staffperson, with the cooperation of the planned giving committee, is responsible for preparing a plan of action that will include the following broad areas of activities:

- Planned giving methods included in the program;
- Policies and guidelines for managing the program;
- Prospect identification and cultivation, and definition of the marketing plan;
- Goals and objectives for the first year;

- Budget for the first year; and
- Donor recognition devices, activities, and plans.

Four procedures can be applied to develop the interest and to secure the involvement of nonstaffpersons who can have an effect on the outcome of the planned giving program. The individuals who should be involved are members of the governing board, the task-force study committee, the planned giving committee, and any other volunteer who might become part of the program. The four areas of procedures are (1) the planning and feasibility study, (2) the process of determining which planned giving methods should be included in the plan, (3) the establishment of policies and guidelines for the program; and (4) the creation of a contributor-recognition program that includes qualifying actions for membership.

Each of these procedures will provide an excellent opportunity for the participants above to develop an understanding of planned giving and the benefits it can provide to the contributor and the values it can bring to the organization. Although opportunities to involve a critical force of constituents as primary advocates of the plan exist, they will not be brought to fruition unless they are captured, channeled, nurtured, and allowed to develop. The pressures to push for quick decisions, approve plans, or accept ideas do not contribute to the program's effectiveness or its value to the organization.

Policies and Guidelines for Planned Giving

The consideration and definition of policies and guidelines is an educational process for both the organization and those principals who participate in this defining task. Each person — board member, manager, fund raising staffmember — benefits by learning more about the potentials and technical requirements of a planned giving program.

Six items require discussion during the preparation of policies and guidelines:

1. Who should be authorized to negotiate the terms of an agreement with the contributor?
2. Which committee should approve the terms of the agreement or contract before any final signing?
3. Who among the organization's staffmembers and officers should be authorized to sign the agreement or contract on behalf of the organization?
4. Should the organization serve as trustee of a charitable trust or should this responsibility be assigned to a bank, investment house, or some other financial entity?
5. What minimum amounts and other limitations should be defined for each of the planned giving instruments? This pertains to the minimum

gift that the organization would be willing to receive to fund a trust, as well as to the maximum payable interest rate.

6. Who should have the authority to accept gifts of appreciated property, particularly real estate: the development officer, the chief executive, or the governing board?

Suggested Policies and Guidelines

The following is an example of policies and guidelines that should govern the planned giving program. By their clarity, they will provide prospective contributors with a clear understanding of planned giving and its value, purpose, and advantages to both the contributor and the organization. Furthermore, they provide adequate guidelines for staff personnel.

Conflict of Interest. In all matters involving contributors or prospective contributors, the organization's interests come second. No agreement, contract, or commitment should be urged upon any contributor that would benefit the organization at the expense of the contributor's interests. No agreement should be made between the institution and any agency, person, company, or organization on any matter—whether investments, management, or otherwise—that would knowingly jeopardize the donor's interests.

Use of Legal Counsel. The organization should seek the advice of legal counsel in matters pertaining to its planned giving program and should execute no agreement, contract trust, or other legal document with any contributor without the advice of legal counsel.

Likewise, any prospective donor should be advised to seek legal counsel for any and all aspects of proposed gifts whether by devise, trust agreement, contract, or other form. In particular, the donor should be advised to consult an attorney on matters relating to both estate planning and the tax liability of a gift.

Confidential Information. All information about donors or prospective donors, including names, beneficiaries, gift amounts, estate sizes, and so forth should be kept strictly confidential by the organization and its authorized personnel unless permission is obtained from the donor to release such information.

Authorization for Negotiation. The board of trustees and such committee and officers as may be designated by it should be authorized to negotiate with any contributor of a charitable unitrust, a charitable remainder annuity trust, or a charitable gift annuity that follows the basic format of the agreements approved by the governing board.

Any agreements that are binding on the organization and that do not follow the approval forms should be approved by the board or its executive committee before final negotiations with the donor are carried out.

When any real estate or real property is exchanged for an agreement of any kind, prior approval of the board or its executive committee should be required before the property is accepted.

When the contributor makes recommendations on the handling of stocks or securities used to fund a trust agreement, these recommendations should be presented to the executive committee for acceptance before the trust agreement is signed.

Any two of the following should have the authority to sign planned giving agreements on behalf of the organization: the board chair, the president, and the treasurer.

Avoidance of Pressure Techniques. The organization should exercise extreme caution against the use of high-pressure sales techniques when negotiating with prospective donors. The task of all personnel should be to inform, serve, guide, or otherwise assist the donor in fulfilling a philanthropic intent; but never, under any circumstances, should the donor be pressured or unduly persuaded.

In keeping with this policy, all persons employed by the organization to administer or promote planned giving should be paid a salary or an hourly wage and should not receive any commission, which might give them an undesirable personal interest in any agreement.

Trustee. The donor should choose the trustee for a charitable remainder unitrust. If the organization serves as trustee, then it may but should not be required to engage the services of a bank, trust company, or other agent to administer any such trust.

Limitation on Trust Agreements. When the organization has been named as trustee, the fixed rate of return on both the unitrust and annuity trust agreement should be determined by agreement with the contributor and be specified in the trust agreement. It must be at least 5 percent, as established by law. It should be the organization's general practice to use the gift annuity rates as established by the Conference on Gift Annuities.

Ordinarily, the minimum amount required to fund a trust agreement should be as shown in the table below:

Agreement Type	Amount ($)
Unitrust	100,000
Annuity trust	100,000
Pooled income fund	5,000
Charitable gift annuity	5,000

If the organization serves as trustee without compensation, and it is competent to serve as trustee, then the terms of each agreement must be manageable and the end result must justify the agreement's requirements. This refers to both the amount used to fund the agreement and the age of the beneficiaries. If the organization chooses to serve as trustee, then the minimum amounts for the unitrust and annuity trust can be reduced to as low as $50,000.

Trust agreements involving more than two lives should have the approval of the governing board or its executive committee. No gift annuity should be made for more than two lives. And no exception should be made to this policy. No gift annuity should be issued unless the charitable gift, as computed by government tables, exceeds 10 percent of the amount transferred by the annuity. No exception should be made to this policy.

Any investment of funds, securities, or property received in a contract for a unitrust, an annuity trust, or a gift annuity should be administered by the board of trustees or such committees and officers as it may designate.

Intervals of Payment. Payments on gift annuities and lifetime-income agreements should be made at the contributor's choice: monthly, semiannually, or annually.

Final Distribution of Planned Giving Funds. Upon the demise of the charitable gift instrument's last income beneficiary, the present value of the gift should be transferred to the endowment fund of the organization unless otherwise determined by agreement with the donor.

Identifying Potential Contributors

The form of planned giving has been defined, and the policies and guidelines governing the activity have been set forth and clarified for staffmembers, volunteers, and board members. The course and the strategies for an interesting fund raising future have been delineated. The exercise now at hand is to begin the never-ending process of identifying prospects or potential contributors. This becomes a serious, continuing task for staff primarily by encouraging support from interested volunteers, particularly those who have already committed to a planned gift.

Constituency development, which was described in Chapter 4, explained the relationship of the L-A-I principle (linkages, ability, and interest) to the task of separating prospects from suspects. The planned giving team— staffmembers and volunteers—will work energetically to isolate prospects from a myriad of suspects and then devote the proper level of energy to convert prospects into planned giving contributors.

Every organization has an established constituency as depicted by the constituency circles in Chapter 4. Many not-for-profits have cultivated the interests of their constituencies by inviting them to give to the annual fund. These organizations are in a favorable position because, by studying their annual giving records, they can identify individuals whose support levels signal an ability to give and whose record of consistent support reflects confidence in the organization and the way that it serves its mission. These are the primary prospects whose interests and dedication should be nurtured. Quite likely, they can become major prospects for planned giving. What is the process? Where to start?

Begin with the family: volunteers at the governing, administrative, and service levels; staffmembers, employees, and current contributors are likely candidates because of their relationship with the organization. Past contributors, those who no longer contribute, can perhaps be reactivated through an interest in the planned giving methods and their benefits. People who are being served as clients sometimes hold potential as prospects, particularly those who are related to such institutions as universities, medical centers, performing and fine arts centers, environmental programs, and so forth.

Renew and revise the list at least annually. Names will be dropped for different reasons, others added. Seek to create a base of prospects from 10 percent of the constituency, including those people who are fifty-five years of age and older, as well as those who have been closely involved with the organization over a period of time. Target this 10 percent base for a continuing cultivation program through the mail.

Marketing Planned Giving

Marketing planned giving has two dimensions: The broad outreach program endeavors to touch the general interests of the larger constituency force and a focused effort informs and motivates suspects and prospects to inquire about charitable giving methods that will benefit themselves as well as the organization. Only a few of the people who could benefit by planned giving methods are aware of either the methods or the distinct benefits they return to the contributor. The organization that provides this information to its constituency will be providing a valuable service and will receive substantial support in return. The elements of an assertive marketing plan are described as follows.

As with any marketing plan, it is essential to know the needs, wants, and desires of the constituency, particularly that segment that contributes consistently. Interest in the organization is an important ingredient for success. Survey constituents; give them opportunities to tell the organization something about themselves and their interests.

Develop a packet of informational materials, three general-purpose booklets, that can be used to inform and educate the constituency about planned giving methods and the benefits they can offer contributors. The first booklet is really the case statement of the organization; it presents the mission, its purpose, and its value to the people the organization serves. The second booklet describes the various planned giving methods that the contributor can use to support the organization's mission. This booklet should emphasize the income benefits and how these benefits will enable the contributor to meet estate-planning objectives.

The third booklet is, in fact, a series of booklets, each describing a particular planned giving method. This booklet is not intended for widespread distribution; it should be directed to the person who expresses an interest in the program and who requires additional information about the program or a specific giving method.

These booklets and other informational materials can be purchased in quantity from a number of providers and imprinted with the organization's signature logo, name, and address. Some organizations prefer to write and print their own promotional materials to ensure that the content contains numerous references to the organization. In this case, it is essential that the content be reviewed prior to printing by qualified legal counsel to ensure accuracy.

Scheduled mailings to selected individuals are a part of the marketing plan. Generally, these mailings are made quarterly; each is concerned with a different issue such as "The Importance of Making Your Own Will" or "Is Estate Planning for You?" Each issue carries a response self-mailer that offers the prospect a chance to seek additional information.

The mailings serve a threefold purpose: They provide information that will be helpful to the reader, remind the reader that the organization has a planned giving program, and provide readers with an opportunity to get answers to their questions about estate planning, the importance of making a will, or how they can make a planned gift. Each piece of mail interaction provides opportunities for continuing personal contact.

Not-for-profits distribute newsletters to their constituents on a regular basis. Each publication should carry information about both estate planning and planned giving, especially about the simple bequest forms that can hold considerable value for the organization.

Professionally prepared videotapes are excellent communication tools, particularly with the national increase in the number of video cassette recorders in the home. This marketing innovation can reach out to a select segment of the planned giving market with information about the variety of giving methods available under the law.

Changes in the tax laws that either enable or restrict charitable giving create opportunities for community informational seminars. Many times, these tax law changes will affect the way people can give away appreciated property, and they will affect how people can make generational transfers of such property in a manner that reduces their taxes. Seminars that explain how the changes in the tax laws will affect people, as well as informational programs on the subjects of wills and estate planning, will attract interest and constitute a service by the organization to its constituency.

To be effective, these seminars or community informational events must be well planned and designed and advertised as an activity in response to the attendees' interests and concerns. Such events must never be offered with the self-interested intent of "informing people about how they can give to our organization." People will not respond to such invitations.

A well-planned event will involve individuals who are highly qualified professionals to serve as presenters, people who can speak authoritatively, such as tax attorneys, financial planners, trust officers, or capable representatives from the organization's planned giving staff. Attractive informational materials should be made available. Careful attention should be given to questions. By recording the questions asked and analyzing the apparent interest of the audience the staff and planned giving committee will discover where best to concentrate their efforts. The estate planning seminar offers double value: the opportunity to communicate information to the constituency and the opportunity to receive direct and valuable feedback. Follow-up is important and should be scheduled among the "things to do" during the immediate postevent period. These additional activities should be considered an important part of the marketing plan.

Workshops should be held for financial and legal advisers—attorneys and other professional advisers who are concerned about keeping up to date on matters that pertain to estate planning and planned giving. Planned giving specialists need to keep informed about changes, particularly in those tax laws that will affect this giving method. The organization can provide a service to professional advisers through some form of information update.

The personal visit or call by staffmember or volunteer is the most effective aspect of marketing. All marketing strategies are designed to bring this about. Practitioners refer to this as the "shoe-leather form of marketing" or the "ultimate transaction"—exactly what it should be.

Donor recognition is an indispensable part of marketing. It is a procedure for thanking and honoring contributors. Done properly and with sensitivity to the needs of the contributor, it can serve the larger, more pragmatic purpose of bonding that person to the organization and thus expanding the advocacy base.

One device that has been used successfully to honor contributors is the recognition club known as the Heritage Club, Foundation Society, Society of Patrons, or similar names that reflect the organization's mission. Many other devices have been conceived to give recognition to contributors who give at the exemplary level. Organizations have used these devices to achieve different fund raising objectives: to honor individuals who commit themselves to make a large gift on a continuing annual basis, or those who enter into one or more planned giving arrangements.

One of five actions should qualify a contributor for membership in a recognition program as it relates to the planned giving program: (1) including the organization in one's will, (2) naming the organization as the owner and beneficiary of a life-insurance policy, (3) creating a charitable trust, (4) participating in the organization's pooled income fund or charitable gift annuity program, or (5) making an outright gift of money or property to the endowment fund.

Creating a Recognition Program

The impetus to creating a program club must come from the planned giving specialist on the fund raising staff or from the chief development officer. The plan for such a club is expressed on paper, cleared with the organization's chief executive officer and then with the planned gifts and development committees, and then presented to the governing board for official approval. Board members' participation in the club should be invited at the outset.

A recognition club brochure is prepared and readied for distribution to a listing of primary prospects. The contents of this important publication should include the name and purpose of the club, a statement of the organization's mission, justification for an endowment fund, an expression of the fund's importance, methods for qualifying as a member, and a statement that explains what action can be taken to become a member. The names of board members and planned giving committee members should be included. If at all possible, it would be wise to list the names of any obliging charter members and other individuals who have already committed to planned gifts.

People who have had active relationships with the organization should receive the initial mailing of the recognition club brochure: board members, staffmembers, past and present volunteers, contributors with a record of support, and other known friends of the organization. Following this action, a "search" letter that announces the club should be sent to selected individuals who have an affinity for the organization.

A charter event is scheduled and charter members are invited as guests of the governing board. The purpose of this activity is to pay tribute to those who have played a major supportive role in the club's establishment. The agenda should include an expression of the club's value in advancing planned giving and the work of the organization.

It should become evident that a program of this definition and financial potential must require an operating budget equal to the scope of its endeavors. The cost of establishing and maintaining a program of this nature must be considered at the beginning of the planning activity. It is an item that should be investigated during the feasibility study period. The lack of funds is an inhibiting force. Some organizations have started programs without providing the needed funds to produce the results expected.

A fund raising staff that can claim success in the production of annual program-support funds or money for capital development should be sufficiently creative in seeking out funds from board members, current major contributors to the annual fund, and possibly from foundations at a level that provides the start-up funds for a planned giving program.

Is There Competition for Planned Gifts?

Often the question is asked, "Should we even consider planned giving when all other organizations seem to be doing it?"

The answer is *yes* if the organization wants to develop the financial resources needed for the years ahead.

The answer is *yes* if the organization wants to take advantage of its constituency's readiness to make such gifts as a result of the encouragement it has received from other organizations.

The answer is *yes* if the organization wants to help its constituency achieve family financial-planning objectives.

The answer is *yes* if relatively little has been done to take advantage of planned giving programs approved by Congress in 1969. Many years have gone by and only now is planned giving reaching maturity.

The answer is *no* if the organization is ready to concede to others the opportunity to cultivate the interest and support of its constituency. This will happen because people tend to respond to organizations that keep in touch and that help them with their charitable and financial planning needs.

Seeking
the Big Gift

There is hardly a governing board member, executive officer, staffperson, or volunteer of a nonprofit organization who does not yearn and express hope daily for the "big gift" that will make a difference in the fulfillment of the mission, goals, and objectives of their human service organization. Any listener would reply, "Whom have you asked? Are you ready to ask? Did you ask enough to compliment the constituent's capacity to make a difference? Did you show how the constituent can be a great philanthropist?"

The big gift may be $500, $1,000, $10,000, $100,000, $1 million, or $50 million. "Big" is relative to the organization's positioning of itself to seek unprecedented philanthropy. Then there must be study and strategy sessions to suggest to constituents with the "appearance of capacity" to provide generous investments in their preferred philanthropies. Big results come from big plans for big human and social impact.

The nonprofit sector lives in a field that needs positive thinking, positive attitudes, and positive motivation of people to share resources small and large to make the shift from the intangible feeling of caring for others to the tangible expression of sharing in positive, unselfish ways.

U Thant, one-time secretary-general of the United Nations, would have been an invaluable governing board member, chief executive officer, resource development officer, or volunteer of any nonprofit organization—and raise a storm—when he said, "It is no longer resources that limit decisions. It is the decision that makes the resources."

Philanthropic success begins with personal attitudes. Attitudes of an entrepreneurial character. Attitudes of a building zeal rather than custodial complacency or abdication of responsibility.

It is remarkable to look at the latent power for human good sitting in a million nonprofit organizations. To apply that power to humanity's needs, they await only the discovery of unhampered vision and release from self-imposed apology for their limited resources. Even contemplating the need for a big gift, fund raising practitioners tend to apologize themselves out of their responsibility to maximize potential by evaluating a value to society, planning for that value assessment, and presenting it to awaiting investors. There is a tendency to apologize for a lack of sufficient resources to maximize the goals and objectives rather than to settle for budgets that lead to excellence. There is no need to apologize for and excuse those who have the influence, affluence, or both to make a difference because of the weakness of the practitioner's vision, drive, zeal, and attitudes to assess the impact and potential of big gifts. Satisfaction comes with the numbers of gifts, rather than the numbers of dollars.

We insure our lives, our homes, our cars, and our valuables, *but we do not insure our values*!

Robert F. Kennedy said it for every philanthropy-bound nonprofit organization when he quoted what George Bernard Shaw wrote in *The Devil's Disciple* (1901): "some men see things as they are and say why? I dream of things that never were, and say, why not?"

Given the increase in the numbers of Americans who have minimum annual incomes of $1 million and the increasing numbers of individuals cited as decamillionaires, one might ask the following questions:

How many of these are on your governing board?

How many of these are among your constituents?

How many of these are in your community?

Who among your board members, volunteers, or staffmembers knows or can talk to these people? If no one, why not?

How prepared are you to invite these people and their spouses to visit your facility or to become involved except at timeworn fund raisers?

How prepared is your organization to invite these people to join your governing board? Why not? Most are the very entrepreneurial types you need.

To what purposes would you suggest their investment of $10,000, $100,000, or $1 million in your organization?

Do you have a design for your earned and deserved destiny, and do you know what that destiny costs?

Would *you* give $1 million to the organization you represent?

Do you still have fund raising "appeals" (which means "begging for a buck") or are you investment counselors for your organization's fiscal stability and security?

Are you still addressing people older than fifty-five only for planned giving when demographics show great wealth and philanthropic potential exist also in thirty- and forty-year-old people?

Are you aware that every living human being in the United States has a will under state law?

Have you prepared an investment portfolio that lists *all* the features in which people can invest through philanthropic commitments of $10,000 to $5 million and more?

Do you know the fifty to one-hundred constituents who hold in their hearts and hands the capacity to benefit the destiny of your organization forever?

Seeking the big gift can be related to the first discoverer of today's space ship odyssey. Even though Robert Goddard of Clark University was imprisoned for a while for suspected insanity, he said, "It is difficult to say what is impossible for the dreams of yesterday are the hopes of today and the realities of tomorrow."

In the Beginning...

In his unforgettable book, *MegaGifts* (1984, pp. 139–140), Jerold Panas reports from big-gift donors what can be called "management preconditions" for great philanthropic productivity. Coordinately, Cyril Houle's book *Governing Boards: Their Nature and Nurture* (1989, p. 232) is mandatory reading. Its advice should be heeded by every current and future board member and every executive staffmember who intends to ensure confidence-building features for great potential philanthropists.

Except for legal requirements, it is not important that a nonprofit organization has a governing board. But it is important *who* is on that board. It is the *who* that communicates confidence that the organization is deserving of big gifts because they will be managed properly by big managers, or the right governing board membership.

Next, in the management context, potential great philanthropists will look for adequate, responsible budgets to fulfill the organization's vision, balanced budgets, debt-free audits, gift and grant policies, and investment policies and retained counselors. Great philanthropists, whether individuals, families, business executives, or foundation executives, know the "management confidence game" and what to look for even though they may not say so.

On to the Future...

Potential great philanthropic investors will also look at the organization's plans for its future. Has the organization designed its destiny and determined the costs of that destiny or is it waiting for destiny to implement its design?

Given the enormous demographic data that are available locally, regionally, nationally, and internationally, and given the reality of *involuntary* forces, issues, and trends afoot, every nonprofit organization must have a plan for its future in realistic terms. These plans must be cost-projected, analyzed, and reviewed each year. The endowment must also contain endowment opportunities. These should relate to features, functions, services, positions, and departments that can be endowed. These elements can be removed from the budget to allow funds for items that never get budgeted.

This ultimate planning process is a marketing procedure for the big-gift constituent to note investments available in a marketing context. Such investment opportunities stimulate even remote interests and concerns that prospect research would never uncover.

Someone once said, "It's amazing in the game of life how many people choose bleacher seats." In the game of big-gift philanthropy, every organization must move out of the bleacher seats and position itself in the front row confidently to attract the unprecedented, confident, and sophisticated philanthropy of large sums through diverse resources.

Research, Research, Research...

Perhaps the greatest limiting factor that restricts confidence to seek big gifts is the absence of or minimal amount of research on prospects. It is the apparent intangibles that affect, positively or negatively, personal decisions to be philanthropic. Even business firms and foundations are staffed by people, and it is crucial to know them; their interests, concerns, hobbies, and eccentricities; education; family history; spouses and children; experience in the nonprofit world; residences; evidence of objective judgment and wisdom; civic, social, and fraternal positions; sports interests; religion (when appropriate); and failures. This is quite an order. But most of this information is public today. Therefore, the prospect research person in the resource development office may just be the most important staffmember.

In the *Houston Chronicle* of June 17, 1990, Cecil H. Green, philanthropist and cofounder of Texas Instruments, sums up in one sentence what giving is all about: "Our giving has been what we wanted to do. We never did it just because we were asked." Mr. Green has donated $150 million in recent years and has vowed to give it all away "down to the last nickel."

The availability or absence of such information sets the agenda for a systematic, progressive cultivation process that moves the potential philanthropic constituent from suspect to prospect to investor. Here prospect cultivation is an art of applied human relations. There exists no formula for successful cultivation. What is required is plain, raw genius for seeking out and interpreting *what is*, and tying it together with studied, creative initiatives for sequentially involving prospective candidates.

Why Give Anything, Anytime, Ever?

No one—no family and no business—is required to share resources. Philanthropy is the voluntary expression of a love of humankind. The rewards of giving are deeply personal, even spiritual. Therefore, the motivation for giving to any nonprofit organization must be expressed in an inspirational case statement or prospectus. That case is the sales story of the organization, its present services and its future in an expanding, dynamic world.

When done, even in draft form, the case should be market-tested in small groups of related big-gift prospects. Such groups of five to seven people are known as "chief executive consultation conferences." After ninety minutes of discussion of the case only, the meeting is closed. Ownership of the plan of the future results!

It is not unusual that certain large big-gift prospects require a special sales document (case) that is tailored to *their* studied interests and concerns. But when provided, they generally foster investments that secure financial stability for the organization.

Why People Give

It just may be that there is no greater sense of frustration, disappointment, or failure than to fail in the personal solicitation of a philanthropic gift commitment. There is, there can be, no standard form or process of personal solicitation to deal with a constituent's emotions, pride, resentments, priorities, or readiness whether the constituent is an individual, a couple, a family, a business firm, a foundation, an agency, or a religious or other type of organization. Each and all are individuals. Each has different attitudes on different days. So do solicitors.

Look at some of the reasons why people give. First, there is quiet, concerned, spiritual love for humankind; or voluntary philanthropic care; or an expression of personal values, ideals, and goals; or a deep gratitude for life, benefits, and services received. Second, there's personal and family pride; the opportunity to join in the organization's success; gratitude for personal achievements; and providing for tributes and memory. The oft-used explanations of greed and fear as reasons for giving are misrepresentations of basic human values.

Tax considerations are seldom—very seldom—the *primary reasons* for giving. If taxes are *the* reason for generosity, then the nonprofit organization may be "used" by the donor without any future consideration that the donor will support the organization again. Taxes constitute involuntary philanthropy.

Why People Do Not Give

Where adequate study has assessed a prospect's potential, there must be reasons—stated or unstated—why there is no favorable response. There may be unfortunate, unstated, and subliminal personality differences between the people responsible for cultivating the prospect or between the solicitors and the prospect. But there is more.

Sophisticated, experienced philanthropic donors and investors will inquire about the management preconditions that must exist—as evidence of confidence—to motivate early and generous commitments. After the actual solicitation interview, they may conduct their own research to answer the questions in Resource A (see page 297).

People with newly acquired affluence who want to be sure that their resources will be properly used need certain evidence of the organization's fiscal management and integrity. They also need answers to the questions in Resource A.

The art of persuasion, which challenges a prospect's ideals, concepts, values, and dreams, rests in the hearts, hands, minds, and talent of only a few individuals. Philanthropic giving is a two-way street. But when two needs meet, investments result.

Prevailing Assumptions

Within each human being is a philanthropist waiting to jump out. But before the door opens, the person must *want* to jump. The big-gift question is, how high?

The height of the jump can be determined by an experienced analysis of human reactions from a philosophical, psychological, theological, or sociological perspective. Then there is the entire matter of management, administration, solicitor training, and fund program preparation. Resource B (page 298) lists some of the factors of human behavior that are believed to be in the hearts and minds of donors and investors.

There are many differences between and among the impulsive donor, the habitual donor of small amounts, and the thoughtful, careful donor who responds to sophisticated, tender, and loving care and yet does his or her own investigation into the organization's validity and competence.

The meeting of organizational needs with prospective donor's needs for personal fulfillment becomes a mutuality of concerns and respect. Thoughtful giving begins with thoughtful asking, which always seeks an understanding as to why people do or do not give.

Deterrents to Success

Because successful big-gift commitments require careful positioning of the organization, marketing of its goals and objectives, market-testing of its case, comprehensive prospect research, volunteer enlistment and training, and strategic cultivation and solicitation processes, much can go wrong.

There are many and diverse reasons why solicitations for large gifts, and sometimes unprecedented philanthropic gift commitments, are not successful. Experienced solicitors must be analyzed in terms of their previous solicitations to determine in advance their characteristics, procedures, and previous results. These factors are covered in Resource C (see page 299).

The solicitation process is a highly specialized art of persuasion to induce participation in an activity that yields the intangible reward of personal satisfaction. It should be prepared for most carefully to achieve success. It must never be approached as a mechanical obligation. Solicitations of $100, $1,000, $100,000, or $1 million in which personal contact is expected first requires that the solicitor adjust his or her attitude. In fact, the attitude is the first element of communication, and it takes place even before a handshake. The manner of seeking the appointment, personal dress, eye-to-eye contact, smile, thanks to a secretary, compliments on the office or home or club — each and all constitute the "first impression" even if the solicitor and prospect have met before.

What the Prospect Thinks

Remember, the prospect is not obligated to give any of his or her resources. The task is to so involve the prospect so that he or she *wants* to be part of the solution, not part of the problem. The next task is to raise that part of the solution to the highest possible level so that the prospect/donor enjoys the greatest possible personal satisfaction in accomplishment. When this is done, participation the next time will be easier for the organization to determine, at greater levels, and with greater donor self-esteem for having participated generously in the organization's destiny, stability, and security.

But what process must the prospect undergo to ascertain his or her part in the program as presented? An interview request immediately alerts a prospect to prepare mentally for "whatever is to happen at the scheduled meeting." It is mandatory that staffmembers and volunteers anticipate the prospect's reactions to the solicitation. Some of these forethoughts are included in Resource D (see page 301).

All of these considerations can be telescoped into a spasm of consciousness lasting fifteen seconds or several agonizing months. But each person must and does weigh his or her own interests and concerns before committing to a relative modest or even generous philanthropic gift.

Therefore, fund program managers must condition each and every volunteer to anticipate the donor's psychological position during an interview. And one of the best ways — maybe the only way — to ensure that volunteers will perform as requested is to obtain their personal commitment first. No personal commitment, no assignment. When committed at the level expected of prospects, the volunteer is armed to be very persuasive and convincing about why and how he or she believes in and supports the organization.

Solicitation Strategy

Given all of the preparation and psychological marketing factors discussed here, what, then, must be the solicitation strategies for each individual, family, business, foundation, agency, or organization? These strategies, techniques, and forms of solicitation and giving are included in Resource E (see page 303).

With the basic solicitation process agenda listed in Resource E, the motivational case or prospectus for the organization is assumed to be the thread linking all parts together. The well-established admonitions for solicitors of knowing the case, giving first, making appointments personally (rather than through a secretary), and so on are given attributes of a well-planned solicitation program. The eventual success of any solicitation depends upon the judgment and sensitivity of the investment sales manager — the development officer — to ascertain the "readiness" of all concerned. The positioning of the organization, the investment sales program, prospect research and cultivation, and solicitor training reflect as much on the development officer as on anyone else.

Considerable time should be spent in ascertaining the best possible solicitation strategy for each prospect. Solicitation success must be designed; seldom is it accidental. There are three essential elements to plan for in the solicitation:

1. The *introduction* establishes common ground between the prospect and the solicitation team by generating charitable feelings about the mission, role, and experience of the organization.
2. The *argument* inculcates sympathetic interests to the mutual satisfaction of the prospect and the organization and its needs and gift opportunities.
3. The *summation* presents specific gift ranges and opportunities and describes the gift's impact on the organization.

When a solicitation team is present, there must be a specific role for each person in each of the three essential presentation elements.

Psychologists would argue that the presentation must proceed from an intelligent reasoning of the prospect's point of view, feelings, and opinion. Use the strongest argument first. Proceed to climax and then to anticlimax. Anticipate all possible counterarguments in advance to disarm possible negative positions taken by the prospect. Obtain a series of agreements from the outset of the interview. Let the prospect spin the dream. Analyze perceived strengths and weaknesses and then proceed positively. Not in defense, not with argumentative tone, but with "Let us look at it this way. . . ."

Asking for the gift commitment is a sales situation. The art of conversation (establishing common ground, making the case presentation, suggesting participation, persuading, responding, and closing) is an individual experience.

Many product salespeople are taught to sell by the book. But they have a tangible product. Philanthropic gift participation offers only the intangible rewards of self-satisfaction, gratitude in being able to share and to help, personal fulfillment, spiritual solace, and quiet pride.

Everyone—repeat *everyone*—who can sell the value, even the indispensability of the institution or organization confidently and enthusiastically *can* ask for a gift—if they realize that the donor innately desires to participate. Why not, then, proceed this way?

"We have discussed the program and how crucial it is that it be successful. I am sure that you know we have been busy studying the strategy for success that you would want assured. And we know that you know that we have discussed your participation.

"It is not my or our mission here to tell you what to do. We do want you to know that we had hoped that you would consider a gift in the range of $1,000 to $5,000 a month as your fair share as part of this program. [Always suggest a monthly commitment that is more palatable for every prospect whether for an annual or a five-year commitment.]

"It just may be that you will wish to have a larger part, or consider a challenging or matching gift, or a special memorial or tribute fund. We just don't know that."

What you feel determines what you say. Persist with simple, short analogy; seldom use emotion. Emotion is a temporary feeling. Appeal to reason. Present options from the bottom to the top of the scale of interests. Suggest a range of interests, a range of dollar commitments, a range of satisfactions—from participation to full underwriting of a gift opportunity.

Compliment the prospect appropriately, frequently, but not to the point of distraction. Draw out business, family, professional, and civic interests for temporary mental diversion. Then reintroduce the mission, the role, and the importance of the prospect and the organization's grateful appreciation.

Encourage follow-up. Suggest other meetings, other events, and other communications. Say "Thank you." "Thank you" is not said often enough and with genuine feeling.

And use a summation. It is far more important to know when to close than when to begin! Do not overstay the requested time period. When that time arrives, be prepared to leave. If requested to stay, then you are on the prospect's time, but do not remain too long.

In summary, recount the argument using fresh vocabulary. Avoid redundancy. Paint a picture—a realistic picture. Cite the hopes and apparent promises of the future. Spin the dream and whenever possible, use the prospect's own words to spin the prospect's own dream. This will give the prospect cause to think or rethink positions taken.

Thus, the introduction, the argument, and the summary in total constitute a creative sales event. It should never be viewed as just another meeting with "old so-and-so." The solicitation process should be designed as carefully as an appearance before a congressional committee, as a commencement address, or as a requested appearance for an IRS audit. If the event is prepared for carefully, then its results will be far more satisfactory than the events just cited.

Should a gift be offered that is so small as to insult the institution, the program, the objectives, and the solicitor, then decline the gift graciously and with the observation that it is inconsistent with the prospect's importance in the community and the organization's importance. Leave a discussion of participation to another time.

After an unsuccessful interview, a debriefing session should be held to plan a resolicitation by a different approach, a different solicitor, in a different environment. But always write thank yous for each interview, whatever the outcome.

Summary

All that we have we hold in trust for others as others have held in trust for us. Therefore, philanthropy and persuasion for philanthropy is a ministry for humankind. According to R. D. Sproul, Jr., in his book *Money Matters* (1985), "Money is not wealth. Money cannot feed, shelter, or clothe man. By itself, money cannot give physical comfort to anyone. . . . Money is a promise for future goods or services."

Webster's dictionary defines *philanthropy* as "goodwill towards one's fellow men especially as expressed through active efforts to promote human welfare"; or as "an act of deliberative generosity"; or as "an organization distributing funds for humanitarian purposes; an institution or agency supported by such contributions."

Webster's also defines *ministry* as "The action of ministering the performance of any service or function for another."

Big gifts result from big designs, big plans, big attitudes, big suspects turned prospects, big strategies, big ideas for big investments. Never planned, never implemented—never accomplished.

A hand not extended in giving is in no position to receive.

Case 1: A Self-Propelled Big Gift

En route to an airport, the chairman of a governing board development committee told of a prospect he knew who was near a decision about providing a $250,000 gift for endowment as a Christmas gift to the institution. I was asked if this kind of commitment could be used at that time to enlist three others for a $1 million gift and whether that would be appropriate. Of course, after my years of experience, I cited concern that each of the four should be prospects for that gift potential. If their gift potential was larger, then this might not provide them with the personal fulfillment they could have through larger personal commitments. I was assured that each had been part of our screening, rating, and cultivation process in the first gift level of $250,000, although known "capacity" was much larger for one or two of them. Although I had some trepidation, I suggested that the effort would be most worthwhile.

Somehow I was suspicious that the first donor cited was the driver himself. We had never discussed his gift, however. The planned capital fund program was scheduled for implementation the following spring. The $1 million gift total would be gifts of confidence and an inspiration for other governing board members, parents, families, and alumni. It would show that what had never been done could be done.

Soon thereafter, $1.1 million was reported as a Christmas gift for endowment!

Later the drive chairman told me that, having gone through the process of case development, capital fund program design, and other elements, he had never wanted to do anything more in his life than to give $250,000 — and to the organization of which he was a trustee. He had never given that much before to any organization. He personified Kahlil Gibran's ideal of giving "unasked, through understanding." In retrospect, the trustee could not have been solicited better, with greater motivation, with greater results, or with greater personal fulfillment. And he became a far greater solicitor because of his commitment. His eventual commitment to the program was $5 million!

This desire, this deep personal wish to be able to actually accomplish a special leadership, a personally fulfilling gift, is the goal of each and every solicitation. To lead the prospect to the point of *wanting* to give, to be part of a program, to gain personal satisfaction from doing so is the first desired result.

Case 2: Citing an Institution's Worth

I was retained by the Nelson Gallery in Kansas City, Missouri, to design a program to raise $10 million for art acquisition by the gallery's golden anniversary in 1983. Counsel told the selection committee that the goal did not befit the integrity of the gallery because the financial goal sought was first a public declaration of the organization's estimate of its own worth and not what it needed to get by. Thus I was retained.

There had been only three trustees since the William Rockhill Nelson trust had been implemented in 1929. There was no business office. There was no resource development office. Only a Society of Friends of six hundred members giving $150 annually were close to the gallery. A Friends of Art organization existed but was separately incorporated.

A management audit restructured the administration. A resource development office and business office were created. Prospect research was begun. A brief community audit resulted in counsel recommending by name nine additional trustees, a board structure, and bylaws. Counsel prepared a long list of endowment investment-gift opportunities from $25,000 to $40 million. The executive director was replaced without public fanfare. A large-gift prospect suggested a change in name to the William Rockhill Nelson–Mary E. Atkins Museum of Art. This also was done with no fanfare.

Counsel recommended a $50 million goal, the largest ever in the Kansas City region. He enlisted and solicited the chairman. No campaign was planned — only an asset-building plan for low-key, high-gift commitments. There were only seven committee members. Individuals and families were the highest priority prospects.

The close of the program reported $58,123,187. The twelve trustees accounted for 58 percent of the total. The trustee who suggested the $10-million program personally accounted for $11 million. There were 14 gifts over $1 million, sixteen of $500,000 to $1 million, and seventy-six of $100,000 and higher. There were only two planned gifts of residences.

There were only 265 rated prospects. In lieu of a campaign, a Golden Anniversary Tablet was created and carried in three special newsletters. Statement of intent gifts of a minimum of $50 per year for five years each placed one name on the permanent tablet when paid.

Of the total, 1,220 individuals and family investors gave 57 percent, ninety-five businesses gave 11 percent, and fifty-eight foundations accounted for 32 percent. Works of art counted for $15,880,628. Total costs, including the golden anniversary gala, were 0.8 percent of written commitments. At the close of the fund raising period, $4 million was committed, although not in writing and not counted. Solicitation had taken one year.

Case 3: Proof — Giving and Receiving

Every executive, volunteer, and staffperson in the not-for-profit sector must elevate him or herself in purpose above necessary but mundane administrative responsibilities. These duties should be interpreted as the administration of philanthropic ministry. Thus each and every constituent can be motivated to care about others and to share with others the bountiful blessings God has bestowed on us.

In the October 15, 1986, special issue of the *New Yorker*, "It's Time to Start Doing Good" (p. 77) reported the real-life story of Tom Anderson, an executive with the investment firm of Bear Stearns. His favorite book is the Bible, and yet he was only a $2 collection-plate donor at his church. He was challenged by reading in the Book of Malachi, "Will a man rob God? Yet ye have robbed me. But ye say, Wherein have we robbed thee? In tithes and offerings." In discussing this with a friend, the friend said to Tom, "Give God more money."

Tom wrote a check for $250 to World Vision. The very next day, an unproductive stock rose unexpectedly and covered the amount of the check. He gave away another $250. The same stock went up the next day. He sent $1,000 to a philanthropy. The stock advanced again. He now says, "I've never seen anybody try to outgive God and come up short."

The whole philosophy of working at Bear Stearns is "We like to help human beings." The firm's managing directors must give away a percentage of their salary and bonus. Here a firm's employees are inspired to be donors — to be philanthropists. The firm is not the philanthropist. Herein is a lesson for treating and crediting all business-firm matching gifts.

PART FOUR

MANAGING THE FUND RAISING PROCESS

An effective organization is a living thing: An organization *is* its people. People breathe life and purpose and energy into an organization. An organization has a manner, spirit, tempo, nature, and character. It has moods, joys, fears, and sorrows. But most of all, an effective organization has a purpose that is shared by all of its members and to which they willingly commit their efforts. People working together can do almost anything (Hayes, 1983, p. 3).

People working together in the independent sector do so out of a sense of service, a commitment to the mission of the organization with which they are associated. They share ideals, a set of values, a feeling of serving a cause that is much larger than themselves, and they draw a deep satisfaction from this service.

Leadership is a part of this commitment. It can be identified as that "something extra" that individuals must have in their spiritual makeup to achieve something truly great. Certainly, individuals involved as leaders in the fund raising profession must possess this special quality to help them perform as effectively as they must to generate the resources required.

The fund raising professional is in the delicate position of having to assert a quiet leadership, of having to accomplish so much through persuasion. Managing the fund raising program is a gentle exercise in helping people work together productively.

The Trustee's Role in Fund Raising

The classrooms of The Fund Raising School have served as a remarkable clinical laboratory since 1974, when the school was founded. More than 15,000 individuals have participated in the training, some from large institutions, many from medium- and small-sized agencies. Class enrollees have included chief executives, fund raising staffmembers, financial officers, program staffmembers, volunteers, and, quite frequently, trustees eager to learn more about fund raising. In classroom discussions or private conversations, many of these enrollees expressed a deep frustration that stemmed from their inability to induce board members to assume their rightful responsibilities in fund raising. The most common problem brought to the formal creative problem-solving session has been that of trustee apathy and lack of willingness to become involved in fund raising.

This chapter will address the need for trustee involvement in the fund raising process, articulate a rationale for this involvement, and explain the role of the trustee as a central force in marshalling the interest and the support of a constituency for fund raising.

The involvement of trustees in fund raising is critical to the success of the programs and vital to the fiscal well-being of not-for-profit organizations in this country. The trustee can be an important moving force for fund raising, its strongest advocate, and its primary volunteer exemplar. The dedication of the trustee can serve as an inducement to others to become involved.

This principle must be heeded if the organization intends to cope with increasing competition in the marketplace or if it expects a continuing high level of financial support from its constituency. It stands to reason that trustees must serve in the forefront of any effort to raise funds for the programs and services that they have reviewed, approved, and put in place as members of the governing board.

A trustee is an individual who is charged with the responsibility of holding the not-for-profit corporation in trust in the public interest and ensuring that it will function in accordance with its statement of mission. "First, the board should keep the overall mission of the program clearly in focus and satisfy itself that the objectives of the particular part of the work or units of the organization are in harmony with the mission" (Houle, 1989, p. 90).

A trustee, therefore, is a steward, a "keeper of the hall," in the Middle English etymon of *stieward*, meaning hall or "keeper of the pig sty" in the Old English meaning of *stigweard* or sty.

As a primary steward or primary "keeper of the hall," the trustee is fully accountable for responsible management of the organization's resources. This is an overview responsibility. Day-to-day management of the corporation is assigned by the board to the chief executive officer and through the CEO to the senior management staff. Final accountability to ensure that the mission is being served faithfully must reside with the members of the governing board.

In this role of primary steward, a trustee must be more than an overseer, a custodian, a casual adviser, a "sometime" participant, an absentee member, a misguided volunteer apt to confuse administration with governance, or a vociferous adversary maintaining steadfastly that gift making and gift seeking are *definitely not* the responsibilities of a board member. A trustee must be willing to espouse the cause of the organization by assisting it in securing the resources that are necessary to support the programs that are required by the statement of mission.

With the steady and increasing emergence of new not-for-profit organizations in an environment that is both complex and competitive, the formation of new boards and the almost frenetic efforts to recruit competent people to fill the positions on these newly formed boards is an awesome phenomenon. New board members who lack experience and any form of training in trusteeship resist efforts to involve themselves in fund raising. Organizations in general are not providing proper orientation for new trustees. There is minimal, if any, discussion of the trustees' responsibilities for fund raising. That there is confusion surrounding this subject is understandable.

Yet willing involvement by board members in fund raising has been the hallmark of successful programs of past decades. This is becoming less and less of an accepted responsibility in the present period despite sometimes frantic efforts on the part of staff to encourage trustees to accept fund raising responsibilities. If trustees continue to decline such invitations, the alternative to volunteer-centered fund raising will be staff-centered fund raising. This means that staffmembers will accept full responsibilities for *all* fund raising activities: planning, organizing, and managing; researching, qualifying, cultivating, and soliciting prospects; acknowledging, following up, renewing, and upgrading gifts of contributors of record; and providing full accountability for the program.

What is wrong with this? The profession is beginning to mature. Many highly experienced, well-qualified practitioners fill its ranks. These are men and women in the profession who are as capable as the trustee in soliciting the large gifts and every variation of the more sophisticated planned gift. So, what is lost by assigning the full task to the professional staff?

Much is lost, in fact, if the effort is not made to involve even the most reluctant trustee in fund raising.

- Trustees can be the magnet that draws the volunteer to work on behalf of the organization. Absence of the trustees creates a void. Other volunteers who question why the trustees are not involved will hesitate to fill that void.
- Trustees as well as other volunteers help to identify potential contributors, involve themselves in the prospect cultivation process, and accept the responsibility to solicit.
- The volunteer's link to prospective contributors may be much stronger than the staff linkage and possibly more of a factor in closing.
- Trustees are the visionaries, the advocates for the organization and its fund raising plans, spokespersons for the urgency of the needs and the validity of the programs. As volunteers without a vested interest, they can give powerful testimony to the worth of the services and thus justify the gift.
- Trustees and other volunteers can serve as "door openers" to facilitate access to prospects for both planned gifts officers and staff solicitors of large gifts. The personal contacts that many trustees have with major prospects are valuable assets for the fund raising program.

Much is written about the place of the trustee in the corporate structure of the not-for-profit corporation. The subject is widely discussed with enthusiasm and with wide variations on the theme of trusteeship. Some believe that only the board sets policy, others are firm in their definition that policy setting is a shared task of a trustees–executive partnership, one of cooperation in an environment of mutual respect. In general terms, it can be said that these are the responsibilities of a governing board as generally accepted:

- to hold the corporation in trust;
- to define and to interpret the organization's mission:
- to review and to set policy that is compatible with the statement of mission;

- to acquire, to conserve, and to manage the corporation's resources in a responsible manner;
- to select, to nurture, and to terminate the chief executive;
- to internalize and to communicate the values of the organization;
- to serve as responsible change agents by encouraging and involving itself in long-range planning;
- to approve long-range plans;
- to approve programs that are responsive to the needs that are central to the organization's mission;
- to ensure fiscal solvency;
- to serve as a body of advocates for the organization, interpreting the mission, and always being accountable to the constituency; and
- to serve as a court of last resort.

The Organizational Triad

Two phrases—"to acquire, conserve, and manage the corporation's resources" and "to ensure fiscal solvency"—emphasize the need for board members to become involved in fund raising. If programs approved by the governing board require financing—and inevitably they always will—then trustees will have to work with and support staff efforts to produce the required revenue.

Each element in the organizational structure offers the potential for synergism. This can be depicted by a triad of interlocking circles with separate circles representing management, programs, and support (see Figure 11.1). The management circle includes governance because both have the task of ensuring responsible management. The second circle, program administration and execution, justifies the organization's existence. The third circle shows the support division, which must direct its total energy to advocacy building, constituency development, fund raising, and community relations. The support division's productivity can be enhanced considerably if the governance–management partnership can demonstrate responsible stewardship of the trust and full and continuing accountability to the constituency that it serves. The division's work can be further served by the responsiveness of a competent, caring program staff that serves the human and societal needs reflected by the organization's mission statement.

Fund raising becomes difficult, if not impossible, if the organization suffers from inept management or if the programs are badly contrived by a staff that is careless, incompetent, and inattentive to the needs that it should be serving. Fund raising can never function apart from the organization, apart from its mission, its goals, and its program and apart from its governance and management structure. Fund raising derives its energy and its reason for existence from the cause it serves. It has no existence by itself. It has no meaning beyond the meaning accorded to it by the accomplishments of the governance–management–program team.

Figure 11.1. The Organizational Triad.

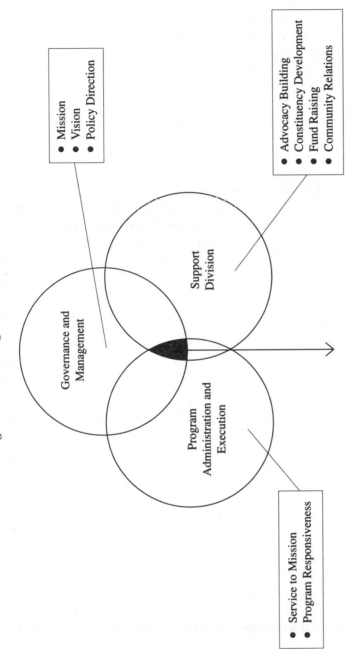

- Mission
- Vision
- Policy Direction

- Advocacy Building
- Constituency Development
- Fund Raising
- Community Relations

Governance and Management

Support Division

Program Administration and Execution

- Service to Mission
- Program Responsiveness

Combines the best creative energies of all three organizational entities

Synergism becomes evident in the triangle created by the intersection of the circles. This union maximizes the creative energies of governance and management, the program staff, and the fund raising staff.

The authority and responsibility for fund raising must be assigned to the governing board. Day-to-day execution of fund raising programs can be delegated to the proper staff by the chief executive. The flag for fund raising must always fly from the flagpole of the board and the senior management office, reminding everyone of the interrelatedness of responsible management, responsive programs, and productive fund raising.

Trusteeship: A Link to the Constituency

The Wheel of Roles and Responsibilities is explained in some detail in Chapter 4. As stated in the description of the wheel, board members fill many roles in the community, opening up opportunities for contacts with people through family, vocation, recreation, church, education, and social and political contacts. Truly, each board member is a window to the world for the organization and in this strategic position is able to facilitate the networking that is so essential for effective fund raising.

An Asker Must a Giver Be. The mere power of gift making moves a person to ask another to give. Gift making reflects a commitment. It states forthrightly, "I believe. I can affirm the values of this program. And because I believe, I have made my own gift, and I am asking you to join with me in support of this most important work."

A solicitor who does not believe in giving or is unwilling to commit a gift in advance of any solicitation is not in a strong enough position to ask others to give.

What is a proper contribution for a board member to make? This can be determined only by the trustee. The only determinant that the person making the contribution can apply is, "Is this gift a true expression of my commitment to this cause? Is this the kind of gift that would be considered generous by a peer?"

These questions do not have to be answered orally. No one has to confess to the amount of the contribution. Commitment communicates itself. If the contribution is truly generous according to the board member's circumstances or set of values, then the gift *is* truly generous and will empower the trustee to ask another person for a similar or even a larger contribution.

If the contribution is at a token level or significantly below the person's ability to give, then this person will find it difficult and even uncomfortable to ask another for a contribution. Generous giving according to ability to give is a major spur to effective solicitation. Conversely, failure to give will and does inhibit many trustees. This is one major block to solicitation by board members. A contribution in the form of time, talent, and energy in the

performance of board duties is not sufficient to accommodate the requirements of true stewardship. The often-expressed rule of stewardship is to "give
of your time, give of your talents, and give of your financial resources." This
counsel is far superior to the crude charge to board members that they
should "give, get, or get off." It is superior also to the convoluted canon that
board members should "give or get $5,000 each." This discourages the person
who is able to give more, and it penalizes the person with limited resources
who can give only $50.

The Myth of Limited Opportunities

A continuing myth that is daunting to trustees and staffmembers alike holds
that fund raising is becoming so competitive that the wells of philanthropy
will soon run dry. The myth is only a myth. George A. Brakeley, Jr., a highly
respected dean of the fund raising profession, reiterated his favorite thesis in
lectures to staff of his early company: "There are uninvited billions to be
raised out there. Your job is to invite them in."

Giving USA reports that philanthropic growth over the past twenty-five
years supports Brakeley's contention that an abundance of human and financial resources is available to organizations of the independent sector that ask
for them properly. Philanthropic support in the form of voluntarily contributed dollars and service will continue to be available to not-for-profit organizations. It is the belief of this writer that by A.D. 2000, total philanthropy in
this country will exceed $225 billion. An awesome 90 percent of that munifi-
cent sum will come from people, providing that there is no cataclysmic
intrusion such as war or depression to interfere with this remarkable growth
in human generosity.

The informed, fully involved, and supportive board member who
understands philanthropy and who can accept it as a force for human
advancement will be the major catalytic force in making all of this happen. A
continuing, magnificent human accomplishment, such philanthropy will
serve as a tribute to the unselfish dedication to values that move and inspire
the human spirit.

Managing
for Results

Fund raising is a complex management function. One of the most important areas within that function is the productive management of the people involved with fund raising. As with effective fund raising, effective *people* management is about *relationships*. In fund raising management, these relationships are diverse and multidimensional.

The People Who Make Fund Raising Happen

Staffmembers. In many organizations, the number of paid development staffmembers is quite small. "One-person shops" are not unusual: Of those who attend The Fund Raising School's basic course, the majority are from development offices of fewer than ten people, including support staffmembers.

The typical development office in a medium-sized institution will consist of a development director, an associate or assistant development director, an administrative assistant or secretary, and professional staffmembers to handle one or more of the following areas: annual funds, major gifts, special events, public relations, planned giving, and capital campaigns. Additional support staffmembers may include data-entry or donor-base managers. Other professional and support staffmembers should be added, as budgets permit, in the areas of greatest need.

Volunteers. To leverage institutional resources, volunteers become an integral part of the "staffing" of most organizations, especially in a one- or two-person office. Volunteer coordination is usually part of the overall management responsibility of the development officer, and systems for encouraging volunteer efforts and productivity have to be developed along with systems for managing staff.

Fund raising volunteers include board members with specific leadership responsibilities (for example, committee chairpersons for development, special events, annual fund, capital campaign, corporate development) as well as board and non-board members of those committees. In most organizations, the development director staffs these committees and has responsibility for arranging meeting times and places and keeping minutes for each meeting. Maintaining good volunteer relationships is pivotal to the success of the fund raising effort.

Donors. The third dimension of the fund raising executive's people-management responsibilities is donor relationships. Although donors are not technically part of the staff and not volunteers, they are all vital to the success of the development effort. The conscientious stewardship of donors strengthens the organization's overall fund raising ability.

Whether staffmember, volunteer, or donor, each individual who interacts with the development department (or executive director if there is no development department or director) can potentially affect the organization's ability to raise funds effectively and fulfill its mission.

Essentials of Good People Management

Most fund raising managers are familiar with basic management principles. There is an enormous amount of popular and scholarly literature on effective management practices, and many theories have been developed about managing people for results. In the midst of all the theories, a few basic practices survive time and trend and form the basis for managing people effectively:

1. respect for one's self and others;
2. open communication;
3. confidence in one's own abilities to manage and lead;
4. personal and professional goals that are clear and achievable;
5. belief in the organization's goals and the importance of seeing them accomplished;
6. trust in others;
7. ability to delegate, reward, and provide feedback;
8. a belief that "systems liberate" — that people function best in a structure that systematizes routine tasks and encourages creative approaches to tasks that are new and unusual;
9. consistency, including standards and expectations that are broadly communicated and understood; and
10. accessibility.

These ten assumptions underlie the material in this chapter.

The development of a management "style" is an evolutionary process. Because fund raising professionals manage multiple constituencies, consistency is important: It is confusing to those who are being managed to realize that different standards and practices are applied to others who are managed by the same person.

Finally, it is well to remember that good management begins with self-management. All of the concepts and theories that apply to effective management of others have value and application in managing one's own energy, output, goals, and effectiveness.

Challenges in Fund Raising Management

Managing the people who make fund raising happen is made even more challenging by problems that lead to development staff and volunteer burnout, including conflicts and problems with other staffmembers or board members and the pressures of meeting fund raising goals.

Fund raising is not a process that can be isolated from the activities and goals of program and administrative staff. Successful fund raising requires and deserves support from the entire organization.

Among the most common problems that face fund raising executives in their people-management responsibilities are the following.

First, the development function is not understood by board members, program staffmembers, and other managers. The development function must be marketed internally. "Internal marketing" is a process in which the development officer and staff provide regular information to board, program, and administrative staffs about the successes of the development effort, the impact of contributed income on program development, the linkages that have been forged with funders in the community, and the heightened visibility of the organization that has resulted from public relations and marketing programs. Strategies for promoting understanding of the development function include:

1. Presenting information at board and staff meetings about the functions of the development office;
2. Communicating regularly about successes in funding proposals, mailings, or events, including "good news" bulletins when major gifts are received;
3. Telling program staffmembers when information they provided for a direct mail letter, proposal, or brochure had a major impact;
4. Letting staffmembers know what the development office can do for their specific programs, interests, and needs by holding monthly brown-bag lunches at which new funding sources are presented and ideas for proposals are discussed; and

5. Linking program staffmembers with donors who are interested in their work and inviting the donors to cultivation activities and events.

Such strategies can ease potential tension, open communication, and promote understanding of the fund raising function.

Second, development is often considered peripheral; when budget cuts are made, they are made in development. To some extent, this is related to the problems of internal marketing. Because it costs money to raise money, and because the investment in fund raising takes time to yield a return, there is a tendency to cut the development budget when finances are tight. Internal marketing of the development function helps counter this and gives fund raising staff a respected role in the budgeting process. When cuts are inevitable, development staffmembers and fund raising volunteers should participate in the planning for downsizing, realizing that severe cuts in program funding alone would diminish essential agency services and ultimately reduce the integrity of the fund raising message.

Third, limited authority is coupled with wide responsibility. Sometimes, against the advice of or without the knowledge of the development manager, decisions are made by board and administrative or program staffs that have major financial impact. When such decisions are made, the fund raising manager should communicate the impact that the decision will have on fund raising. For example, if a new program is to be launched that will require considerable seed funding, then the development officer should ask for assurances about the amount of institutional support that will be available to meet the additional responsibilities.

Other situations have lesser impact: The board chairperson and/or executive director may make inappropriate appointments to development-related committees, or they may commit the board or staff to an activity or project that falls outside the development plan. In instances such as these, the fund raising executive should exercise professionalism in conveying a firm response to the decision and expectations about future involvement in such matters.

Fourth, key relationships must be developed. The earlier list of individuals (staffmembers, volunteers, and donors) with whom the fund raising executive interacts does not cover all relationships within the organization. *Vertical relationships* must be developed with the CEO or immediate supervisor, with the board chair and trustees, key volunteers, major donors, top prospects, and development staffmembers. *Horizontal relationships* must be built with program staffmembers, clients, vendors, and other professionals in similar organizations and professional societies. The fund raising manager must concentrate large amounts of time on these people-intensive functions.

Fifth, a "professional stance" must be modeled. A professional stance is a major management concept, one that reflects self-respect, self-confidence, confidence in the organization, and a belief in personal and organizational goals. It evolves from an ability to use professional skills, to project a positive attitude, to enroll others in a vision that will move the organization to the next level of achievement, and to act on one's own principles and ethics while upholding those of the profession. There are three major reasons why a professional stance has become such an important aspect of a development manager's responsibilities.

1. The fund raising executive is often the "face" of the organization in the community. He or she is a primary contact with board and community members and other not-for-profit and professional organizations.
2. The response of external audiences to an organization's management integrity is important in the overall advancement of the institution's goals in the community.
3. Constituents—from board members to those who attend events only occasionally—assess the organization by the professionalism of its development staff.

A professional stance conveys a posture of pride rather than apology. This is basic to the success of the fund raising process, and it affects the attitudes that volunteers have about working with organizations to raise money.

There is an internal dimension to professional stance. Not only does it enhance the organization's perception among nondevelopment staff and external constituencies, but also it provides inspiration to development and administrative staffmembers. Those just entering the field or having recently joined an organization will practice the performance standards and behavior demonstrated by their managers. A professional response to personnel and other organizational issues empowers staffmembers, deescalates conflict, encourages leadership, and provides important role modeling. A professional attitude characterized by discretion, confidentiality, ethics, and integrity is vital to both the internal and external images of the development function.

Two threats to a professional stance are goal and functional displacement. Development officers are frequently hired with the admonition that they will have to "raise their own salary" in the first year—or every year—to justify their jobs. In accepting such a condition, development officers diminish their own professionalism. A board or executive director, by framing the job in these terms, is encouraging *goal displacement*, one of the major obstacles to effective fund raising management. Such displacement diverts the development officer's professional focus from fund raising for the programs that are meeting the needs of the community to fund raising for his or her own salary. When this happens, energy and incentive are drained from the fund raising effort and the public may perceive a self-serving motivation in the fund raising effort.

Functional displacement also erodes professional confidence. In this practice, organizations load the development manager with many other tasks and functions that fall outside of development and still expect the fund raising goals to be met. Fund raising practitioners must set limits on the tasks that can be performed outside of the development function unless there is a clear understanding by the executive director or board chair that certain fund raising assignments will have to be delayed or left undone. This is not to say that the development officer should refuse to be helpful in times of need or crisis, but functional displacement becomes a problem when it is chronic or when no consideration is given during evaluation to unrelated assignments that may have delayed achievement of the fund raising goals.

Although these challenges place pressure on fund raising managers, certain key practices and strategies foster productive interaction among staffmembers, volunteers, and others who are vital to the fund raising process.

Strategies for Managing People Effectively

Developing a Workable Fund Raising Plan. A development plan provides the basis for leading staffmembers and volunteers, balancing priorities, working with major donors on funding priorities, and responding objectively to the demands placed on the fund raising professional staff. The plan is based on the long-term vision for the organization, and it must be consistent with the organization's mission (see Chapter 5). A plan is a road map for staffmembers and volunteers and a source of institutional credibility to donors. The planning process is nearly as important as the plan itself. Broad involvement by staffmembers, board members, volunteers, key constituents, major donors, and others who are primary stakeholders in the organization will engender feelings of ownership and responsibility for the plan. An annual day-long planning meeting that involves a broad representation of organization staffmembers, board members, volunteers, and donors will encourage consensus on priorities. The planning session is enhanced when the fund raising manager has prepared an evaluation of the previous year's plan.

Fund raising plans should include goals (general) and objectives (specific, measurable). Supplementing the fund raising plan are specific action plans that break objectives into smaller tasks to be assigned, with a time line, to individuals in the organization. Each person involved in a particular action plan receives a copy of the entire action plan so that there is a full understanding of the various tasks and assignments. Samples of fund raising goals, supporting objectives and time line, and an action-planning form are shown in Exhibits 12.1 through 12.3.

The fund raising plan is the principal resource for setting and communicating priorities with staff and volunteers. Although successful managers adhere to the basic direction laid out in the plan, they are also flexible, responding to the changing fund raising environment and the emerging needs of the marketplace. They realize that the development plan is a dynamic tool that should be reviewed, evaluated, and revised on a regular basis.

Exhibit 12.1. Fund Raising Goals.

1. To identify, cultivate, and build a strong and diverse annual donor base for the support of all programs.
2. To arrange and implement special events appropriate to the organization's purposes and resources.
3. To establish a planned giving program appropriate to the organization's resources and needs.
4. To expand volunteer participation in organizational fund raising efforts.
5. To develop and implement a public relations program that will enhance fund raising strategies.

Practicing Open Communication. Every staffmember, volunteer, and donor is an *investor* in the organization. Open communication of successes, challenges, accomplishments, concerns, and opportunities is the best encouragement for continued commitment to an organization and its management.

An open-door policy is as much a state of mind as an actual door that is open. Staffmembers, volunteers, and donors work more effectively when they feel they have access to the fund raising manager. Issues that are brought directly to the manager for resolution are much less apt to fester and become sources of gossip and dissent. While there are times when a manager's door must actually be closed for certain confidential meetings or telephone calls, at other times people should feel as though they and their concerns are welcome.

A great deal of organizational communication occurs in and around meetings. The following are suggestions for improving meetings and keeping communications productive.

1. Post or circulate the agenda for meetings in advance and invite additions or comments on the agenda.
2. Set a meeting calendar well in advance so that staffmembers, board members, and volunteers can be there. People feel excluded and resentful when they are repeatedly notified of meetings at the last minute.
3. Make sure that all meetings are held openly, or that the reasons for certain confidential sessions are understood.
4. During the meeting, be sure that all viewpoints are acknowledged. Encourage discussion and discourage escalated conflict. Become adept at problem-solving techniques and apply them to decisions that require broad consensus.
5. Post the minutes from staff, board, and committee meetings, or mail them to individuals who were unable to attend.
6. Deal immediately, usually right after the meeting, with difficult issues or people who have disrupted the meeting or have indicated their displeasure or distress over a particular decision. Do not let such situations fester.

Exhibit 12.2. Supporting Objectives and Time Line.

Goal 1: To identify, cultivate, and build a strong and diverse annual donor base for the support of all programs.

Objectives: Individual Donors

1. By September 1, 199–, information about United Way Donor Option giving to be promoted among existing donor base through newsletter or direct mail.
2. By September 5, 199–, staff to complete analysis and assessment of existing donor base and convert record keeping to new software.
3. By October 1, 199–, board and fund raising committee to review assessment and analysis and prepare preliminary fund raising goals based on existing donor base and projected return from direct mail (see next objective).
4. By October 1, 199–, staff and fund raising committee to arrange for rental of psycho-graphically compatible list(s) from reputable mail house for a direct mailing of approximately 5,000 pieces from which a 1 percent to 2 percent yield should be realized.
5. By November 1, 199–, staff and fund raising committee to develop, approve, and print a direct mail fund raising letter with appropriate brochure and remit envelope.
6. By November 1, 199–, staff and fund raising committee, working with the board, to select from the donor base those prospect listings and rented lists of individuals who should be solicited by techniques other than mail (personal solicitation, group cultivation or presentation, and so on) and develop strategy for carrying out these solicitations.
7. By November 5, 199–, staff and fund raising committee to make all assignments for one-on-one solicitations, mail or phone solicitations, and other volunteer involvements.
8. By November 10, 199–, staff and fund raising committee to sponsor a "PS-athon" for board members, committee members, and other volunteers to add personal notes to the direct mail piece.
9. By November 15, 199–, staff to release first-class presorted direct mailing.
10. By December 15, 199–, fund raising committee to plan and implement a minimum of one "Friends of the Organization" non-fund raising event in city, county, or both.
11. By December 20, 199–, board and fund raising committee to implement year-end mail and phone solicitation to selected previous donors and prospects.
12. By January 31, 199–, staff to develop and implement a process for ongoing prospect research and tracking.
13. By February 10, 199–, staff and fund raising committee to plan and implement a "thank-a-thon" for all year-end donors involving volunteers, including but not limited to board members and committee members.
14. By March 1, 199–, staff to prepare, with board and fund raising committee input and approval, a report on mail and phone results to date and a strategy for completing the renewal and acquisition cycle, including follow-up on "Friends" cultivation events.
15. By April 1, 199–, staff and fund raising committee to implement Objective 14 strategy by mail, phone, or personal solicitation.
16. By May 15, 199–, staff and fund raising committee to implement strategies for final follow-up on outstanding solicitations, including an additional or follow-up "Friends" event in city or county.
17. By June 1, 199–, to complete follow-up of outstanding solicitations and contacts for analysis during summer.
18. By September 1, 199–, staff and fund raising committee to evaluate previous September-to-June fund raising cycle and develop strategies for next year's cycle.

Objectives: Corporations

1. By the time of preparation for individual donor mailings (direct and select) and no later than November 1, 199–, staff to refine and tailor list of corporations that will match gifts to arts and social or human service organizations.

Exhibit 12.2. Supporting Objectives and Time Line, Cont'd.

2. By October 15, 199–, fund raising committee and staff to develop a plan for outreach to small businesses in the city and elsewhere in the county based on visibility to be gained and benefits of involvement. Plan to be presented to the board at the November meeting.
3. By October 15, 199–, using donor analysis, staff to prepare list of current and prospective corporate donors.
4. By January 1, 199–, fund raising committee to appoint corporate-development sub-committee. Subcommittee will be responsible for exploring corporate giving markets and preparing a recommended plan for cultivation and solicitation to be presented to the board at its March meeting.
5. By April, 199–, board to approve and subcommittee to target a financial goal and begin implementing a corporate-development program that will include strategies for approaching corporations in neighboring communities, with initial emphasis on [City 1] and [City 2].
6. By June, 199–, corporate-development subcommittee to sponsor a minimum of one corporate-cultivation luncheon, during which time executive director will explain the program, a video will be presented, and appointments can be arranged for one-on-one visits.
7. By June, 199–, fund raising committee and staff to report on growth in small business and corporate giving as a result of increased efforts.
8. By September, 199–, staff and subcommittee to evaluate small business and corporate giving and set budget figure for 199– budget.

Objectives: Foundations

1. By July 1, 199–, staff to conduct research into new foundations with potential for supporting organization.
2. By August 1, 199–, staff to prepare a comprehensive report on these foundations for purposes of fund raising committee review.
3. By September 199– board meeting, fund raising committee to present foundation market assessment to board for review and discussion.

Developing Job Descriptions for Staff, Board, and Volunteers. Job descriptions clarify the roles, relationships, and expectations within the organization (see Exhibit 12.4).

Employee job descriptions are the basis for effective performance appraisal and objective setting, and should include the following information:

- Title of job
- Basic responsibilities
- Reporting relationships
- Qualifications required
- Performance expectations (how the job should be done, as well as what should be done)
- Salary or salary range offered

All job descriptions should be reviewed annually to ensure that they accurately assess what is actually being done by employees. Sharing of job

Exhibit 12.3. Action Plan.

Date _____ Project _____

Page _____

Task or Responsibility	Responsible Person(s)	Date Due	Date Done	Comments

descriptions (exclusive of salary) builds respect and understanding of responsibilities within the organization. Occasionally, it is helpful to do a full departmental (or institutional) review of responsibilities to check for redundancies in assignments or gaps that need to be filled. When a staff position is created or becomes vacant, it is a good idea to assess all related positions and meet with the individuals who will work with the new staffperson. Restructuring positions and responsibilities can often boost employee morale and provide new opportunities for growth and advancement.

Volunteer job descriptions, including those for board members, detail individual and committee assignments and are vital recruitment and management tools (see Exhibit 12.5). Clearly defined expectations can help volunteers and staffmembers work together more productively, as well as serve as a basis for building respect for institutional goals and standards. "Full disclosure" through descriptions of expectations is a key aspect of successful volunteer enlistment and retention.

Maintaining Motivation When Staff Compensation Is Limited. Motivating without money is something many not-for-profits have learned to do well. Many of the principles for nonmonetary incentives are derived from a tradition of working with volunteers.

Recognition is one effective tonic for burnout. It can be administered in many ways and in many forms, and it should be consistent with how the person likes to be recognized. Recognition may take the form of special rewards that can be donated by businesses in the community (a weekend getaway, a basket of fruit and cheese, a gift certificate, and so on). The "employee of the month" may be rewarded with a special parking place (highly valued during winter or rainy months). Often, a personal note is all that is required: something that says "Thank you for making a difference." Sometimes, more formal public recognition at a board or staff meeting may

Exhibit 12.4. Job Description.

Title: Director of Development

Reports to: [Title of Chief Operating Officer]

Position Concept: The Director of Development is charged with the responsibility of managing activities related to the analysis, planning, execution, control, and evaluation of fund raising and selected public relations programs. The director works with and through the [board, development committee, foundation board, and so on] for all fund raising programs including public relations activities designed to support fund raising. Public relations programs that are designed to enhance and support the overall mission of [name of organization] are conducted under the auspices of [committee name] in concert with the administration, the board, and employees. The Director of Development also serves as the administrator's chief liaison with the [auxiliary or other support group], assisting it in its support role to [name of organization] in fund raising, community relations, and in-service programs. The Director of Development also serves as a member of the [management council name] by attending meetings as necessary for proper communication and coordination of responsibilities.

Principal Responsibilities:

1. Provides administrative and executive staff support to the [name of community fund raising committee or foundation] in all of its activities.
2. With input from board committees and staff, creates appropriate record-keeping system(s) for tracking donor participation, identification and cultivation of prospects, and volunteer involvement in programs.
3. Trains and supervises paid and volunteer support personnel in establishing and maintaining the record-keeping system(s).
4. Analyzes the need and opportunity for general public relations programs, works with volunteer and staff committees and task forces, and recommends programs that will enhance and advance the mission, goals, and objectives of [name of organization].
5. Manages the implementation of most of the public relations programs as they are approved, including serving as coordinator with outside consultants or contract services in the creation of specific projects. (Note: Some programs may be assigned to other administrative staff for implementation.)
6. In concert with the appropriate committees, prepares or initiates preparation of all content and materials needed for approved fund raising and public relations programs, including proposals to donors and donor prospects, gift recognition and acknowledgment materials, appeal letters, and so on.
7. Researches or initiates research and data compilation on potential individuals, corporate and foundation donors identified by board members, staffmembers, and volunteers by virtue of their gift history to similar organizations or activities.
8. Keeps up to date on current fund raising and public relations programs, practices, and procedures being used in the not-for-profit sector and informs the board, volunteers, and other leaders of matters that would benefit and interest them in their work on behalf of [name of organization].
9. Prepares detailed plans of action for all approved fund raising and community relations programs, including budgets that support their implementation.
10. Works with the [name of special support group or auxiliary] board of directors in analyzing the fund raising programs and planning for future activities.
11. Assists the [name of auxiliary or support group] and [name of organization] in identifying and developing opportunities for in-service activities.
12. Works with staffmembers and volunteers to ensure that all fund raising and community relations programs are consistent with both the overall mission and the philosophy and concepts of each program and service.

Exhibit 12.4. Job Description, Cont'd.

Staff Supervision: One secretary or administrative assistant

Volunteer Supervision: Part-time volunteers who assist in record-keeping and maintenance functions on a regular basis plus others who work on special projects in fund raising and public relations.

Volunteer Coordination: Works directly with the board of directors and [names of committees or groups involved in fund raising and community relations] to coordinate their development activities. Frequently serves as the [title of chief executive officer or spokesperson] and liaison to other committees, task forces, and organizations.

Exhibit 12.5. Board Member Job Description.

Board members of [name of organization] are our links to the community and as such are essential and important volunteers. A commitment to serve on the board carries with it certain expectations, both formal and informal. The organization's commitment is to make your board service rewarding and enjoyable and to help you exercise your special skills and talents on our behalf.

Board Member Responsibilities:

1. Attend meetings.
2. Participate on one or more committees or in an ad hoc manner as requested by the board chair, president or CEO, or development director.
3. Be aware of and execute the formal, legal core of board roles and responsibilities [attached to the description].
4. Support the organization financially at an appropriate level.
5. Fulfill commitments within agreed-upon deadlines.
6. Participate in board orientation to ensure organizational knowledge.
7. Provide candid, open, and honest feedback and evaluation when appropriate.
8. Take initiative in informing the organization about opportunities for funding or program development.
9. Identify individuals in the community for volunteer participation or funding support.
10. Support the organization and its officers in times of controversy or crisis.
11. Provide sensitivity and support to staff members and other board members as they perform their duties.
12. Exercise loyalty towards [name of organization] and confidentiality regarding its internal affairs as discussed at board meetings.
13. Provide leadership within the board and in the community on behalf of [name of organization] and its programs.
14. Serve as an informal advocate for [name of organization] in the community.

Staff Support of Board Member:

1. Attends to details of meetings and so on and informs board members in a timely manner.
2. Provides adequate preparation for meetings in which board members must play a leadership role.
3. Provides complete, concise, and accurate information as required or requested.
4. Uses board member's time judiciously.
5. Meets agreed-upon deadlines or notifies promptly if deadlines cannot be met.
6. Provides prompt response to requests for information.
7. Returns phone calls promptly.
8. Demonstrates candor and respect in individual and organizational relationships.

be the way to encourage the employee to continue being a valued contributor to the organization.

Providing employees with a sense of their growth opportunities is another nonmonetary incentive. If they feel they can move up or expand into new areas that will enhance professional growth, then they are more apt to remain satisfied and experience less burnout.

Regular and thoughtful performance appraisals encourage growth, build confidence, and solidify an organization. Appraisals must be based on both the job description and mutually determined objectives, and they should include both personal and professional goals. Separate the appraisal process from the salary review. Although performance is often the principal basis for salary increases, the two are distinct functions. Appraisals are provided to review and evaluate past performance; discuss current needs, concerns, and aspirations; and set future objectives. They are thus totally tied into the relationship between the employer and the employee. Salary reviews must take other factors into consideration: the organization's total financial resources, the comparative earnings of others in the organization or in the profession, the individual's years of experience, as well as the previous assessed performance.

Other motivators include the use of informal techniques such as one-minute praisings or reprimands (Blanchard and Johnson, 1982), or more formal strategies for tracking successes and shortcomings that provide feedback to the employee between appraisals.

Because people are motivated not by what *we* want them to do but by what *they* want to do, effective managers take the time required to find out what tasks motivate their employees. This does not excuse employees from tasks they do not enjoy: It means there is an effort made whenever possible to assign responsibilities that match the employee's interests. Two relatively easy methods—asking and observing—can determine what motivates someone.

Uncovering employee aspirations, interests, and concerns is one of the pleasures of managing. Through consistent communication based in trust and respect, a person's motivations unfold. In the challenging environment of fund raising management, this purposeful communication is time well spent for a manager. Although the professional relationship implies that a certain distance be maintained between manager and employee, one of the attributes of the not-for-profit sector is the breaking down of artificial hierarchal barriers. When the mission is understood not only by those at the top but also by those who carry out program, fund raising, and administration, then the vision is more easily shared. Talents and skills emerge in this environment of acceptance and encouragement. People are encouraged to contribute, and in so doing they are motivated.

These same principles also apply to volunteer management and donor relationships.

Staff Management and Accountability

Public and board demands for accountability and professionalism are key expectations against which management standards must be set. Little was known or understood about the sector several decades ago, and the mystery permitted certain lax management and financial practices. Contributors were moved by the perceived sincerity of causes and responded to their own felt need to help. They made donations and asked few questions.

In the late 1960s and through the 1970s, the proliferation of not-for-profit agencies stimulated societal awareness of their work. However, those years were characterized by substantial government funding of these agencies, a factor that helped to sustain the public's lack of curiosity about management and accountability. Heavy government funding also meant that the size and number of gifts expected from the general public was much smaller.

Today, in an era of scaled-back government funding and flat or diminished corporate and foundation giving, the expectations of the individual donor are significantly greater. As a result, prospects and donors are requiring more information, more accountability, and better stewardship of their philanthropy. For the fund raising manager, this growing trend will create new demands for effective and productive management of the fund raising staff. Increasingly, individual and organizational professionalism will be a key standard for prospects when making decisions about significant investments of time or money in the not-for-profit sector.

Personal and Organizational Professionalism

This challenging issue in staff management extends also into volunteer and donor management. The image of the impoverished organization with staffmembers who are more eager than trained is fading. The sector is moving toward a new posture, one in which personal and organizational professionalism is emphasized while the special qualities of not-for-profit organizations are preserved: commitment to mission, a supportive environment, an emphasis on teamwork, and the importance of nonmonetary incentives.

Professionalism is a key issue for debate among practitioners and scholars in the not-for-profit sector. The discussion isolates issues as far-ranging as ethical management practices and whether fund raising is a profession at all. For the most part, this discourse is not the general public's concern. Its concern is whether not-for-profit organizations—and their managers and leaders—are professional. To meet these concerns, there has to be an adherence to standards, ethics, and sound management practices that survives close examination. If the imposition of inappropriate external standards is to be prevented, then the profession must become self-monitoring not only within each organization but also across the profession.

Strategies for Reflecting Professionalism

The not-for-profit manager needs to model leadership, set standards, and discourage individual behavior and practices that diminish the public perception of the organization. Leadership and team building are addressed in depth in Chapter 13, but professionalism is a management issue as well.

First, at all board, committee, and other meetings of volunteers and staff, the manager's preparation, attitude, and participation signal the degree of his or her professionalism. That professionalism is manifested in behavior that focuses on solutions, not problems; in an attitude that is positive even in times of crisis or difficulty; in actions that support and enhance relationships; in a willingness to provide essential information or personnel to get a job done; and in the capacity in all decision making to adhere to the vision and mission of the organization.

Second, professionalism is reflected in the way that managers deal with conflict. Conflict is inevitable, and yet it can be productive. *Escalated* conflict, however, erodes organizational stability. Not-for-profit managers need to deal creatively and positively with minor conflict and ensure that it does not escalate and divide the staff or board.

To deal with conflict early and effectively, isolate the source of the difficulty, work *directly* with the individuals involved, provide a nonthreatening environment in which they can confront one another with the difficulty, and provide a positive solution that capitalizes on the value of each person's position. At the same time, the manager must promote an overall environment in which people understand that escalated conflict is not acceptable and that avenues for problem solving and conflict resolution are available. Conflict is often the last resort of employees and volunteers who feel they are not being heard. Good managers are good listeners.

Third, when participating in professional society meetings, civic luncheons, conferences, or other meetings in which people from the not-for-profit sector or the community are present, managers must remember that they *are* the institution they represent. Leave the dirty laundry at home. Never air organizational difficulties in a public environment, and keep complaints about board members or staffmembers to yourself or to appropriate individuals who can help you resolve the issue. Rumors multiply, and gossip undermines personal and institutional stability. The capacity of an organization to fund raise and attract volunteers is severely diminished when the public perceives organizational strife. Professionalism includes loyalty to the organization and discreet silence about confidential matters. If an organization has problems that are already public, then managers should be coached in their responses to public and media questions. Responses to such questions should be honest and to the point: They should not elaborate beyond what has been asked for. And as for "off the record" comments, they seldom stay off the record. Avoid making them.

Specific Techniques for Managing Volunteers

Larger organizations may have a paid (or volunteer) volunteer coordinator, whose primary responsibilities are to enlist, train, and reinforce volunteers and to keep track of volunteer hours and projects. Smaller organizations that do not have this management resource will assign those tasks to one or more staffmembers or volunteers. Most organizations involve volunteers in a variety of staff-relieving and important tasks; the focus in this section will be on volunteers who assist with fund raising.

Volunteers can play many roles in the development process. The first and most obvious is in the direct fund raising process itself: the identification, qualification, strategy development, cultivation, solicitation, follow-up, stewardship, and renewal of donors. At each stage in the fund raising process, there is a role for volunteers — even for those who absolutely *refuse* to ask for money. Volunteers are essential in the first three steps of the process, because they are the link to the community and are more knowledgeable about prospects. The cultivation process also involves volunteers who can host events, take prospects to lunch, and provide thoughtful monitoring of the growing relationship between prospect and institution.

In the solicitation itself, volunteers are critical. Whether working in teams or alone, they provide the vital linkage and represent the community investment in the organization. Once a solicitation is complete, other roles are available to volunteers: in follow-up if further meetings are required before a gift is confirmed; in stewardship of the donor after the gift is received; and in renewal or the upgrading process.

In addition to involvement in the full solicitation process, there are other volunteer opportunities within fund raising: special events, gift acknowledgments, clerical and secretarial support, phone appeals, "PS-athons" (in which personal messages are added to large mailings that will be sent first-class presort), and direct mailings. The list is only limited by the time and willingness of staff managers to enlist, train, and encourage volunteers.

In addition to volunteer job descriptions (described earlier), a volunteer contract can be developed. In this practice, a letter or contract summarizing the expectations of the organization is given to the volunteer for signature. Limitations to this practice include the inability of the organization to exercise significant leverage if the volunteer chooses not to complete the contract. A middle ground, which is suggestive of the contract but less binding, is a letter that summarizes the understanding between the organization and the individual. It does not require a signature, and it is maintained in the volunteer's file for reference. A sample letter might read as follows:

Thank you for agreeing to serve as chair of our annual antique auction and wine tasting. We are confident that this year's event will be the best yet, and we look forward to working with you to ensure its success.

To review our shared expectations, we have prepared the following. Please review it carefully and let us know if it reflects your understanding of our conversation.

You have agreed to:

1. Enlist a committee for the event.
2. Schedule regular meetings for the committee.
3. Work within the agreed-upon budget for the event.
4. Make timely reports regarding progress.
5. Attend board and other meetings as required for reports.
6. Be available for media and other interviews.
7. Mobilize your committee to work with you on the following:
   a. Overall production of the event.
   b. Development, production, and printing of the invitations.
   c. Review of lists from our data base to select those who will be invited.
   d. Addition of other names to the list from other sources.
   e. Contact in-kind donors for food, wine, and so on.
   f. Work with the facility to ensure appropriate setup.
   g. Oversee all activities on the day of the event.
   h. Provide an evaluation of the event that includes an accurate budget.

To support you, we will:

1. Provide information from the data base on request.
2. Secure underwriting, with your assistance, for the event.
3. Provide lists of potential in-kind donors.
4. Troubleshoot problems with printers, the post office, and so on.
5. Provide you with a desk and telephone.
6. Be there for you when you need us.
7. Assist you in any other way we can.

Many thanks for taking this on. We know it will be a huge success.

To make this a more formal contract, the following sentence can be added: "Please sign below and return one copy to us, keep one copy for yourself, and keep one copy for the committee."

Managing Board Relationships

For board members, one of the most productive practices in clarifying roles and communicating expectations involves an annual individual meeting with the board chair and the executive director or the development director or both.

During this meeting, the accomplishments of the previous year and the board member's contributions toward those accomplishments are reviewed and the plans for the coming year outlined. A commitment is gained from the board member about the nature and extent of his or her anticipated involvement in the forthcoming year, and an annual gift or pledge is made. As a follow-up to this meeting, a letter is sent to confirm the commitment and thank the board member for the gift or pledge. This letter becomes part of the file and is used when assessing board effectiveness and renewal of board terms. The following is a sample letter.

> Thank you for agreeing to serve another term on the board of [organization name]. Your board membership is important to us, and we appreciate your willingness to spend the time to make this an effective and productive relationship.
>
> The board member job description we reviewed is enclosed, along with current materials about the organization. The board orientation is scheduled for [date] from [time] to [time]. We know you will find this a productive review of information about our organization.
>
> Your commitment to make an annual gift this year of $1,000 and a capital campaign pledge of $6,000 payable over three years is greatly appreciated. We will send you pledge reminders, as you have requested, and understand that your annual gift will be received before December 31.
>
> Your continued participation on the development and finance committees is also greatly appreciated, and we have notified the chairs of those committees of your willingness to serve again.
>
> You are a valued and important member of our board and we feel fortunate to have your involvement. Thank you for all you have done and all you will continue to do. And thank you for your generous financial support.

Volunteers are demanding more from their volunteer experience. They want their time to be well spent and their labors to be well directed, and they want to support an organization that is well managed. Job descriptions and contracts or letters of agreement increase the organization's professionalism and heighten a volunteer's sense of importance about his or her assignment.

People remain motivated as volunteers when they feel they are making a difference, when they are appreciated, when they are learning new skills or meeting new people, when they can be involved in important work including problem solving and decision making, when they can advance to leadership positions, and when they can participate in meaningful workshops or sessions. They *lose* motivation when they are confronted with unreal expectations, fail to receive appreciative feedback or support, when their initiative or creativity is blocked by staffmembers or other volunteers, when they perceive no real reward, and when they are offered little variety in tasks. To motivate volunteers, here are some useful techniques:

1. Create mutually agreeable expectations and objectives.
2. Create cross-teams of staffmembers and volunteers to provide wider perspective on solving common problems.
3. Include volunteers in the fund raising planning process.
4. Share exciting, responsible jobs with entry level volunteers, and then share the recognition for success with them.
5. Emphasize the *mission* and how the volunteer's contribution is helping to address the social needs reflected in that mission.
6. Provide a pleasant place to work.
7. Start a volunteer-recognition program.
8. Keep volunteers informed about key organization accomplishments and successful fund raising.
9. Resolve conflicts immediately and creatively.
10. Provide training in and resource materials about your organization's programs. Increase the volunteer's "product knowledge."

Stewardship of Donors

The third dimension of the fund raising manager's people management-responsibilities concerns donors. Traditional notions of stewardship refer to the gift and ensuring that it is spent wisely and in accordance with the donor's wishes. An increasingly competitive marketplace and increased donor expectations have created an expanded sense of stewardship, one that includes continued relationship building with the donor.

This new view of stewardship lets people know on a regular basis that you care about them, respect their support, appreciate their gifts, and want their interest and involvement. At the end of its $1.1 billion centennial campaign, Stanford University identified enhanced donor stewardship as a primary postcampaign goal. The numbers of new and increased donors to the campaign warranted an intensified program of outreach and communication to which the university committed itself. All organizations should have the same goal, whether they are emerging from a campaign, anticipating a campaign, or just wishing to increase the numbers and commitments of their annual donors.

Implementing a stewardship program may require additional volunteers or paid staffmembers and a new allocation of funds. Although boards and administrators acknowledge the importance of stewardship, they frequently balk at the cost of providing events and opportunities that have no direct fund raising impact. Because of this, not-for-profit managers must educate those within their organizations about stewardship as a function of the development process.

Implementing a Stewardship Program. A key aspect of stewardship is accurate information. Donor record keeping and prospect-list management provide the basis for all effective fund raising, including building key relationships with consistent or potential supporters. But stewardship is more than list maintenance or newsletter publication. It is a sophisticated process that should become part of a skilled manager's priorities.

First, treat all donors as prospects. Cultivate donors and work tirelessly to let them know how important they are to your work. Seek their opinions as well as their money. Provide major donors with drafts of case statements or brochures and ask for their response. Call and invite them to special meetings or presentations by professionals in the program area of their interest who may be visiting the organization or the community. Some regional theaters have instituted "play support groups" that provide opportunities for donors (and prospects) to become part of the theater production from first reading through opening night, including dinners and meetings with the performers at appropriate times.

Second, remember that a donor, who has been brought into a relationship with an organization, has become an investor in that organization. As an investor, the donor should be provided with regular information that assures that the gift has been used properly and is making a difference. Because fund raising is based on the principle of values exchange, be sure that the "return" your investors realize is the affirmation of those values. This forms the basis of stewardship.

Third, get to know your donors: Fund raising is a contact sport. Personal outreach to your donors will increase your ability to meet their needs. Their enhanced sense of involvement with your organization will galvanize their commitment and help you reach your fund raising goals.

Fourth, have a regular schedule of "host opportunities" for board members and other active volunteers to continue the cultivation and stewardship of donors. Publish this list of opportunities on a quarterly basis, and be specific about how people can bring guests to these activities. Such opportunities may include lunches with the executive director or key program officers, tours of the facility, special receptions before a performance or an event, and invitational dinners during which awards or presentations are made to others who are involved with the organization. These lists can be distributed at board meetings with follow-up provided by the development or administrative office.

Fifth, stewardship requires thoughtful attention to the donor's interests and concerns. In addition to "host opportunities," provide time for one-on-one involvement with donors about key issues concerning present and future plans for the organization. A key value that motivates much giving is that of wanting to belong. In its 1990 membership brochure, the Oregon Shakespeare Festival related the following: Berthold Brecht once wrote that he chose one place over another not because the first hadn't a delectable menu, but because the second invited him into the kitchen. In the one he was an honored customer; in the other, a participant. He belonged.

Stewardship encourages participation and a sense of belonging. It can help institutions build the kind of relationships on which successful fund raising is based.

Summary

Fund raising managers have the responsibility to effectively manage staff members, volunteers, and donors in such a way that communication is encouraged, productivity is enhanced, personal growth is stimulated, and institutional goals are accomplished. In the environment of a rapidly changing sector, and given the pressures of the profession itself, these tasks have become even more important. The development officer must be a team builder and a team leader working with volunteers, professional staff, support staff, and donors in ways that empower and involve them most effectively. When this happens, organizations and individuals are able to realize the full potential of their abilities and provide leadership and direction to the not-for-profit sector.

Leadership
and Team Building

Of all the factors that contribute to sustained success in fund raising, none may be more important than creating a cohesive and effective development team. Sustaining such a team requires leadership, vision, and a commitment to the value of team effort in achieving organizational goals.

There are challenges to working with a fund raising team of staffmembers and volunteers. Although it is widely understood at a theoretical level that volunteers and staffmembers *share* the responsibility for fund raising and that *all* board members should participate in some aspect of the development process, difficulties emerge when theory is put into practice. Similarly, the hope that board and staff will pursue fund raising as a team with a common purpose, guided by a shared vision of what the organization can do and become, is not always realized. The leadership skills required to develop, motivate, and maintain the fund raising team are best understood when the composition and function of such teams are examined.

A Strategic Force: The Full Development Team

A distinction is made here between the development team and the development committee. The *full* development team includes the development committee and other professional and support staff, as well as the core team members; the *core* team involves key leaders of the organization as strategists and implementers. The core development team comprises the CEO, the development director, the development committee chairperson, and the board chairperson. These individuals transmit the vision and create the structure that motivates and maintains the development function. The importance of the development function is validated by the involvement of these leaders in the fund raising process.

Development staff (professional and support), members of the development committee, certain other members of the board and staff, and other volunteers make up the full development team. Depending on the size of the organization, the following individuals or groups also may be part of the full team:

1. Fund raising support staff (clerical, data-entry)
2. Auxiliary or guild leadership
3. Volunteer coordinator
4. Finance committee chairperson or finance staff
5. Program staff as its expertise is required for cultivation of major donors and proposal writing
6. All members of the board as participants in the solicitation process.

This expanded view of the development team helps to support and advance the fund raising program, and it provides wider understanding and acceptance of the complexities of the full development function.

There has been a movement among some organizations—principally colleges, universities, and hospitals—toward "staff-driven" fund raising, thereby minimizing the need for a full development team that involves board members and other volunteers. In this approach, development staff members initiate and execute the vast majority of the fund raising responsibilities, including major donor solicitations. Volunteer participation is limited. Although this may seem advantageous as a simplified form of fund raising management, there are strong disadvantages to this model: an absence of peer-to-peer linkages, diminished community involvement in the organization, and the decline of long-term relationship building in the community—which is the basis of fund raising. The traditional structure, involving a full development team, draws its strength from the empowerment of many to be effective advocates for the organization's mission.

The Development Committee

The development committee carries out the principal functions of the development team. It should comprise board and non-board (community) volunteers. The chairperson should be a member of the board and serve on the executive committee. In smaller organizations, this committee may be responsible as a working team for executing all development functions (for example, annual fund, special events, phone appeals, and mailings). The committee may function as a group in all aspects of fund raising, and may be as large as ten to twelve people.

In larger organizations, the development committee often will be constituted as a steering committee, comprising the chairpeople of several subcommittees responsible for the various fund raising activities cited above. With the steering committee model, the membership is usually smaller (five to seven people). In addition to the sub-committee chairpeople, there should be several "at-large" members (usually non-board volunteers from the community) on the development steering committee. Both types of development committees are staffed by the development director (or, by the executive director if there is no development director).

The development committee is responsible for working with the development officer to analyze financial needs, prepare the development plan, and put the plan to work. A committee job description should be prepared and used in the enlistment of committee members. The development director serves as *staffperson to*, not as *member of*, the development committee. As a staffmember, the fund raising executive can exercise objectivity, authority, expertise, and guidance.

Community involvement on the development committee has a number of significant benefits: fresh perspectives, an opportunity to involve new people in the organization, an objective source for validation and revalidation of mission and vision, and a potential source of future leadership. Strategies for enlisting these individuals are discussed in the section on leadership later in this chapter.

Functions of the Development Team. The full development team has many important functions within the organization. The core development team defines these responsibilities at the policy level, and the development director (or executive director) structures the various responsibilities. These are delegated to staffmembers or volunteers, according to the size and policies of the organization. Among these responsibilities are the planning, implementation, and evaluation of the following:

1. The strategic and long-range development plan
2. Annual giving programs, including mailings, telephone-appeal materials, and personal solicitation strategies
3. Major gift solicitations
4. Foundation and corporate appeals
5. Continuous "prospecting" to identify new prospects, qualify them, and develop strategies for solicitation
6. Special events
7. Marketing and soliciting planned gifts
8. Institutional marketing and public relations, including a community newsletter (if no separate department is responsible for this function)
9. Capital or endowment campaigns

The success of the development team in carrying out these functions depends greatly on the partnership between volunteers and staffmembers, as well as on the quality of institutional leadership. The leadership balance in most organizations is delicate and often difficult to attain. It begins with a commitment to recruit, enlist, and grow leaders.

Factors in Attracting Fund Raising Leadership

Individuals with fund raising leadership experience or potential are attracted to organizations that position themselves around the following:

1. A compelling, convincing, and well-articulated mission statement that captures the importance of the human or societal need the organization is meeting in a way that motivates people to help solve the problem.
2. An inspiring vision statement that clearly conveys what the organization hopes to achieve and which invites people to become participants in the dream.
3. Documentation about the stability, competence, and reputation of the organization, which ensures not only past performance but also continued ability to address the mission and achieve the vision.
4. Evidence that the special leadership qualities of each individual already involved with the organization are used effectively and rewarded appropriately, and that those who join as staffmembers or board members will enjoy similar appreciation for their unique skills.

Perceptions of Leadership. The factors cited above are conveyed to the community through external materials, including case statements, brochures, public relations releases, and public speaking opportunities. Much is also conveyed to those already on the staff or the board through internal memos, meetings, and other communications. Current members of board and staff have considerable influence on the success of leadership recruitment. Because of this, the content of internal as well as external communications should be evaluated regularly, using criteria such as the following:

1. Do external published materials convincingly convey the organization's mission and vision?
2. Is the public relations program providing the media with adequate information not only about the organization but also about the problem being solved or the need being met?
3. Are current board members and staffmembers enthusiastic advocates for the organization? Are their accomplishments and rewards well publicized?
4. Is there a solid institutional plan and budget based on carefully developed and accurate assumptions that can be shared with potential leaders?
5. Is there a reputation for fiscal responsibility? If there have been problems

in the past, are people aware that they have been resolved and the organization has turned the situation around?

6. Is there a perceived atmosphere of cooperation, open and honest communication, and shared vision? Is there an absence of escalated conflict and political tensions that detract from the fulfillment of mission and goals? Do management practices stimulate organizational and personal attainment of goals?

7. Is there a spirit of renewal that acknowledges new ideas and yet affirms basic organizational practices and values? Is this renewal tied in to a constant monitoring of the needs of the community?

Success as a Magnet for Leaders. Another key factor in attracting leadership is success. People like to be on a winning team: They find deep satisfaction in belonging to organizations that are perceived to have positive impact on local, national, or international issues. Once involved, they will offer their leadership to help maintain that success.

Fortunately for those organizations that have experienced financial or organizational problems, the success factor has another side. Organizations that need new leaders to bring them out of difficult times often discover that some individuals are attracted by the *promise* of institutional achievement or by an understanding of how they can be pivotal in the shaping (or reshaping) of a new (or reemergent) organization. These leaders—both staffmembers and volunteers—thrive on such opportunities and derive their rewards from the rebuilding and eventual repositioning of an organization. It is not uncommon, however, for leaders who step forth in times of crisis to move on to another organization in need when the problems have been solved.

Other Factors Influencing Leadership Recruitment. Community perception of an organization is shaped strongly by the perceived quality of its leadership. Some organizations seem to be able to attract *all* the leaders to their boards, while others search vainly for one. These same organizations also seem to be blessed with a succession of capable leaders on their management teams—individuals who promote the organization's needs, raise funds, and invite community participation and recognition.

In leadership recruitment, a determining factor for many individuals is whether they feel comfortable with and committed to the mission and purpose of the organization. An organization can have an excellent reputation for delivering quality services, solid staff leadership, financial stability, and an outstanding board and still not be able to attract certain people as employees or volunteers. When this happens, it is most likely a matter of personal or professional judgment that this is not a cause for which they could be effective advocates. In such cases, be appreciative of their interest and grateful for their honesty: It is far better for an individual to decline the invitation to become involved with an organization than to sign on and later decide to leave.

When the mission and purpose are compatible with their needs and interests, potential volunteers or staff leaders will make their decision by evaluating some or all of these benefits of joining the organizational team:

1. community recognition;
2. opportunities for achievement, prestige, and power;
3. meaningful work that is rewarded appropriately;
4. opportunities to resolve issues, solve problems, or promote values that are important to them;
5. camaraderie with other leaders and the chance to serve as a mentor to individuals who have leadership potential;
6. an environment that is supportive and stable; a place where creativity and initiative are encouraged;
7. an organization that encourages institutional renewal and does not stifle organizational change;
8. a strong institutional vision that is widely shared; and
9. ample opportunities for personal and professional growth.

All recruitment for both board and staff should be done systematically, using job descriptions and a matrix of required tasks and skills. In the process, however, keep the above factors in mind.

Encouraging Leadership and Team Building

The most powerful function of a leader is that of inspiring others to be part of the leadership team. Leadership flourishes where there are opportunities to share vision and goals with others. Leadership is supported when staff and volunteers are trained in their leadership and team responsibilities. Commitment to leadership principles and institutional leaders cannot be demanded: It must be encouraged and reinforced through trust, respect, and communication of the institutional vision throughout the entire organization.

Leadership and Empowerment. It is not enough to recruit individuals who have leadership experience and potential. If they are to become part of the fund raising and organizational team, then they must be empowered by the existing leadership structure. Empowerment involves people throughout the organization's leadership.

This transfer of power from one or few to many involves the delegation of tasks and the sharing of responsibility. But there is more. It also includes the sharing of the organization's vision and goals. When the vision and goals are conveyed to all employees and volunteers, there is a greater sense of participation. This is especially important in fund raising. Most people's reluctance to become part of the fund raising team stems from their fear of the process and their lack of training.

The following are strategies for empowering the full development team:

1. encourage participation in the planning process and the setting of fund raising goals and objectives;
2. provide fund raising training that focuses not only on effective strategies but also on underlying principles, including the importance of substituting pride for apology;
3. offer coaching and practice to reduce anxiety about making the solicitation call;
4. invite and respect their observations and opinions on development-related issues;
5. keep them informed of successes and failures and ask for their support on key issues;
6. team them with a staffmember, experienced volunteer, or other expert witness for solicitation visits; and
7. remind them as much as possible of the mission of the organization, and of the community needs they are helping to meet.

There are many positive results of empowerment. People feel more significant: Their knowledge and expertise are important to the organization. They have a heightened sense of belonging and teamwork, both of which can lead to increased commitment and productivity.

Empowerment—and leadership that builds leaders, not followers—sometimes requires a suppression of ego on the part of the board member or staff leader. A major university, whose volunteer fund raising team is one of the most effective in the United States, coaches its professional staff in techniques for making volunteers not only feel good, but also look good. Successful staffmembers in this environment are those who can relinquish their own need to receive credit for a gift (in whose solicitation they shared) in order to accomplish the longer-range goal of building a solid volunteer and staff team.

The Scope of Team Building for Fund Raising

Team building for fund raising extends beyond the development office. One of the potential obstacles to achieving a workable level of teamwork for fund raising is the need to blend the talents and motivations of a diverse group of employees and volunteers in a way that capitalizes on each individual's strengths. Program and administrative staffmembers may be peripheral to the development process, but they are a leadership resource as expert witnesses when proposals are drafted or key solicitations are made. Fund raising leaders must keep them involved and feeling appreciated so that they will be there when needed.

Similarly, certain board members may not feel as though they can play a leadership role in fund raising. However, when they are trained in the total solicitation process and have their own leadership skills validated, they will often find a role for themselves in the identification or cultivation of prospects or in the stewardship of donors.

Some people resist teamwork because they fear it will detract from their sense of individual achievement. They need assurance and evidence that teamwork—in the planning and in the implementation of the fund raising process—offers ample opportunity for recognition of individual contributions to the team's success. To build an effective fund raising team requires management and leadership skills, as well as an abundance of patience, fortitude, and flexibility.

Learning About Leadership

Two aspects of leadership are especially important to fund raising managers: to be perceived as a leader and to encourage leadership in others through team building.

Fund raising managers who have not had courses in leadership or team building may wish to familiarize themselves with general information about leadership, especially the tasks of leaders. An understanding of various leadership tasks provides a helpful framework for evaluating one's own leadership skills, and it offers guidance for instituting practices that heighten others' perception of leadership.

Analyses of these tasks vary, and some are more pertinent to fund raising leadership than others. John W. Gardner (1990), founder of Common Cause and cofounder of INDEPENDENT SECTOR, has identified nine leadership tasks: envisioning goals, affirming values, motivating, managing, achieving workable unity, explaining, serving as a symbol, representing the group externally, and renewing (pp. 11–22). The first eight are self-explanatory; the ninth may be a new concept. *Renewing* requires that leaders interweave continuity and change. Gardner cites it as a vital force in institutional and personal leadership; it has the power to renew and reinterpret values, liberate energies, reenergize forgotten goals, achieve new understandings, and foster the release of human possibilities (1990, pp. 122, 124).

To "encourage the heart" is another task that has special significance for fund raising leadership. This concept, which can help promote a system of rewards, reinforcement, and other nonmonetary incentives within an organization (see Chapter 12), is described by Kouzes and Posner (1987, p. 239): "Leaders give heart by visibly recognizing people's contributions to the common vision. With a thank-you note, a smile, an award, and public praise, the leader lets others know how much they mean to the organization."

Other books on leadership, such as those by Batten (1989), Bennis (1989a, 1989b), Bennis and Nanus (1985), Conger (1989), Hersey (1984), Lundy (1986), and Waterman (1987) provide stimulating sources from which fund raising managers may develop their own insights about appropriate leadership practices for their organizations.

Fund raising executives who want to develop strategies for becoming more effective leaders and encourage leadership and teamwork in others can draw on the insights of these scholars and practitioners, applying them appropriately within their own organizations.

Board and Staff Leadership in Fund Raising

Fund raising leadership is modeled by staffmembers and transferred to the board through standards, performance, and example. Staff leaders who become frustrated with the absence of board leadership may need to review their own attitudes and actions to determine whether they are modeling the kind of leadership they expect from others. Neither board nor staff should have to carry the leadership responsibilities alone. When this happens, the capacity for fund raising is diminished. In the absence of volunteer leadership, community support will fade; without staff leadership, trust in the organization will diminish.

Because this leadership balance is reciprocal, a decline in leadership by either staff or board will lead to a subsequent decline in leadership by the other. Fund raising managers are challenged to sustain a level of leadership on board and staff that will enable fund raising and organizational goals to be met. This requires a continual leadership recruitment and building process on both staff and board.

The ability to attract and grow leadership in the staff, in the board, and in volunteer committees is a distinguishing aspect of excellent organizations. Organizations that are willing to acknowledge the importance of these functions and set organizational priorities around the essential tasks of leadership can get and maintain a leadership advantage.

Leaders and Teams

Because they are able to share their vision and empower others, successful leaders can build effective teams. They realize that it is more important to build new leaders than to maintain followers. Although teams need designated leaders to take them through specific tasks and projects, a team can comprise only individuals who are leaders. And these leaders bring their authority, experience, shared vision, and common goals to a team. Their confidence — in themselves, the organization, and the team process — is a catalyst to accomplishment and change.

Occasionally, organizations will constitute special committees or teams to meet extraordinary needs. These teams draw from the leadership of the organization and the community. In major capital campaigns, the campaign steering committee always comprises campaign leaders: other committee chairpeople, staffmembers, consultants, and major donors. When convened by the chairperson of the campaign steering committee, these leaders function as a team. The budget or long-range planning committee of an organization is also made up of leaders from the board and staff who function for this purpose as a team. When leaders combine in this way to form a team for a special or continuing purpose, the true benefits of team building emerge.

Benefits of Team Building

The benefits of building teams far outweigh the time it takes to organize and work with individual members. Obvious benefits are the synergy of many ideas, the feeling of empowerment and participation, and the increased opportunities to motivate team members as their strengths and interests are revealed. Commitment, and the willingness to encourage commitment in others, is often heightened through participation in the team decision-making process.

Because not-for-profit organizations must provide programs and conduct fund raising in an environment of change, teamwork can provide a sense of collective strength, unity, and purpose that reinforces the determination to achieve institutional vision and goals—even in times of chaos and disruption.

Coalescing the Development Team

The characteristics of effective development teams are no different from those of other kinds of teams: high morale, effective task performance, a clear understanding of their relevance to the organization, shared goals, respect for leadership and one another, strong orientation to task, trust, productivity, and a sense of team spirit. What distinguishes the development team from others is its sense of purpose and how that purpose relates to the institutional mission and its goals.

The strength of the development team is influenced by the quality of teamwork throughout the organization. From the board itself to the smallest task force, teams take their cues from the way in which they are supported and encouraged by the institution. Gail Ginder, organizational consultant and faculty member of The Fund Raising School, developed the following list of tasks for building board–staff teams—not only for development, but also for comprehensive institutional purposes. The list is used as a worksheet for The Fund Raising School's advanced course, "Maximizing Fund Raising Results Through Leadership." As a checklist, it asks, "To what extent do board and staff work together to. . . .

1.   identify community needs (mission building)?
2.   define and realize agency purposes and priorities?

3. identify and develop financial resources and other forms of support for the agency?
4. give leadership to development of programs and services?
5. develop an organizational structure that supports the program?
6. give leadership to policy formulation and review?
7. evaluate the agency in terms of program effectiveness, board functions, and overall management?
8. create an atmosphere for change?
9. value and promote teamwork?
10. maximize the contributions of all involved: board members, other volunteers, and staffmembers?
11. maintain, describe, and share the institutional vision?
12. develop and maintain a sense of trust and confidence in one another?
13. resolve problems effectively?
14. arrive at decisions that both board and staff can support and for which both accept responsibility?"

These issues form the basis for a successful partnership and stimulate team building for fund raising and other institutional goals.

What Makes Teams Work?

Certain benefits of team building have been suggested. What makes teams *work* is more difficult to describe, although a sort of chemistry occurs when people of like mind and purpose get together. Some call it "team spirit." Its presence is not measurable, but its absence is unmistakable. Observable qualities of highly productive teams—including development teams—are important to note and are as follows.

1. *Highly productive teams have developed and can communicate a shared vision.* They give life to a vision and enroll others in it. This is one of the strongest aspects of effective teams.
2. *There is an absence of hierarchy.* Every team member can help make the idea or plan work, and there is strong cooperation. Communication is open and nonthreatening and based in trust and respect. With few exceptions, no one pulls rank.
3. *There is organizational support for the team.* Team building is part of an institutional culture in which each person adds value to the process. Organizations that pay lip service to the notion of teamwork are eventually revealed, and staff and board expectations for sharing in the vision or achieving personal and professional growth are diminished in the discovery.
4. *They practice empowerment and can coalesce the team while making each individual stronger.* The whole is greater than the sum of its parts. Synergy,

cooperation, interaction, and resolved conflict are by-products of an effective team approach.

5. *They encourage open communication and reduce misunderstandings.* As a result, individuals may work toward and accept new ideas. The potential for change is heightened, and institutional renewal is stimulated.

The value of teams that evidence these qualities is apparent. Unfortunately, not all teams adhere to these principles and some teams—and some leaders—collapse in disarray.

The Disintegration of Leadership and Teams

At the root of crisis in many organizations is an inability to view leadership as a shared responsibility. When this happens, blame and finger pointing cause deterioration of trust, respect, and initiative, and each element within the organization waits for another to step forward and take control. The results may be a power play, a leadership void, or the disintegration of the organization's fabric.

When either board or staff begins to fail in its leadership role, it is a sign of organizational dysfunction. Before the imbalance becomes critical, it is imperative that one or more individuals from board and staff step forward together to model the kind of leadership skills that will correct the situation. Otherwise, a predictable cycle may begin, one leading to the loss of valuable people from board and staff and diminished organizational strength. The following five-step destructive scenario has been enacted in far too many organizations.

First, conflict or competition erodes the concept of shared leadership, and no one models the kind of behavior that will reverse the erosion. The energy and enthusiasm of key individuals begin to wane.

Second, frustration grows over the lack of synergy within the organization, the level of politics that has emerged, and the lack of wide involvement in critical decisions that have created the crisis. Attempts to intervene or provide solutions are disregarded or thwarted. Excuses are offered instead of solutions; suggestions for resolving issues are ignored.

Third, the sense of purpose and involvement diminishes: Board members stop coming to meetings, staffmembers lose interest, and rumors and gossip run rampant inside and outside the institution.

Fourth, board members resign and staffmembers seek leadership opportunities elsewhere—or they coalesce with other board members or staffmembers who are similarly frustrated, becoming an invading force intent on restructuring the organization.

Fifth, the invasion—or the evacuation—leaves the organization shaken and damaged. Leadership has to be reconstructed, the vision revitalized, and massive repairs to internal systems and external relationships must be done if the organization is to flourish again.

Preventing Team Failure

Leadership practices that encourage communication, discourage escalated conflict, and keep the mission foremost in people's minds will help discourage this scenario. Clandestine meetings, inappropriate memoranda, stormy meetings, and failure to meet one anothers' expectations for performance and support all violate the leadership's responsibility and contribute to the downward spiral of organizational stability.

Organizational strife has a strong negative impact on fund raising. Donors from all constituencies become reluctant to invest, perceiving that the focus of the organization is not on its mission, but on its own institutional problems. Those who support not-for-profit organizations do so because of the inherent values exchange. The fallout from team and leadership failure is a public perception that the organization's vision and mission — and hence its values — are no longer worthy of investment. In a competitive environment, the advantages of strong leadership and team building become more apparent.

Leadership fails most often when leaders lose sight of the mission and become obsessed instead with issues related to the organization as an entity separate from its purpose. When this happens, the big picture is replaced with narrow or tunnel vision, and the need to unite behind community needs is obscured by the fracturing of the institution.

Team work and leadership is essential in all not-for-profit functions, but it is especially important in fund raising, where so much public trust is invested.

Summary

The full development team is institutional in its scope. Broadly drawn from the board, staff, and community, it applies the leadership standards and practices of the institution to fund raising. For this reason, development practitioners must be familiar and comfortable with all of the tasks and aspects of leadership. Organizations can attract people with leadership potential or experience, but they must assess the image projected into the community before beginning active enlistments.

To maintain and grow organizational leadership, especially in fund raising, requires an understanding of the characteristics, qualities, and benefits of team building and the ability to empower others.

Thinking Strategically About Information

Development professionals would do well to take seriously Thoreau's dictum to "simplify, simplify, simplify." Thanks to modern technology, we can now store more information in less time and in less space than ever before. But here, too, Murphy's Law is fully operative: first, the more information stored, the more difficult to achieve focus; second, the not-for-profit across the street is just as likely to collect staggering amounts of data; and third, targeted donors are bombarded by sophisticated (and not so sophisticated) fund raising appeals.

It is ironic that out of today's computerized efficiencies, volumes, and "personalization," the old-fashioned handwritten letter or note has emerged as today's ultimate status symbol because it is ultimately personalized.

How well not-for-profits make productive use of strategic information almost certainly determines success or failure in the pursuit of philanthropy.

All Information Bytes Are Not Equal

One of the hardest fallacies to conquer is that "bigger" and "more" equate with success. Nothing could be further from the truth; in reality, both are counterproductive. The beginner tends to equate size with progress; the seasoned veteran knows beyond question that success is continual prioritizing and then acting on those priorities.

And although insightful information can make all the difference in the world for an organization, information gathering must not become an obsession. It is essential to find a happy medium.

Figure 14.1. Information and Relationships: One Depends on the Other.

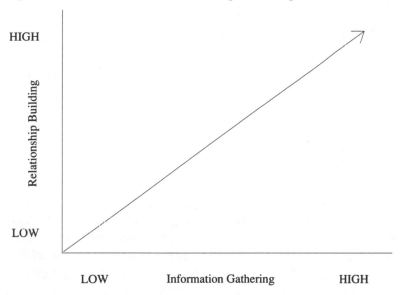

This model shows that a decision to increase the investment in information gathering must correlate with the organization's ability to achieve the same growth in the relationship with the donor or prospect. It would make no sense for the development office to collect extraordinary amounts of information on the richest family in the country if the organization had no connection to it through constituents or board members.

Development professionals and volunteers must avoid getting bogged down thinking they have to fill in every detail and find every little piece of information before they *do* anything. One must not be like the salesperson who has the best prospect list in the company—detailed, alphabetized, and immediately accessible—but who ends up spending time improving the prospect list instead of making any sales calls!

Elements of Successful Fund Raising

There is a fascination about miles of computerized printouts that is difficult to resist. Surely, all those names, addresses, and information units will automatically translate into a higher and higher level of success. Not necessarily so: One must keep in mind that *information gathering for its own sake costs money but does not raise any.*

Whether it is called development, advancement, attracting philanthropic resources, cultivating voluntary support, or friend raising, the key to fund raising success is *relationship building.* This process of building relationship is supported by and works with information gathering (see Figure 14.1).

The challenges of the future will require identifying, building, and maintaining relationships with an organization's most important prospects and contributors—and doing these better than ever before. No longer can organizations afford to invest the majority of their time and effort on donors and prospects who end up being one-time contributors. Continued success (and in some cases continued *existence*) will depend on the ability to develop and maintain a close relationship with "the few" who have the ability and the willingness to make a difference for the organization.

How few? Strangely enough, their numbers continue to shrink. For many charitable organizations, 80 percent of their dollars have traditionally come from 20 percent of their donors; this rule of thumb is becoming obsolete. For many charitable institutions today, 90 percent of their dollars come from 10 percent of their donors; in some, 95 percent comes from only 5 percent of donors! In a few instances, 98 percent of the money has been contributed by 2.5 percent of the donors, and the amount of money these increasingly fewer donors annually account for continues to skyrocket.

One would think that with this reality professionals working in philanthropy would be in the throes of profound information-gathering shock as everyone restructured development procedures and priorities. Instead, for most it remains "business as usual." Yet for not-for-profits to live up to their potential, a new order of things must be explored.

Determining the Essential

Fund raising futurists see the 1990s as a crucial decade, one that mandates a new order based on the premise that effective philanthropic endeavors are *not* heavily dependent on the solicitation of a mass of donors; rather, they are dependent on the practitioner's ability to develop and maintain the kind of relationship with the few who will spawn higher and higher levels of success.

What this all means is that a higher priority exists than being a great team player and office manager. It means that profuse green foliage does not count, only harvested fruit.

It means that directors of development must so allocate time and energies that the 5 percent to 10 percent of the donors or prospects who have the potential to deliver 90 percent to 95 percent of the needed funds are carefully and tenderly cultivated, and that they are never far from mind.

It means that, in spite of the daily blizzard of paper, these professionals must find a time and a place, away from the telephone, away from *everyone* and *everything*, and there dream, plan, conceptualize, and prioritize. It means constantly breaking through the barrier of the *routine* to accomplish the *essential* so that voluntary financial support can become all that it can and should be.

And not a week should go by without significant attention being given to the care and cultivation of those at the top of the major donor list!

Information Gathering: An Investment

"Investment" implies that resources, adequate budget, time, staff, and staff effort must be invested in the information-gathering process. As will be true of all major expense categories, the dollars spent to create, develop, use, analyze, and retain information about donors should be continually scrutinized. Just as it would not do at all to scrimp on the concrete in the foundation during the construction of a new home, it is equally inappropriate to fund the information-gathering process inadequately.

In addition, an investment in information gathering means an investment of energy, a pervasive and constant awareness of information that surrounds the philanthropy professional.

Whether it is scanning the business and social columns in the newspaper, reading trade magazines aimed at the industries from which funding is being sought, asking for information while networking with colleagues, or picking up on a signal from the donor, relationship building is a process that knows no time boundaries, keeps no office hours, and never stops.

A development officer was visiting with a foundation executive and his wife in their home. The man, who used his home as his office, had responded to the development officer's request for an appointment to discuss a forthcoming proposal. While in their home, the development professional, an accomplished pianist and musician, spotted a beautiful piano in the living room. She remarked about it and her interest in music. A lively conversation ensued. The participants talked about their favorite types of music. The hostess, upon declaring her love for ragtime, pulled out a piece of sheet music and asked the development officer to take it home with her and return in the near future to play it.

When relating this story, the development officer admitted, "I confess that I could never do justice to ragtime. So during my next visit, I offered to play another piece, a specially arranged version of 'Amazing Grace.' They seemed so very pleased. I had no idea that all those years of practicing the piano could add to my repertoire of fund raising skills!"

And the foundation executive and his wife? They still rave about the fund raiser who played the piano for them. They are just as pleased about the $500,000 challenge grant they were able to give her institution.

Will music continue to be a topic in their conversations? Does this experience and information contribute to relationship building? Without a doubt!

In travels, this same development officer has been known to pick up a souvenir or item with particular meaning for a volunteer or two (such as the chocolate tennis balls from Ghiradelli's for her tennis tournament chairman) before she shops for her family!

It's Not the Same for All

Basic information gathering is the same for everyone. Institutional development offices need to know correct addresses and how people like their names
to be listed in recognition publications. Donor histories are a must for all.
Each donor receives information about the organization in the form of
newsletters, publications, or annual reports. But that is where the "sameness"
stops.

As we have observed, a disproportionate share of the needed funds is
likely to come from 5 percent to 10 percent of the donors. This fact alone
underscores the importance of the judgments made when it comes to investments in information gathering, cultivation, and nurturing of donors. Although it is important to attract gifts of all sizes (and new donors whatever the
gift level), organizations can no longer afford to treat everyone the same.

Of course, all donors receive appreciation. All donors deserve a
"Thank you" for gifts, both large and small. However, one of the development
officer's most important jobs in making productive use of strategic information will be knowing where to shift levels in nurturing groups of donors and
individuals in a special way.

The development officer has a fiscal responsibility to allocate
information-gathering dollars wisely, remembering always to direct such
funds to channels where the ratio of return per dollar is at a maximum.

Where to Invest in Information Gathering

A decision to move a particular donor to a higher information-gathering
status will depend on the type of gift that the donor is capable of making
(see Figure 14.2) and the method of fund raising that will be used to solicit
the gift.

Paul E. Wisdom developed this idea when he wrote:

> Development is not only contact-intensive but paper-intensive.
> Prospects must learn a good deal about the institution, its
> programs, and its people before they will support it. They need
> to know what it is, why it's important, its quality, what it will do
> for them and for others, and why the institution needs their
> support. Conversely, the fund raiser also needs to know a great
> deal about prospects in order to maximize chances of success.
>
> You should target much of the consequent information
> gathering on discovering whether or not an individual qualifies
> as a major donor prospect (MDP), someone having the capacity
> to make a one-time gift of $5,000 or more. Once a person is
> identified as a MDP, the research efforts and contacts accelerate.
> Development officers need to find out as much as possible about
> each individual, in order to devise and develop a successful

Figure 14.2. Giving Is Built on Relationships.

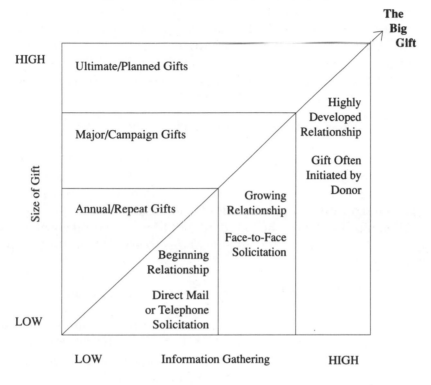

This model illustrates the dependence of big-gift fund raising on information gathering and relationship building. The higher the gift (or the anticipated amount), the more one invests in the types of activities that build relationships and the more essential it is to gather appropriate information.

cultivation strategy. Ultimately each prospect will be asked for a major gift, ideally at the right time for the right purpose in the right amount at the right location and with the right person or persons asking.

A recent national survey of senior development professionals and consultants suggests that an average of nine separate cultivation activities should take place before a major solicitation. The cultivations can take place in a variety of ways and settings. They may include such things as a personal letter from a faculty member, an alumni volunteer, a dean, a development officer, a vice president, a department head, or the president; a phone call from any of the above; a personal visit at home or at the office; an invitation to lunch or dinner; attendance at an athletic event or play; a visit to an art exhibit; or even a suggestion for a golf match or a fishing trip. The event may not even be university- or college-related, as long as an institution-related person is involved. The nature and style of these events depends on the ongoing research that determines the interests of the prospect, what he or she might or might not attend, what might entice an interest and what would not. All of the events are designed to develop a good person-to-person relationship that ultimately will bring success (Fisher and Quehl, 1989, pp. 148–149). Copyright © 1989 American Council on Education and Macmillan Publishing Co. Reprinted by permission.

Facts and Figures: Not Much by Themselves

For major donors and for those who are on the cultivation track for ultimate gifts, one must go beyond facts and figures to discover the *essence* of the donors' interests and participation. Why do they give? How must organizations present additional opportunities for action?

This information can be found in both likely and unlikely places. One of the most likely and most dependable places to learn about the prospect is *from the prospect*.

The Donor Is the Best Source of Information

It is not difficult to obtain information about prospects from public sources or even from peers, friends, or associates. But what differentiates successful development programs from less successful ones? *Listening* to the donor and listening well makes all the difference in the world. By "tuning in" to the prospect, professionals can tailor requests and proposals to the prospects' likes and interests, even knowing the amount to ask for or whether to name a "hoped for" amount.

A corporate giving officer may talk about the sizes of gifts that his or her company usually gives. A foundation representative may expound on the board's philosophy and desire to make a national impact by awarding small grants over a wide geographic area. Still others may talk about focusing on a few projects and awarding large gifts to "really make a difference."

By listening intensely to what the prospective donor is saying, the development professional can pick up on small items, almost indiscernible directives that will help in the cultivation and solicitation process.

Not all donors will be as direct as one foundation executive encountered by a young development director early in her fund raising career. Because two gifts had arrived in the office on the same day for the same piece of equipment, she asked for an appointment with one of the donors. She thanked him for the gift and asked whether the hospital had permission to use the $3,000 grant for a different piece of equipment also needed by the surgery department.

The donor graciously said that the gift could be used accordingly, but continued by saying something the young woman will never forget.

"You know," he said thoughtfully, "I was disappointed that you didn't ask for more." She mentally picked herself up off the floor and stuttered an apology. "That may be because I'm new to this, and I certainly will try to do better in the future," she promised.

Rest assured, she saw to it that the foundation executive *never* had that problem again! The development director nurtured that relationship, asked thoughtful questions, and continued to "tune in" and listen to that executive. The foundation's support grew and eventually totaled several hundred thousand dollars, including a grant that is the largest gift ever given by that particular foundation, before or since.

Really listening also means using "intuitive listening." An example of this is told in the words of a chief development officer: "During one casual conversation with a donor, we talked about likes and dislikes, tastes and eccentricities. He mentioned that, while he probably doesn't know a good cup of coffee from a bad cup of coffee, it drives him crazy to drink out of a styrofoam cup.

"'I don't care what it tastes like, but I want to drink out of a *real* cup,' he remarked with a chuckle.

"A little thing? Insignificant? Maybe. Maybe not. But you can be sure that if any member of our staff offers refreshment to this particular donor, it will be served in a *real* cup!"

Never Assume You Know the Answer

Development professionals should adopt the motto, "When in doubt, take the direct route." Ask the donor about preferences when preparing a request letter for a foundation or a corporation, then ask questions such as:

- "Do you prefer that I send you a formal or informal request?"
- "Do you prefer that we ask for funding for one piece of equipment or shall we include a choice of several items for your committee?"
- "May we send you a proposal asking for consideration of a gift in the $50,000 to $60,000 range for the XYZ project?"

If the gift range is unrealistic, the prospect will give an indication.

Notice that these questions are not vague. Questions should not imply that one is on a "fishing trip." One does not say, "Could you give us your ideas of what our organization should ask you for?" The donor should *never* be asked to define the needs: The donor does not know the organization's critical needs, only the organization does.

After a lengthy cultivation process and several modest gifts from one foundation, the development director realized that the funding committee might consider a *much* more significant gift. A conversation with the foundation officer revealed a key piece of information that shaped the institution's approach to the grantmaker. The foundation executive asked, "What do you think of challenge grants?" The development director answered with a smile, "We like them!" "Well, I think they're good, too," the foundation officer replied.

Of course, the proposal requested a challenge grant. By meeting the foundation's conditions of raising $500,000 in cash from other donors, that hospital qualified for a dollar-for-dollar matching grant.

As a result of development professionals using listening skills and asking carefully phrased questions, corporate executives have been known to offer their help in critiquing proposals and actually helping to rewrite portions of those proposals before they are forwarded from the local corporate branch to the national headquarters for funding.

Make Information Gathering Everyone's Job

Every staff member, and every volunteer, for that matter, must play an important role in gathering information. Bits and pieces of information, learned by various people in various ways, contribute to the overall picture *when the information is incorporated into the donor file.* If it does not get into the donor file, it does not become part of the basis for cultivating that donor.

Making everyone in the development office an information gatherer also enhances team building. It prevents situations such as the one at an institution whose director of development did not want to let his staff have passwords to the computer or add information to the donor files without him looking over their shoulders.

When everyone on staff is an information gatherer, it is a natural step to make everyone a prospect cultivator, to make everyone a thank-you sayer — to make everyone a fund raiser.

Information as an Obligation

In the fund raising business, odds are that a development officer will not be in one institution or position for an entire professional career. The information trail that is left will be one of the key criteria by which careers will be judged for years to come.

Just raising a lot of money is not enough. The information trail, validating one's work, outlining donor relationships, detailing the next steps for future cultivation will clearly demonstrate *how* those dollars were raised. Dollars raised without good record keeping and documentation and without top-notch donor files can lead organizational leaders to the assumption that "it was a fluke" or "most of that money would have come in anyway."

The highest praise that one development professional can give another is to say, after joining an organization, "The person I replaced did a *fantastic* job. I could tell exactly what had been done with the major donors every step of the way. It was easy to continue those relationship-building steps, because of the information I had at my fingertips."

Leaving a legacy of information and tip-top record keeping is not an optional exercise. It is integral to the professional fund raiser's life and work.

A Special Note About Leadership

The organization's president or CEO is ultimately responsible for the information-gathering activities of the development staff. The staff cannot be expected to maximize fund raising without the tools and access needed. All of the computers and software programs in the world will be of no help if there are barriers to *accessing* information.

In some organizations, the barriers exist simply because the development function is never a high enough priority to get attention and programming time from the data-services department.

Making sure that the development officer is in the "inner circle" in receiving administrative and institutional information will not only enhance the organization's ability to attract gifts but also will save some embarrassing moments. For example, one development officer was about to submit a grant request for an existing program (the proposal had been approved by the administration a few weeks before) when the news came that the program had been eliminated.

Information can also help the CEO to assess the productivity of the development program, but only if the right questions are asked. Consider the following:

1. Do you know how to tell if your development program is making progress, and do you play a key role in cultivating donors?
2. Have you requested information from your development officer lately on donor trends and renewal rates in addition to dollars raised?
3. Do you know how to judge if goals are "stretch" goals?
4. Is your involvement in and evaluation of the development process as thoughtful and as consuming as a joint commission review or a visit by the accrediting committee for your organization?
5. Have you gathered enough information and done enough intuitive listening to figure out what makes your development officer tick?

If the CEO cannot answer with a resounding "Yes!" to these questions, mixed messages are being sent to volunteers, donors, and staffmembers.

Information Helps to Profile the Donor Base

All of the information in the world will not help raise money unless time is spent analyzing it as well as planning the cultivation process needed to get repeat gifts, upgraded gifts, special gifts, major gifts, and—ultimately—planned gifts.

If the donor base is not on a computer with software that allows analysis of this information, the organization will also have to grapple with the decision of "to computer or not to computer."

According to Eugene P. Schulstad, president of Master Software Corporation in Indianapolis, not-for-profits can consider several things when investing in fund raising software. Although volume is a consideration, the number of names on a mailing list alone does not determine whether computerizing is essential. Rather, it depends on how much the organization *does* with the donors and the level of activity in the program.

Many offices computerize to provide accessibility of information to several staffmembers. Many newly founded organizations computerize from the beginning to save time and thus avoid the monumental effort of computerizing "after the fact" a few years down the road.

The organization also may purchase donor-tracking software to achieve consistency of records. Donor-tracking software (or fund raising software) is especially helpful to the new development officer who is just learning the field. It provides a starting place and a format for keeping records.

Whether selecting fund raising software for the organization for the first time or just inheriting a system along with a new job, the practitioner must be informed enough about the data and the way the software works in order to help streamline the work of his or her staff. It is important to know, for example, when it is better to enter five hundred biweekly employee-payroll deduction gifts as simple annual contributions (with a code indicating the payroll-deduction method of giving) instead of processing 500×26 pay periods = 13,000 transactions per year. One yearly entry per contributor will save initial staff time as well as computer-processing time on all future reports for which the computer must "read" individual history records.

One does not have to be a computer expert to become "computer literate" in addition to providing the tools, the training, and the resources for making the computer system work for the institution.

Some organizations have learned the hard way about performing regular computer data "backups." One development office lost three weeks' worth of work when its system had a problem. Says the director: "It was discouraging having to do the work all over again, but it was our own fault. If we had done daily 'backups' of the information we would have lost only one or two days' worth of work.

"Now, not only do we 'back up' the data regularly, we also take a copy 'off-site' so that donor histories are not irretrievably lost to fire, like one development office I know of on the East Coast. . . . Another thing, if someone says, 'We can hire my brother-in-law, the computer programmer, and develop the software ourselves for half the cost' — my advice is to run for the hills."

Debriefing by Dictation

Ultimately, all information gathering should lead to one thing: *the process and practice of taking the donor's view in cultivating the philanthropic partnership with the organization.*

Reviewing major donor and major prospect files and information constantly, especially before making an appointment, visiting, or soliciting, gives continuity to the efforts of volunteers and staff.

One development professional performs a *debriefing by dictation* (DBD) after every visit with a major donor prospect. A DBD takes the form of "Notes to the File" and includes a summary of the visit, new items learned about the donor during conversation, and general and specific thoughts about the next steps to be taken in the cultivation process.

Some of the notes on donors remind the professional about a person's pace or "style." For example, one foundation executive, after a quick and friendly greeting, likes to get right down to business. Another executive likes to chat for a while about the community, about family, or about the organization in general. It sometimes takes fifteen or twenty minutes to get to the meeting's appointed topic.

Reviewing the file before the appointment also helps the solicitation professional match the pace of the prospect or donor, to anticipate conversations and questions, and to make that time as full of relationship building as possible.

Tracking the Cultivation of Major Donor Prospects

Besides the at-the-fingertips types of information available on the "giving history" screen of the computer, the development office will need to keep individual hard files for major donor prospects. The Milton Murray Method (M^3) for tracking cultivation for major donor prospects uses two file folders for each prospect. One contains data and information: items that range from newspaper clippings to IRS-990 forms. The second, a correspondence file with the most recent information on top, details letters, contacts, conversations, and visits.

A sheet inside the front cover of the correspondence file lists one-line entries that summarize the documents contained in the file. This kind of file and this much detail is only kept for donors who have made or have the capability of making a major or "ultimate" gift to the organization.

Those intimately involved with the organization can define what determines a major gift. Some organizations only "start counting" when gifts are $10,000 or more; for others, a gift of $1,000 is considered a leadership gift.

Whether a gift is major is not determined solely by its amount. Rather, the relevancy of the gift to the overall well-being of the institution and the capability of the giver are paramount. In this vein, there are no "big" or "small" campaigns. Instead, there are only "tough" and "tougher" campaigns.

Information Goes Both Ways

Information is really a two-way proposition. Collecting information and gathering facts and figures about donors and prospects is an incoming process. Information is also an outgoing function that is concerned with the concept, frequency, and method of communication with donors and the centers of influence in the organization's service area.

Besides using information as an institutional voice (see Exhibit 14.1, "Information Treasure Chests"), there are a multitude of ways to use donor information in a manner that builds and validates relationships. As the maxim says: People rarely give to causes or institutions; people give to people. Credibility must be first established before any serious thoughts of giving manifest themselves. Information and astutely orchestrated dialog (written and oral) will gradually build solid foundations for donor relationships.

In the early stages of a donor relationship one can always acknowledge the anniversary of a gift. For example, "It was one year ago today that your gift helped to culminate our capital campaign. We just wanted to tell you again how much that gift has meant in influencing others to give."

Acknowledgments of birthdays and anniversaries might be included as the relationship grows. Successful fund raisers know that prospects must also be involved in nonsoliciting experiences for gift requests to be positively received.

Only if development professionals feel deep inside that the relationship with the donor is more important than the gifts requested can they be truly effective. Such sincerity shines with laserlike clarity.

Information must travel up and down in the organization, as well as back and forth between the institution and its donors. Development officers should make information accessible to those who need it, making sure that vital information is passed along to the right people above and below them. Donors will feel much more comfortable about investing in an organization whose leaders "have it together," who are communicating from the staff level all the way to top volunteers and administrators.

Donor Information: Handle with Care

Keeping information confidential does not necessarily mean keeping it secret. Rather, it refers to the sensitive gathering and sensitive, judicious, and ethical use of strategically important information about top prospects. In the wrong hands, detailed information could possibly hurt either the prospective donor's reputation or the institution's. Consequently, the bigger the donor, the more essential to safeguard confidential files.

A case in point: Researchers in a certain college development office routinely ordered business profiles from Dun and Bradstreet to research alumni donors who owned businesses. But they failed to provide adequate safeguards to maintain confidentiality and process. One day, instead of directing the corporate information to the appropriate researcher, a student worker inadvertently mailed the information to the donor himself. Outraged, the alumnus called the college development office.

"If you want to know something about my business, all you have to do is

Exhibit 14.1. Information Treasure Chests.

If you are new to your organization, you need to immediately assess what information is available to you. Quickly assemble some basic information to have at your fingertips. If you are not new to your organization, it's a good idea to use this section as a checklist and periodically run your information files through a "relevance review."

1. *Information on the Organization.* Such information would include the organization's history, who it serves today, and its philosophy (vision statement). You also should be able to access (within seconds) a copy of the organization's mission statement, articles of incorporation and bylaws, statistics on clients served, and plans for the future. A one-page fact sheet about the organization may be the item you use most.
2. *Information on Needs.* The "never-finished" case statement that is constantly revised and updated is a sign of a vibrant and dynamic organization. But if your agency has a "never-started" case statement instead, you have some work to do! Also, can you (or anyone on your staff in your absence) pull out a list of named gift opportunities upon request?
3. *Information on the Fund Development Effort.* Such information should include current and historical annual plans, evaluations and accomplishments based on the plan, project reports for special events, results from and examples of direct mail projects, development audits and studies done over the years, and charts and graphs showing the growth (or need for growth) of annual and capital funding efforts. Also add pie charts to show the sources of contributions in comparison with national trends.
4. *Information on Successes.* Gifts received, challenge grants met, people served, families helped, children educated, lives saved—all should be part of this file. Also include human interest stories that illustrate how your organization has made a difference in the community.
5. *Information on Donors.* Besides the information covered elsewhere in this chapter, consider collecting written comments on the reasons that donors have given to you. Were they or a family member dramatically affected in some way? The major donor with eye problems who designated gifts for the ophthalmology department, the community leader whose volunteer work started in speech and hearing because she had a deaf daughter, the businessman whose life was turned around when he was a young student by a caring teacher at his alma mater—all of these are examples of important pieces to be included in the information treasure chest.
6. *Information on Solicitors.* If you have enumerated solicitors' likes and dislikes, interests and hobbies, you will do a better job matching them with potential givers. You may also need to record who should *not* be assigned—such as the overenthusiastic volunteer whose brash manner turns your current donors into former donors!
7. *Information on Key Institutional Players.* Make sure you have copies of the CEO's resume and information on other prominent players (physicians, professors, researchers, and scientists, for example) who are affiliated with your organization. Keep a current list of board members handy along with business address, home address, phone information and spouse information.
8. *Information on Your Not-for-Profit Sector or Industry.* Establish a clip file on education, health care, the arts, social services, children's issues, or whatever it is that your organization is about. Then find ways to share pertinent thoughts and issues with your volunteers and donors.
9. *Information on Giving and Philanthropy.* Professional organizations serving not-for-profit and fund raising interests publish a plethora of information about giving and philanthropy. Stay current with the trends and find a way to share "big picture" information with your donors and volunteers. Don't scrimp on your resource library. When new books on fund raising hit the shelves (or the mail-order catalog pages), buy them and *read* them.
10. *Freestyle Information.* In addition to the above, you will want to develop resources on topics that particularly appeal to you. I collect quotes on philanthropy and volunteering. Some of my colleagues collect cartoons about fund raising, giving, special events, and so on, and I contribute to their collection. I also find myself latching onto any

Exhibit 14.1. Information Treasure Chests, Cont'd.

---

article I can find about trusteeship and what makes a good volunteer — not for the sake of filling a file folder, but always with the thought of how the information might be shared with our volunteers and used to expand the strengths of our efforts.

11. *Personal Information.* Get into the habit of keeping information on your own personal and professional development and accomplishments in fund raising. Keep track of your contributions to professional organizations (service, writing, or chairing committees, for example). This information makes the process of applying for and maintaining your professional accreditation much simpler. *And* it lends itself to establishing a periodic "personal audit" of accomplishments, plans, sources of satisfaction, and the next goals to be set!

---

ask me," he announced angrily and hung up the phone. Needless to say, the carelessness of a few seconds irritated the donor and damaged the work of many years.

Information Helps to Identify the Right Solicitor

Gathering information on committee members and volunteers, particularly those who will solicit gifts for the organization, is another important piece of the information pie.

Is the prospective solicitor pleasant? Persistent? Is the solicitor sensitive to the right time to ask? Confident to *do* the asking? Does the solicitor have good taste, a sense of appreciation for the donor, and the ability to cultivate and nurture the prospect? Will the solicitor express gratitude appropriately when the gift is made?

Good fund raisers have extreme sensitivity to nuances, those almost imperceptible gradations of expression that no true professional ever disregards. These individuals well realize how easy it is to undo years of toil. Those who do not possess this sensitivity should never be unleashed on a donor or prospect.

During a joint multimillion-dollar capital campaign being conducted by several hospitals in a Southwestern metropolis, a small group gathered to evaluate the giving ability of potential donors.

When Mr. Prospect's name came up, one of the committee members expressed his doubts that Mr. Prospect would give to the campaign. "He's been in town for thirty years and has never done anything for the community."

A second committee member commented, "Well, I think he might give $2,500 if he were asked in the right way."

A third committee member spoke up. "I met Mr. Prospect as he got off the train when his company in New York sent him out here. I know him fairly well. Although it is true he hasn't done much, I think if he were asked in the right way, in due time he might be convinced to give $25,000." Of course, the third volunteer was designated to cultivate Mr. Prospect!

At this juncture, a young development officer was assigned to the volunteer to help him educate, cultivate, and inform Mr. Prospect. The staffmember went through his calendar and wrote the name of the volunteer down on his calendar every four to six weeks. He communicated periodically with Mr. Volunteer about Mr. Prospect. Whenever a campaign milestone was reached, the development officer made sure that Mr. Volunteer had the particulars about the news to share with the prospect.

Occasionally, Mr. Volunteer would take Mr. Prospect to a baseball game. Over a period of time, this volunteer visited with Mr. Prospect, communicated with him, and even enlisted Mr. Prospect's daughter's support for the cause.

About a year-and-a-half after those initial conversations, Mr. Prospect became Mr. Donor when he gave a gift of assets to the campaign. It was immediately converted into a cash total of $800,000!

The development officer declares, "That experience taught me the value of matching the right solicitor with the right prospect, and how the development staffer sets into motion the notes, calls, and visits which, in combination over time, impact the relationship that is built with a resulting contribution."

Putting It All Together

Managing fund raising information to support relationship building is demanding yet exciting. This brief introduction can but scratch the surface of this rapidly changing field.

Fund raisers must continually ask themselves these questions: "How much information should we gather? How much cultivation should we do? How long does it take to build a relationship for a lifetime gift?"

At a gallery, an artist was asked, "How long did it take you to do that painting?" Without batting an eye, he replied, "Thirty-one years and three hours." The entire span of his artistic career was focused and condensed into each painting he created!

Likewise with nurturing donors: The process spans years, and each experience and exchange is woven like a different colored thread into the relationship tapestry.

A proverb says, "Kind words can be short and easy to speak, but their echoes are truly endless."

Just so, information gathering has far-reaching effects on the relationship building that will propel not-for-profit organizations toward success!

Assessing
Costs, Risks, and Results

Not-for-profit businesses suffer from a unique characteristic in the world of business—the lack of a profit motive. The implications resulting from this difference are significant in many areas of the organization's operations, but never more apparent than in the fund raising arena.

People are drawn to the not-for-profit sector of society because they care about other people, about animals, about the environment. Money and personal gain are not their primary motives. The issue of fund raising for a cause poses a dilemma: How does a person, drawn to this caring arena, balance the desire to help others with the very real need to obtain the funding to support that effort?

One obvious answer for humanitarians is to hire someone else to do the organization's fund raising. There is a problem with that approach. Although development people abound, good development people are few and far between. Why? Because good development people are made—not born. And once having learned their craft, good development people apply those skills carefully and maturely in organizations that can appreciate and best use those qualities.

Who are these good development people? They are the humanitarians who, through sufficient dedication to their cause, set aside personal fears and awkwardness about asking for money and force themselves to plow through the uncharted fields of fund raising.

Many successful development people learned through trial and error. Immersed in the organization's financial needs of the moment, these fledgling fund raisers probably started off with an event fund raiser, which soon was followed by a poorly strategized direct mail approach. Next might have come the grant-writing cycle, interspersed with presentations to clubs and groups to explain the organization's good purposes.

Some fund raisers may have found these efforts to have produced sufficient revenue to support their small-scale volunteer programs. More likely, however, these enormous volunteer efforts brought small returns, and the cause wilted and died for lack of sufficient funds or sufficiently enthused volunteers to continue fund raising. Other fund raisers may have been heartened by the slowly increasing revenue and begun to recognize a pattern emerging in their fund raising efforts.

Unbeknownst to the fledgling developer, fund raising is a field that has already been charted. Unfortunately, the discomfort surrounding fund raising and the immediacy and urgency of the need combine to create an emotional blindfold that prevents a clear view of the field, camouflaging the path to proven and documented approaches to success. So trial and error prevails.

A trial-and-error approach can be very creative, but it can also cost effectiveness. One of the most significant drawbacks to a trial-and-error approach is its tendency to develop fund raising efforts around personalities, rather than strategy. The more outgoing personality may claim the group's attention with the idea of a "fun" event fund raiser. Other personalities align their own involvement with those task areas that fit their personalities and interests. Potentially hard-working volunteers will suddenly find their time and energy absorbed by a fund raiser whose income potential is far less than the needed revenue, which creates the need for another fund raising effort. But the organization's volunteers are exhausted from the last effort and are not so easy to rally to the cause.

Paper Versus People Fund Raising

Fund raising can be categorized by specific areas of approach. One such categorization differentiates between "paper" fund raising and "people" fund raising. Simply stated, paper fund raising means that paper—in the form of brochures, direct mail pieces, invitations to fund raising events, grant writing, and personal letters requesting donations—is used as the primary tool in the solicitation process.

The people approach infers that personal contact is made between the potential donor (the prospect) and the fund raiser. People contact includes person-to-group presentations, telephone contact, or one-on-one (eyeball-to-eyeball) contact in the solicitation process.

Indirect Ask Versus Direct Ask

There are various ways to let potential donors know of the organization's need for financial support. An indirect approach alludes to the fiscal needs of the organization without an outright request for funding. A demonstration before a group indicating the service the organization provides would be considered an indirect ask. In demonstrating its service to the club or group, the organization lets all who are present understand that a need exists to continue its work. If the presenter were to indicate that the organization needed financial support, the approach would still be categorized as an indirect ask. In both examples, support of the organization would need to be initiated by the club's membership.

If, in the above example, the presenter were to include a specific request of the club or group to make a donation to the organization, this would be a direct ask. A direct ask, therefore, reflects a simple change in semantics—from making a vague allusion to a need to making a direct reference to the need and a specific solicitation of that person, club, or group.

No Close Versus Close

Another important category in fund raising relates to the existence or lack of a "close." A close uses a direct ask and requires a response by the person, group, or club being solicited. It is one thing to ask for a donation on paper, on the telephone, or in person. It is quite another to phrase that ask in a way that requires an answer.

Financial Risk Versus Financial Return

Each fund raising endeavor that an organization attempts can and should be assessed in terms of the "financial risk," or the fund raising activity's up-front costs as well as projections of staff and volunteer time (which are also assets of the organization that need careful management). This financial risk should then be compared to a realistic potential "financial return."

Financial risk versus return is relative and must be analyzed in terms of the fund raising activity's goals. If a pure profit motive is indicated, then the highest net-profit margin potential is a crucial criterion for selecting the fund raising activity. However, if public recognition or donor recognition is part of the net result desired, a lower profit margin may be acceptable.

Much research has been done into the differences in costs of various fund raising activities. The cost of an activity can readily be reduced to cost factors per number of people involved. Return is not as easily determined. Factors that must be considered include such issues as the size of the organization's existing and potential contributor base, the enthusiasm of the contributor base for organizational activities, the amount and type of volunteer involvement, the organization's public profile, the creativity of the approach, and the planning methodology.

Personal Comfort Zones Versus Personal Risk Factors

Another assessment that is often overlooked but just as important to the success of the fund raising activity is the personal risk factor. Fund raising activities involve people, and many of them will put their egos on the line for the organization. Each person involved in the fund raising activity has a personal comfort zone that must be considered when determining which fund raising activities can be most successfully achieved.

To better illustrate this concept, consider an event fund raiser. First, the gregarious and outgoing personality sells an event fund raiser to the group. Next, individuals within the group are assigned specific roles to manage the event. Without proper planning and assignment of roles, personalities will determine the outcome. It may well be, for example, that the person put in charge of ticket sales may be most comfortable with (and thus sees the role as one of) marketing the tickets through advertising and media blitzes, while a more successful sales strategy would have required door-to-door solicitations.

A dedicated staff or volunteer group or a highly motivated individual may be willing to sacrifice personal comfort in favor of a more vigorous fund raising campaign. This is frequently the case in a start-up organization, and it is this scenario that "makes or breaks" a fund raising person. The danger in this fund raising activity is its dependency on staffmembers' or volunteers' willingness to break out of their personal comfort zones. If a quiet but highly motivated person has agreed in the enthusiasm of the moment to solicit door-to-door but withdraws as the day draws near, then the campaign may be stifled.

The not-for-profit sector of society is known to attract and employ the services of sensitive, caring, loving, and altruistic individuals. These people, so willing to give of themselves, so willing to share their lives with others, frequently find asking from others a very difficult task — a personal risk out of sync with their good intentions and personal comfort zones.

Because all not-for-profit staffmembers and volunteers are fund raisers in one sense or another, they are called upon to help in fund raising activities. Rather than assign or expect all fund raisers to be equal, it is helpful to indicate the tasks involved and ensure that each is assigned to someone who is willing and able to carry it out.

An Eclectic Approach

To be successful, an organization's overall fund raising goals need to be met with an eclectic approach that uses careful and strategic planning. Through planning, tasks can be identified and assigned to staffmembers and volunteers to ensure a "good fit," one that takes personal comfort zones into account. Accountability is high when the fit works.

Each of the previously mentioned fund raising approaches—paper versus people, direct versus indirect, and close versus no close—are necessary components of an eclectic fund raising plan and should be strategically combined for effectiveness. The key to fund raising is knowing when, where, and how to apply each and whom to use in the solicitation process.

Paper fund raising and fund raising without a close are generally less personally risky than the eyeball-to-eyeball solicitations that use a close. However, a personal letter to an acquaintance asking for a specific donation may be higher on the personal risk scale for some than giving a presentation about the organization to a club or group. The personal risk factor implies what is personal to each individual. Soliciting a donation even by paper from a friend may be more personally risky to one individual than giving a presentation to a group of people the individual does not personally know. For someone else, the opposite may be true.

The Fund Raising Risk Scale

The fund raising risk scale in Figure 15.1 is meant as a guide to help organizations assess their fund raising activities for financial risk versus return as linked to the personal risk factor.

Key elements in the graph in Figure 15.1 target the categories previously mentioned: paper versus people fund raising, indirect versus direct ask, and no close versus close solicitations. Within each category, the latter rather than the former approach generally involves the most risk for the fund raiser. Generally, too, the latter almost always produces the most income for the lowest cost.

Categories to the right of center in the graph require greater risk taking on the part of the fund raiser to be successful. The greater the distance between the dotted and solid lines (when the dotted line is on top), the greater the net profit for the organization.

The number and letter combinations in parentheses following the categories under the graph correspond to the numbers and letters in the outline titled "Explanations of Fund Raising Approaches."

Explanations of Fund Raising Approaches

I. Sales of Items
    A. Advertisements in newsletters, papers, or magazines
        1. Category: People, indirect, no close
        2. Cost versus return: Fairly high expense involved in both purchasing the items to sell and commercial ad costs if used. Return depends on appeal of items and creativity of sales approach.
        3. Personal risk factor: Low
    B. Booths and showcases

Figure 15.1. Fund Raising Risk Scale.

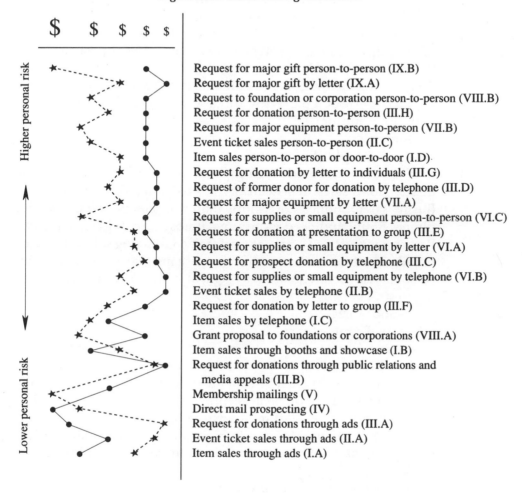

$ $ $ $ $

Higher personal risk

Lower personal risk

Request for major gift person-to-person (IX.B)
Request for major gift by letter (IX.A)
Request to foundation or corporation person-to-person (VIII.B)
Request for donation person-to-person (III.H)
Request for major equipment person-to-person (VII.B)
Event ticket sales person-to-person (II.C)
Item sales person-to-person or door-to-door (I.D)
Request for donation by letter to individuals (III.G)
Request of former donor for donation by telephone (III.D)
Request for major equipment by letter (VII.A)
Request for supplies or small equipment person-to-person (VI.C)
Request for donation at presentation to group (III.E)
Request for supplies or small equipment by letter (VI.A)
Request for prospect donation by telephone (III.C)
Request for supplies or small equipment by telephone (VI.B)
Event ticket sales by telephone (II.B)
Request for donation by letter to group (III.F)
Item sales by telephone (I.C)
Grant proposal to foundations or corporations (VIII.A)
Item sales through booths and showcase (I.B)
Request for donations through public relations and
  media appeals (III.B)
Membership mailings (V)
Direct mail prospecting (IV)
Request for donations through ads (III.A)
Event ticket sales through ads (II.A)
Item sales through ads (I.A)

| Solid line | ———————— | Potential financial risk or cost of the fund raising effort |
| Dotted line | ------------ | Potential financial return of the fund raising effort |

1. Category: People; indirect or direct, depending on staff approach; close or no close, again depending on staff approach
2. Cost versus return: Fairly high expense for acquisition of items. Return depends on the aggressiveness of staff sales approach, popularity of cause, and booth location.
3. Personal risk factor: Low to medium; it is difficult for shy people to work a booth, but if passersby are expected to initiate communication, risk is minimized.

   C. Telephone sales
   1. Category: People, direct, close
   2. Cost versus return: Fairly high expense for acquisition of items, but in telephone sales items can be ordered after the sale is made. Business telephones cost more than volunteers' personal telephones would and need motivating atmosphere to prove effective. Return depends on competence of staff conducting sales effort and popularity of items (item rather than organization is emphasized).
   3. Personal risk factor: Medium to high, although less so when speaking to strangers.

   D. Door-to-door sales
   1. Category: People, direct, close
   2. Cost versus return: Again, the expense in buying the product for resale is high, and a motivated staff is critical in door-to-door sales. An enormous effort must be expended in finding and training this contingent. Returns will be in keeping with the quality and number of door-to-door sales staff minus expenses.
   3. Personal risk factor: Medium to high, although the sales product tends to act as a buffer between sales representative and prospect.

II. Event ticket sales
   A. Advertisements and invitations
   1. Category: Paper, indirect, no close
   2. Cost versus return: Development of good ads and nice invitations costs money; ad space, large printings, and mass mailings add to those costs. Returns depend heavily on the event's previous popularity, the advertising required, the attractiveness of the invitations, recognized "name" draws, and general interest in the event or organization.
   3. Personal risk factor: Low

   B. Telephone ticket sales
   1. Category: People, direct, close or no close, depending on skill of telemarketer
   2. Cost versus return: An all-volunteer force is both inexpensive and conducive to a high level of success when the organization and event are well known; cost thus is limited to follow-up invitation mailings. Return is small relative to other fund raising mechanisms, but should do well in net profit margin.

      3.   Personal risk factor: Low to medium

  C.   Ticket sales person-to-person

      1.   Category: People, direct, close

      2.   Cost versus return: The primary strategy in an "event" ticket-sales campaign person-to-person is not to sell the ticket, but to gain a major donation to underwrite the event's cost so that general ticket sales generate a profit. The cost of this endeavor is minimal: It is usually predicated on prior cultivation of targeted event "underwriters." The return is generally as high as the organization can stretch its influence.

      3.   Personal risk factor: High

III.   Request for Donations

  A.   Advertisements and public-service announcements

      1.   Category: Paper, direct, no close

      2.   Cost versus return: Ads and public-service announcements take money to produce and compete with nationally known organizations. The return is minimal. Although they do bring attention to the organization, essentially they are only a beginning step in any fund raising campaign rather than a financially successful end.

      3.   Personal risk factor: Low

  B.   Public-relations and media appeals

      1.   Category: People or paper, direct or indirect, no close

      2.   Cost versus return: The cost of a radio or television appearance is usually limited to staff time in arranging for, traveling to, and appearing on a broadcast. Even with a savvy staff person who can ensure that the media coverage includes a bonafide ask, the returns remain very limited. The audience is not necessarily primed or selected for its willingness to give to the organization's cause.

      3.   Personal risk factor: Low to medium, depending on camera shyness

  C.   Telephone requests to prospects

      1.   Category: People, direct, close

      2.   Cost versus return: Again, business telephones cost money to use, and staff time can be expensive. Although dedicated volunteers may like to talk to people who know nothing about the organization, generally they are not motivated to tell about the organization *and* ask for a donation in the same breath. Returns depend on the capability of telephone marketers.

      3.   Personal risk factor: Medium

  D.   Telephone requests to former donors

      1.   Category: People, direct, close

      2.   Cost versus return: Staff time and business phones cost money, but volunteers at home cost only the time to manage them and the telephone campaign. Cost may also involve sending out follow-up literature. Returns are probably higher in number from low-end

donors using this method than any other employed, although direct mail runs a close second.

3. Personal risk factor: Medium when the caller experiences less opposition to his or her request from the organization's own support group. The risk is still there, however. Higher when the fund raiser actually knows the person being called.

E. Presentation to groups
   1. Category: People, indirect or direct, no close
   2. Cost versus return: Generally the up-front cost is low or covered in part by the group being solicited. Staff time costs money, however. Even with a competent person making a direct appeal for donations, the return usually is very limited because many groups preplan their large-gift allocations during their annual budget and planning sessions. A presentation is primarily a cultivation tool to be followed by a large and purposeful request later (see "F." below)
   3. Personal risk factor: Medium to high; risk is primarily based on ability to speak to a group, not the awkwardness of a potential rejection for funds.

F. Letter or proposal to group
   1. Category: Paper, direct, no close
   2. Cost versus return: Writing a proposal or letter requesting a donation is as inexpensive or costly as the person and time used in creating, packaging, and sending it. If this request is made after sufficient cultivation of prospects, then the return should be worth a lot more than the effort expended. Most organizations fail to follow up on these potentials.
   3. Personal risk factor: Low to medium

G. Letter to individuals
   1. Category: Paper, direct, no close
   2. Cost versus return: Again, an inexpensive process. A more effective tool than a direct mail piece, although the potential that it will be tossed, set aside and forgotten, or generally ignored certainly is higher than a direct person-to-person ask. Still, it is more effective — when cultivation has been done properly ahead of time — than other paper forms of fund raising.
   3. Personal risk factor: Low to high, depending on relationship that letter writer has to prospect. For some people it is more difficult to ask a friend for support; for others it is more difficult to ask someone they do not know.

H. Person-to-person
   1. Category: People, direct, close
   2. Cost versus return: Undoubtedly, whenever possible person-to-person fund raising is best. The cost is in the prior cultivation and the planning, time, and travel for the visit, but the returns are by far

the greatest. If one has the means, it is much harder to say no to a face-to-face appeal from a sincere representative of the cause. This is definitely where the money is.

3. Personal risk factor: Medium to high, depending on the amount of funds requested and the fund raiser's perception of the prospect's ability to give and the perceived value of that amount to him- or herself.

IV. Direct Mail Prospecting
   A. Category: Paper, direct, no close
   B. Cost versus return: Direct mail prospecting is expensive and generally considered effective if it breaks even. The value is in increasing the donor base for the following years' solicitations. Costs include purchasing of lists and creating, printing, and sending mail pieces. Returns depend on the appeal of the piece, the strength of the market, and the organization's general name recognition.
   C. Personal risk factor: Low

V. Membership Mailings
   A. Category: Paper, direct, no close
   B. Cost versus return: Membership mailings are essentially direct mailings to the current donor base. Although attrition (the loss of some donors) always exists, a nice profit margin often is realized. Costs include generating mailing labels and creating, printing, and mailing the piece—and, of course, sending thank-yous. Returns are usually low-end donations, although in volume, and basic support for the organization that uses this technique.
   C. Personal risk factor: Low

VI. Request for Supplies or Small Equipment
   A. Letter
      1. Category: Paper, direct, no close
      2. Cost versus return: Cost is limited to writing the letter and making the case; return varies because of the time constraints of small-business people. Generally, the return is high when followed up by a personal appeal, low if not.
      3. Personal risk factor: Medium
   B. Telephone
      1. Category: People, direct, close
      2. Cost versus return: Cost again is limited to the people contact time and probably the time spent picking up the item. The intervening variable that makes this more difficult is the time factor. Usually, supplies or small equipment are needed more immediately, and waiting becomes a problem. However, if this is a planned request and time does not matter, then the return is usually significant.
      3. Personal risk factor: Medium
   C. Person-to-person

     1.   Category: People, direct, close

     2.   Cost versus return: More effective than telephone if the organization is not known to the prospective donor, but about the same if the donor already supports the cause.

     3.   Personal risk factor: Medium to high

VII.   Request for Major Equipment

  A. Personal letter

     1.   Category: Paper, direct, no close

     2.   Cost versus return: The cost is generally minimal: staff time in researching prospects, creating the case, and writing and mailing the letter. The return depends on to whom and from whom the letter is sent; that is, was prior cultivation of this donor done? Returns vary, but generally are not as good as a direct person-to-person appeal. Paper in this case is a good door opener.

     3.   Personal risk factor: Medium

  B. Person-to-person appeal

     1.   Category: People, direct, close

     2.   Cost versus return: The cost is limited to the prior planning, travel, and visitation time. However, the returns usually are good when the product is manufactured by the prospect. Well worth the effort!

     3.   Personal risk factor: High

VIII. Request to Foundations and Corporations

  A. Grant proposal

     1.   Category: Paper, direct, no close

     2.   Cost versus return: Grant proposal writing requires research, study, making the case, and putting it all in a form that is attractive and acceptable to the foundation or corporation for whom it is intended. This is a somewhat time-consuming process and thus costs staff time in printed matter production, planning sessions, and writing. Fortunately, some of that work can be duplicated for other grant proposals. The return is in direct relationship to the breadth of the research and effectiveness of the prior cultivation and the grant proposal itself. Well worth the effort when it is not a scatter approach.

     3.   Personal risk factor: Low

  B. Person-to-person

     1.   Category: People, direct or indirect, close or no close

     2.   Cost versus return: Many requests to corporations and foundations require a written proposal. That does not preclude an attempt at person-to-person contact, however. And as with all other fund raising avenues, person-to-person works! It may be used strategically to initiate a grant proposal or it may be the final step before receiving a gift. Do not bypass this important step because a few calls are rebuffed. Certainly greater returns are realized if this method is available.

      3.   Personal risk factor: High. Because foundations and corporate foundations are in the business of giving away money, however, this risk factor, even though person-to-person, may be perceived as less threatening by some.

IX.   Request for Major Gift

  A. Letter

      1.   Category: Paper, direct, no close

      2.   Cost versus return: As with all letter appeals, the cost is minimal, although prior cultivation is a must and can be expensive in staff time and activity. Returns are limited to the degree the approach captures the attention and interest of the prospective donor. In most cases, the return would be less than what would result from a person-to-person appeal.

      3.   Personal risk factor: High

  B. Person-to-person

      1.   Category: People, direct, close

      2.   Cost versus return: Costs again are limited to prior cultivation, planning, travel, and staff time. With proper research and selection of prospects, returns are inestimable in that they are probably far above the reader's current expectations. This is the crème de la crème of fund raising, and it is to this level that all organizations should aspire. However, this is not the only answer; a varied, balanced approach that incorporates all manner of fund raising puts the organization on a much safer footing.

      3.   Personal risk factor: Extremely high

Conclusion

Paper fund raising in the form of printed materials is the least threatening medium to the personal comfort zone of fund raisers because they can easily distance themselves from the ask. Even though they are a form of paper fund raising, letters are a more personal form of communication and thus increase the personal risk factor. In general, paper fund raising costs more with lower returns than does people fund raising.

     People fund raising is certainly more of a threat to the personal comfort zones of most fund raisers, but it inevitably brings the greatest returns. Note, however, that it is almost as difficult to ask for a small donation as for a large one, which implies that if resources (that is, fund raisers whose personal comfort zones will expand to include person-to-person asks) are limited, perhaps research and cultivation are best spent on big-gift prospects.

     Indirect asks are frequently more comfortable to the fund raiser than direct asks, irrespective of the medium of approach. This gentle technique is more effective in public relations than fund raising because its primary effect is to raise the prospect's consciousness. However, the message "to give" can be ignored more readily with an indirect ask. Indirect approaches also can cost more because some other form of communication (ads, invitations, direct mail) must be used to get the direct-ask message across.

Lack of a close does one of two things: (1) It leaves the gift potential totally in the hands of the prospect without the fund raiser's presence to negotiate a successful outcome; or (2) it allows the prospect to string the fund raiser along indefinitely without a conclusion.

A close, on the other hand, opens the door to negotiation and positive communication between the fund raiser and the prospect, thus allowing for greater understanding between the two parties — and greater potential for success.

Fund raising operates under premises similar to those of sales: (1) have a good product, (2) package it well, (3) educate staffmembers and volunteers on the value of the package to ensure a good fit between the specific solicitation approach and the fund raiser, (4) see that the product is presented to potential donors (preferably face-to-face), and (5) close.

The last and most golden rule in fund raising is to follow up! If the donation did not come through as hoped, keep up the cultivation efforts and try again. If the donation did come through, thank the donor immediately and profusely. Follow up with continued cultivation of this donor, building for future gifts.

How to Select and Use Fund Raising Consultants

Paying someone—an individual or a company—to manage or to consult about the fund raising activities of a nonprofit organization presents important challenges. This chapter is designed to take away the mystery that surrounds the client–consultant relationship and to suggest specific steps to create strong, positive ties. The topics discussed are:

- what a consultant is
- what consultants do for nonprofit organizations
- how to hire a consultant
- how to make the client–consultant relationship work
- what steps to take should the relationship not work out

The client–consultant relationship should be mutually rewarding. Satisfaction is possible only if there is respect on both sides and if an effort is made to create a true partnership, rather than an "us versus them" situation. This point of view permeates all that follows in this chapter.

What Is a Consultant?

Definitions are awkward. To take a living and breathing entity, freeze its activity for one moment, and then describe it is a process that loses the nuances of the "real thing."

With this caveat, Webster's *New World Dictionary* describes a consultant as "A person who gives professional or technical advice, as a doctor, lawyer, engineer, editor. . . ."

The National Association of Attorneys General (1986) provides legal descriptions of *counsel* and *solicitor*: "Fund raising counsel refers to a person who for compensation plans, manages, advises, consults or prepares material for, or with respect to, the solicitation. . . of contributions. . . . A paid solicitor refers to a person who for compensation performs for a charitable organization any service in connection with which contributions are, or will be, solicited. . . by such compensated person. . . ."

A typical quip asks, "What is a consultant? I can best tell you about one by describing the typical behavior of the species. When you ask a consultant what time it is, he borrows your watch to tell you."

Taking a bit from Webster's and another idea from the attorneys general and keeping in mind the perceptions behind the last cynical observation, a fourth view is offered. A fund raising consultant works with key staffmembers and board members to resolve fund raising and related organizational issues. The exact methods and services vary from consultant to consultant.

A consultant can be viewed as the best friend or the worst enemy and still help the organization to achieve desired goals. One might see very little of this person, or the consultant might virtually live with the organization. A consultant can be tall, short, fat, thin, young, or old. The person can free creativity or put everyone into a total rage.

The Fund Raising Business

Fund raising consulting is one business in which chemistry between the client and the consultant must be strong and supportive. The consultant must be flexible to meet the organization's needs and have enough experience to help the organization work through its problems. The development team must have faith in the consultant and not work counter to an agreed-upon strategy.

Fund raising consulting is a relatively young industry. Although the philanthropic and voluntary spirits are part of the fabric of our American heritage, systematic fund raising did not develop until the late nineteenth century. It was an innovation of the YMCA. Colleges and hospitals quickly learned the new skills, and by the turn of the century they were designing and initiating special fund drives (Raybin, 1985, pp. 2–3).

By 1920, a handful of consulting companies were formed to provide services to the growing number of not-for-profit organizations that wished assistance with fund raising. Fifteen years later, a small group of these companies established the American Association of Fund-Raising Counsel (AAFRC), which has been dedicated to maintaining standards in the fund raising field and to supporting the needs of consultants.

From a few firms in the 1920s, the industry has grown to exciting proportions today. Thousands of individual practitioners and firms are ready to meet the diverse needs of a burgeoning not-for-profit community. New ideas, new products, and new techniques abound.

It is impossible to have a fund raising or related management need and not be able to identify a consultant who can provide the not-for-profit organization with a unique service. What are those services? They can be sorted into four broad categories: (1) capital and special campaigns, (2) operating and annual campaigns, (3) other direct fund raising activities, and (4) support services.

Patricia McNeill, vice-president of J.C. Geever, Inc., describes a capital campaign as the "process of raising a lot of money from relatively few people in a fast time frame." A consultant will usually recommend that a feasibility study be undertaken before an organization commits to a capital or special-purpose drive. A series of interviews with individuals and with persons representing foundations and corporations are undertaken by the consultant. An analysis of the data thus gathered provides the not-for-profit with information about the interviewees' feelings toward the proposed capital or special plan, the dollar goal, gifts from interviewees, and leadership for the drive. With this information in hand, the not-for-profit organization can be more certain of success. The consultant's service after the study will be full-time at the organization, full-time elsewhere, or only guidance with the not-for-profit organization implementing all phases of the drive. Whether a consultant remains involved for the entire campaign can always be negotiated. The campaign can be completed by the organization's staff and volunteers.

Frequently, organizations simply need money to operate, to keep the doors open. Consultants can be very helpful in these operating or annual campaigns. They may manage the full drive, work on certain pieces, or provide consulting assistance. Usually the campaign targets are individuals, foundations, corporations, and government entities. An operating campaign will have a time frame for specific types of activities, although some outreach may be ongoing through the fiscal year.

Formal capital campaigns and ongoing fund raising for operating support are supplemented by other direct fund raising activities that many consultants will either teach to the staff or undertake for the organization. These include telemarketing, planned giving, special events, and direct mail. Each is a specialty. Each can contribute to the organization's annual or special fund raising efforts.

In addition, consultants offer an array of other *support* services. These range from audits of the development effort to development office redesign. Training, board development, executive search, prospect identification and research, market analysis, the design and development of fund raising materials, and public relations are among the services that fund raising consultants provide today.

No two firms or practitioners offer exactly the same services or provide them in the same manner. Part of the excitement of working with counsel is discovering a firm that meets the organization's exact needs.

How to Hire a Consultant

Eleven steps should be followed when considering whether to hire a consultant and what type of consultant will best meet the organization's needs:

1. Determine the agency's needs.
2. Build a list of prospective consultants.
3. Refine the list.
4. Arrange face-to-face meetings.
5. Prepare for the interviews.
6. Check references.
7. Manage the interview.
8. Select the consultant.
9. Negotiate a contract.
10. Start work.
11. Communicate with the noncontracted consultants.

While one step leads to another in this process, it is important to discuss the particulars of each.

First, *determine the agency's needs.* As discussed in the preceding section, fund raising consultants can provide many different services. But what does the organization need and what can it afford to spend? Time must be spent making these decisions before searching the network for recommendations or spending time on the phone with prospective consultants. Writing in the Better Business Bureau's publication *Insight* (1989, p. 2), Lisa D. Heltne says, "The first step in choosing a fund raiser begins internally. It is important for an organization to keep in mind that any fund raising effort should be envisioned as a long-term process and investment that will affect the organization long after a given fund raising program ends."

In sum, know exactly what the consultant is to do for the organization and how much can be paid for the service, adjusting both objectives, if needed, as the process unfolds. Work from a position of knowledge rather than reaction.

Second, *build a list of prospective consultants.* Talk with other nonprofit executives and directors of development, funders, and board members about their experiences in using counsel. Whom can they recommend? Also contact the American Association of Fund-Raising Counsel for its list of members as well as the local chapter of the National Society of Fund-Raising Executives for its list of practitioners.

Although some individuals and firms may be named repeatedly, try not to make snap decisions at this stage. Let the list be inclusive. It can be refined as the search proceeds and with more direct contact with the consultants.

Third, *refine the list*. Put the needs of the organization in writing and solicit a written response from each consultant on the list. The request for materials can run the gamut from a simple response to a formal proposal.

With this data in hand, it can be easily determined which consultants are of greatest and least interest to the organization. The organization's representative can then call each of the remaining consultants. To prepare for the calls, it is helpful to have a checklist of general questions to ask the consultant, such as what services will be provided, the total cost, how the effort will be staffed, and what level of supervision will be provided. The written materials also will suggest specific questions for which explanations are required. The tone of the conversation will provide further ideas about whether the organization and the consultant are well suited to one another.

With the written information in hand and the added telephone feedback, final selections can be made about which consultants to meet face-to-face. Create this short list and share it with the board, other key staffmembers, and the network to gather final comments.

Fourth, *arrange face-to-face meetings*. Keep the interview group small. Try to see all of the consultants on the same day or within the same week. Give each one sufficient time to make a full presentation to the group and to answer questions. Allowing time for the interview and holding it in an appropriate setting treats the professional with respect and gives the organization's representatives a reasonable opportunity to gain an understanding of the consultant's philosophy and working style.

Fifth, *prepare for the interviews*. To begin, recruit a group of interested board members and staffmembers to participate in the interview process. This committee should consist of the board president, the development committee chairperson, the organization's CEO, and key development staffmembers.

Next develop a series of questions to be asked of all consultants about services, cost, and staffing. Also have specific questions for each consultant generated by their written materials and previous contact with them.

Then hold a briefing session with the organization's search committee. Be certain that committee members are aware of the full process followed to date, the complete list of consultants contacted and why specific ones were deleted from the final interview group, the fund raising need faced by the organization, and how each interviewee can assist.

In all instances, be objective and keep the committee from making snap decisions without hearing each finalist. Determine who will lead the discussion and who will ask which questions. Be in agreement that the focus of the discussion is on the consultant and the related services to be offered and not on the organization and its needs. The latter point should have been sufficiently covered in the materials and conversations.

Sixth, *check references*. The committee should make a decision after the interviews, so it is critical that a reference check is made for the individuals or firms who are participating in the final interviews. Talk to a broad selection of the finalists' current and former clients. Be sure to add specific questions to any lists when an issue is raised by a reference that needs further exploration with the consultant.

Seventh, *manage the interview*. At long last, the time has come for the committee to meet the consultants. Time the presentations so that the practitioners are not meeting their competitors in the hall.

Be certain that the discussion facilitator makes appropriate and full instructions. Allow the consultant the agreed-upon amount of time to present credentials and proposed services. Pursue friendly dialogue and questions. Remember to allow the consultant enough time to make a full presentation, but do not allow the consultant to lead the committee in a soul-searching discussion. Committee members may feel very satisfied as a result, but they will not have gained critical information on the consultant's services and policies.

When the representative of a firm makes a presentation, the staffmembers who will be assigned may or may not be present. The organization has the right, however, to meet this person or these persons before a contract is signed. It is appropriate to determine how the firm will react if a change in the personnel assigned to the not-for-profit is requested.

Eighth, *select the consultant*. Do not let the committee postpone its decision. While the committee is in one room and the information about the consultants is fresh, force a decision. Perhaps the decision will be not to go forward with the plans in the foreseeable future. Nevertheless, make a decision! A failure to act at this point, if the process has been followed thoroughly, indicates a lack of commitment on the part of key board members and staffmembers to what had been planned. No consultant can make up for that lack of leadership commitment. If the consensus of the group is to move ahead and one consultant is a clear choice, communicate with that consultant as quickly as possible. Now the real work begins on both sides!

Ninth, *negotiate a contract*. A legally binding contract forms the basis for the relationship between the not-for-profit organization and the consultant. State and local regulators often dictate the content of contracts and require their filing and review with the proper authority before work can commence.

Work cooperatively with the consultant to develop a document that adequately reflects the proposed relationship. The document should include:

- detail on the tasks to be performed by the consultant;
- the date when the contract becomes effective and the date of its expiration;
- a cancellation clause that can be exercised by either party with a specific number of days notice, usually not less than thirty or more than ninety;

- a statement of ownership of property such as direct mail lists, artwork, and the like;
- a mechanism for final approval of written materials, scripts, and so on by the nonprofit's representative;
- information on the total amount that the consultant will be paid, when and if payment is tied to delivery of the product;
- data on out-of-pocket expenses or a deposit for which the client may be liable; and
- a provision for the contract to be signed by the practitioner or officer of the firm and an officer of the nonprofit.

Keep in mind the following points. The organization should be represented by legal counsel. A lawyer can be present for contract negotiation but should at minimum review it to protect the agency's rights. Do not consider any comments made orally to be binding on either side. Put them in writing. And do not accept a preprinted contract.

How consultants should be paid for their services—flat fee, commission, or percentage—is a very complicated issue today. Be guided by ethical and not only legal considerations. Be sure the consultant will not take short cuts to increase compensation. Such shortcuts could hurt the organization's fund raising in the long term.

Tenth, *start work*. As soon as the contract has received the necessary regulatory approvals, the not-for-profit and the consultant are ready to begin a relationship that should bring long-term fund raising benefits to the organization. Do not expect overnight results. Keep the dialog going with the consultant and do not be afraid to be critical or to explore problem areas.

Eleventh, *communicate with the noncontracted consultants*. A brief letter should thank all of the consultants contacted for their time and indicate who was hired.

How to Make the Client–Consultant Relationship Work

The organization and the consultant have now created a relationship that each wants to be mutually productive. It is now appropriate to explore what is at stake for both the not-for-profit organization and the consultant, as well as the formula for success.

What should the organization expect? The organization wants to raise more money in the short term and enhance its long-term support. Concurrently, it may have to solve related problems that are preventing the organization from realizing a maximum financial return. But this also should be a learning opportunity. Part of the goal should be to come away from an intense relationship better able to think through and address organizational issues. This does not mean that the organization should sever ties with the consultant as quickly as possible. On the contrary, as staffmembers and volunteers achieve a more sophisticated understanding of the issues of the organization, they will be even more adept at properly using the consultant.

And what does the consultant expect? First, to take the challenge the organization has presented and to succeed. The drive to create order out of chaos, to take a problem and solve it, is very strong in individuals who pursue consulting work. Second, the consultant wishes to do a good job that will lead to more work with the organization and to a strong reference.

There is a desire on both sides for the relationship to succeed. What has to happen to bring that goal to fruition? These four simple steps should be followed.

1. Have the organization's key leadership actively participate with the consultant. All too often, not-for-profit organizations retain outside counsel with the explicit purpose of turning everything over to the expert. This is dangerous. Key leaders must work with the consultant to implement the plan. A team consists of the board president, the board member who chairs the fund raising committee, the chief executive officer, the staffperson responsible for fund raising and external affairs, and the consultant. Together they guide, direct, and effect the effort.
2. View the activities as cooperative. Simply put, the effort will not succeed if there is an "us versus them" overtone to the organization's relationship with the consultant.
3. Respect the skills and opinions of the consultant. It is not necessary to always agree with the consultant, but it is critical to respect the skills and opinion that the person brings to the relationship. If confidence is lost in the consultant or if the advice provided is deliberately not followed, prospects for success are diminished.
4. Create opportunities for open and honest communication. There must be a constant dialog with the consultant about activities in progress, proposed next steps, problems that have developed, and the successes and failures in the work to date.

In the process much is learned from the consultant and the consultant receives feedback — positive and negative — about the work in progress.

In sum, the client–consultant relationship should be mutually beneficial. The organization will be stronger. Staffmembers and volunteers will become more sophisticated in their understanding of problem solving. The consultant will have the satisfaction of a job well done and of a good reference from a satisfied customer.

Steps to Take If Things Do Not Work Out

Chemistry plays a big role in the relationship between the organization and the consultant. If personality conflicts or lack of trust in the person's judgment develops, or if an organization feels that the services obtained are not what was expected, then it is time to have a candid chat with the consultant.

See the consultant alone but alert a supervisor if there is one. Then, if the situation worsens, ask to see the supervisor as well. In any conversation be clear and specific. Articulate the problems and where expectations are not being met. Provide ideas how the situation can be remedied. Allow the consultant an opportunity to respond to the points that have been raised. A plan that corrects the legitimate concerns should result from such a meeting. Put these decisions in writing and provide a copy to the consultant's supervisor.

If matters do not improve, it is time to ask for the supervisor's input or for a second meeting with the consultant about the concerns. In any instance, make it clear that specific changes must occur within a specified time frame or that there is an intent to use the cancellation clause in the contract. If the proposal is not acceptable to the consultant and a counterplan does not create satisfaction, then it is time to sever the relationship. Make sure that in the concluding days the organization is fully briefed on the work in progress and the next steps that must be taken.

In the meantime, start the search process again. Go back to the short list and select the consultants who were liked and were able to do the work. Be certain to review the reasons why those consultants were not selected in the first place. Can the organization live with what was perceived at one time to be a problem or shortcoming?

Sometimes, in a desire to rectify the fund raising problems facing a charitable organization, its representatives can be overanxious and hear what a consultant says with a biased ear. When this occurs, it is very possible that the relationship with the consultant will hit rough spots. Recognize the likelihood of this happening. Be prepared to act when it happens. Be committed to resolving the problems even if the result is the cancellation of an agreement with a consultant who is liked and admired.

Fallacies and Misconceptions

Certain assumptions must be dispensed with by not-for-profit organizations that enter into arrangements with consultants.

What You Might Be Thinking	*Reality*
1. You can easily switch from one consultant to another.	It is true that legally you can break a contract with one consultant and retain another, but you will lose momentum and valuable insights learned by the first consultant while with you, and if done frequently, "good" consultants will not want to work with you.

2. Bigger or cheaper is better.

It is better to find the consultant with whom you and your organization can work regardless of size and fees. In the long run, a more expensive consultant may cost you less, and a bigger consultant may not have the special expertise that your organization needs.

3. We'll interview a lot of consultants and figure out how to do it ourselves.

In all likelihood, you will feel that many of the things consultants tell you can be done yourself. But consultants bring expertise from many years in the field and from working with many different kinds of organizations. You cannot replicate this internally. The consultant is trained to help you face your organization's challenges. Furthermore, the consultant keeps up the pressure, which frequently brings results from volunteers.

4. You hire the consultant and turn all your fund raising over to that person without a worry.

The effort is doomed to fail. No consultant can single-handedly solve a problem or create a successful campaign. You are abdicating your fiduciary and legal responsibility to your organization if you ever allow any consultant to simply "take over" some aspect of your fund raising without key board members and staff members participating in the effort.

5. The more you interview, the better.

Wrong! This will cause the selection process to become interminable. Without preselection and screening, your volunteers will become very confused and unable to make a final selection. An endless interview process is very unfair to the consultants who invest a great deal of time and money on your project.

6. Chemistry does not matter. We can always make things work later.

If you do not feel good about the ideas, philosophy, appearance, and general attitude of the consultant during the interview period when

7. The consultant must have empathy for our cause.

everyone is on his or her best behavior, what makes you think things will get better? In fact, as pressure increases, the differences will become more apparent and you will lack confidence in your counsel. The consultant must have the skills to help your organization. That is first and foremost. If the consultant also agrees with the work you do, it can make the learning curve faster and easier. Someone who is too close can fail to be objective and hard-nosed with you.

8. The consultant must have worked on a similar project and for the same kind of organization.

Again, innovation and fresh ideas frequently will come from a consultant who has not run an exactly similar campaign or worked for exactly the same kind of organization. Fund raising consulting skills are easily transferable.

9. We can hire someone on a percentage basis. Any funds raised are plus for us.

But in the process what has the organization lost? Fund raising is a slow and careful process of building relationships with long-term supporters. Any shortcuts can damage the potential for your organization. Unfortunately, it is more likely that a professional working on a percentage will take shortcuts.

Conclusion

Consultants are fine people. They have committed themselves to a life of service to the not-for-profit community. They use honed analytical skills to solve the fund raising and management problems of our charities. They are driven, hard-working, and concerned.

On the whole, consultants charge fees commensurate with other professionals who serve the charitable world. A few negative stories have made the press from time to time, but when weighed against all of the good that consultants do for not-for-profit organizations, they are aberrations. More than 1,200 organizations are successfully served by AAFRC firms each year. The number of awkward relationships is few, while the percentage of successes is high.

The not-for-profit organization should expect to find a consultant who can meet its needs. Both parties should anticipate that the relationship will be constructive and beneficial.

As Gene Dorsey, chairman of INDEPENDENT SECTOR, said in his opening remarks to the Center on Philanthropy's 1990 Third Annual Symposium, "Taking Fund Raising Seriously," "I believe the potential for expanding the financial support of the nonprofit sector is enormous. But it will require strong, well-managed nonprofits that communicate effectively about their activities and employ professional, ethical fund raisers to solicit their prospects."

PART FIVE

HOW TO RESEARCH AND ANALYZE GIFT SOURCES

As reviewed in Part One, there are "vehicles" in fund raising. There are also "gift markets" in the jargon of fund raising practitioners and their volunteer counterparts. Gift markets can be defined as potential sources of funds. These sources are individuals, corporations, foundations, associations, and government. It is the responsibility of a fund raising officer to be generally knowledgeable about all of these gift sources, as well as quite proficient in the understanding of the few that will make a difference to the organization seeking funds.

Prospect research, or prospect development, is one important part of the fund raising officer's routine responsibilities. It is essential to the process to know as much as possible about potential giving sources. It stands to reason that if a source is to be asked to contribute to a cause, the asker must know a good deal about the source to ask properly. This is the purpose of prospect research.

Is it ethical, is it morally proper to carry out research on an individual? Does this constitute an invasion of privacy? Yes, research is proper. No, it is not an invasion of privacy. It is an honest, ethical procedure to secure information relevant to the solicitation process. All information that is secured is already in the public domain. Obviously, it would be quite foolish to do anything that would offend the person who will be approached.

Phyllis A. Allen   Chapter 17

How to Research and Analyze Individual Donors

Prospect research is the systematic acquisition and recording of data about donors and prospects that provide the basis to establish, maintain, and expand the "exchange relationship." It is a primary goal of the development program to establish long-term gift relationships with as large a percentage of the organization's constituency as possible. The ultimate goal is to develop as many donors as possible into major-gift relationships.

What is meant by "exchange relationship"? The donor brings his or her largess to the program or project and thereby enhances the community well-being. The institution or organization provides the donor with a sense of worth, value, belonging, and making a difference. Such gifts save lives, mount prized exhibits, provide desperately needed community services, stage theater and musical productions, strengthen youth programs, and the list goes on.

Why is it important to conduct research? The success in developing a major-gift relationship — one that brings in significant amounts over long periods of time — will depend upon the ability to make and maintain a "match" between the organization's mission, goals, and objectives and the donor's roles, responsibilities, and satisfactions. Research provides the information to make that match. Research supports the development of the philanthropic exchange relationship.

Effective fund raising requires the accumulation of accurate data. The intent is to know as much as possible, and profiles are built upon data supplied by individuals or researched from public resources. The process,

conducted within board-established guidelines and policies, is neither im-
moral nor illegal. The process identifies the prospect, discovers as much
information as is readily available about the prospect, and then leads to
cultivation and solicitation strategies with the highest potential for successful
gift getting.

Individuals provide more than 90 percent of the revenue in virtually all
fund raising operations. This is supported elsewhere in this book's references
and is important to remember. The gathering of accurate, detailed, and
continually updated information on selected individuals from the organization's primary constituency makes up the baseline from which the most
effective fund raising will flow. John D. Rockefeller, Jr., said it best in a classic
statement that has been printed and reprinted by many organizations in
their fund raising materials: "It is a great help to know something about the
person whom you are approaching. You cannot deal successfully with all the
people in the same way. Therefore, it is desirable to find out something about
the person you are going to—what are his interests, whether he gave last year,
if so, how much he gave, what he might be able to give this year, etc.
Information such as that puts you more closely in touch with him to make the
approach easier."

A good researcher, it has been said, has the soul of a Sherlock Holmes,
possesses a photographic memory, and experiences the "thrill of the chase"
to a high degree. A review of the literature in the field shows frequent
comparisons to the arena of private investigation. Articles are sprinkled
with words such as *sleuth*, *detective*, and *private eye*. These references con-
note diligence, persistence, and cunning rather than any sort of shady
characteristics.

These qualities are best exemplified by a story about a hospital foundation researcher whose photographic memory is legendary. In seeking foundations that would be interested in supporting a particular medical specialty,
she found a Chicago address for one that stirred a faint memory. She followed
her hunch and discovered that the address for a certain private family trust by
a different name was the same. A quick phone call uncovered a strong family
link and it became an important element in a proposal that resulted in
"sister" grants—one from the public foundation, another from the family
trust.

Shadow any experienced, successful researcher for a day and one hears
a number of stories about the seemingly incredible coincidences that bring
about major breakthroughs in knowledge about a prospect's linkage to the
institution, the ability to give, and the areas of interest—any combination of
which may prove crucial to the identification, cultivation, and successful
solicitation of that individual.

Basic Research Principles

There are two aspects to prospect research: "People" research is the gathering
of information from individuals during one-on-one sessions or in the

prospect-identification and prospect-rating meetings that are held with a small committee for just this purpose. "Book" research uses any and all resources from libraries, the institution's own bookshelves, and the vast array of other sources that are reviewed later in this chapter. It is during the people research that the development officer frequently finds the most valuable information.

How does the organization identify those who might give? Who are the members of the constituency? To begin at the beginning, list all the groups that make up the organization's "family." Among them will be:

1. board members
2. alumni (graduates, former patients, and so on)
3. volunteers
4. staff leadership
5. professional affiliates (professors, physicians, and artists)
6. former donors
7. gift-club members
8. those known to believe in the organization's work.

Use the above list only as a start; each development department will derive its own specialized list. For instance, a university may have town-and-gown lectures on biotechnology advances. It is a ticketed series that brings forth a subscription list. These names become part of a long list. This long list is then divided into segments that fit the needs of the organization, beginning with board and former board members. Add those known donors who have a history of gifts over time or who have made recent significant gifts. Only a relatively small portion of the initial list will be candidates for fully developed research profiles.

One method is to divide the list into three categories: The A list are those with the strongest ties, the B list are those who have some linkage and who are thought to have the ability and interest in giving, and the C list includes those who will, over time, graduate to groups A or B.

Working first on the A list—those who have the highest potential to give, who have many strong links to the institution, and who have probably given before on a regular basis—begin a file on each individual. Discuss each name with long-time affiliates of the institution, either staffmembers or selected board members of considerable experience. Record as much information as possible. Identify areas of specific interest. Knowing the organization's funding needs and priorities will help to establish linkage and interest levels.

Check and recheck data to ensure accuracy. Use both book sources and information gathering from other individuals. Stress the confidential nature of the research process with those involved. Many offices mark hard-copy files "CONFIDENTIAL." Computer data files will most often be accessed only by confidential codes, the use of which is restricted to only one or two individuals, such as the researcher and the development officer.

Linkage, Ability, and Interest

Of primary importance is establishing how closely related the prospect is to the organization. What is the relationship? Is he or she a member of the board? A professional providing service to the organization such as a physician, musician, clinician, professor? Is the prospect the daughter of the founder? A graduate of the university? Has that person been a member of a giving club for the past few years? At what level? Is there another close family member with ties to the organization?

What is the ability of the person to make a significant contribution? The development officer or key board members may have knowledge of the person's ability to give. If that individual is a community leader, there will be a general perception of his or her wealth. The social and business press will have reported on the person's gifts to other organizations, attendance at special events, and new developments within his or her corporation or business that have bearing on personal fiscal health. Detailed notations to their files, copies of press clippings, and call reports help to accumulate knowledge and provide accurate updates of basic information.

How interested is the prospect in your organization? What is the specific area of interest? Perhaps the symphony subscriber has a passion for violin and can be approached to underwrite a portion of a scheduled concert by a visiting virtuoso. The person whose triple bypass saved her life may be the one to endow a permanent fellowship in cardiac surgery. The successful alumnus of the law school may establish a chair in his name.

Levels of Data Collection

Starting with the immediate family is an important first step in gathering information. If comprehensive profiles are not available, they must be developed. And if such profiles are on file but are more than a year old, proceed as if they did not exist. A simple format, easily completed, with a request that a formal curriculum vitae or biographical sketch be attached, is mailed to the board members with a cover letter from the chairperson that stresses the importance of accurate information and a request for a timely reply. A business-reply envelope is enclosed for convenience.

The form should be as complete as possible with information that is known to be accurate. Other line items will remain blank. It is a thoughtful courtesy to have the person's name and other information already included. Ask for the following items:

Name
Title and position
Business address and telephone number
Home address and telephone number
Fax number
Cellular telephone number
University
Community affiliations and positions
Other community board memberships
Corporate boards
Spouse's name
Children, ages, and schools

It is the staff's job to follow up this process until files are complete. Be prepared to glean information from the person's secretary or administrative aide. The same format may be used during all meetings of the prospect-identification and prospect-evaluation committees. Extend the exercise to include all major donors (a single gift of significant size to your organization or an equal cumulative total of small gifts during one year).

Profiles should be completed for volunteers, small donors, and other constituents who have a deep interest in the organization and who may have family, business, social, or civic affiliations that provide them with linkages that could be helpful in the fund raising efforts. Additional candidates for in-depth profiles will include those prospects with whom the organization has strong links, *plus* information on the compatibility of their interests in the work and verified indicators that they are capable of making a major gift.

The Prospect-Identification and Prospect-Evaluation Session

A key aspect of information gathering will be the convening of small, informal, shirt-sleeved work sessions involving carefully selected people. The responsibility of this group is to develop adequate prospects and research data on prospects to achieve the organization's major-gift fund raising objectives. This includes an assessment of prospects' abilities to make gifts at specific levels and, if possible, a suggestion on cultivation and solicitation strategies.

The committee membership is usually composed of key staff members: in particular, the development director and the researcher; a chairperson selected from the governing board, preferably someone with long service; and five to seven people who are in a position to know the community's financial resources and who have links to the charitable organization. At the beginning of an intensive annual or special campaign, this group will meet frequently until all names on every prospect list have been reviewed. During these sessions, additional names will surface for consideration. In each worker's packet include a file form for each name to be discussed during the session, complete with as much data as is already on hand, and several blank forms.

A comfortable feeling of confidentiality is the order of the day, and only information that benefits the cultivation and solicitation process is maintained on file. There will always be certain elements of gossip, and it is incumbent upon the chairperson and staff to keep such information off the record. Good judgment and a sense of ethics are expected in these sessions. The researcher will bring the results of book resources to the meeting and, in many cases, will be an astute reader of the various press and thus able to contribute information on economic and demographic trends.

Prepare a list of basic questions that will serve as the discussion guide. Convene the meeting at an hour convenient to the committee. Serve light refreshments. Have someone record all relevant information. Provide pencils. Encourage note taking. Identify each person's folders with his or her name. Collect all folders and forms at the end of the meeting. All information is kept secure in the development office. Assign staffmembers to review and summarize the data. Determine what information needs to be expunged or kept in a separate, locked file. Within the context of such meetings one can learn of new marriages, divorces, deaths, terminal illnesses, and so on.

Schedule a wrap-up meeting to review results and recheck accuracy. Encourage committee members to call the staff if they learn about additional important information. Prospect research is a never-ending process. It continues as long as the donor or someone associated with him or her has a relationship with the organization. Good research is accumulative. One piece of information usually leads to another. Or it can disclose something else that may be available and how to go about finding it.

Book Sources

Background research from publicly available resources is also essential to the information-gathering process. Use all available reference sources and directories that can add to the collection of data. A suggested source list is shown in Exhibit 17.1.

In smaller or start-up development offices, expensive reference volumes and directories may not be within the budget. However, good research can begin with a call to the public library. The Junior League office in most cities also carries a well-rounded and up-to-date reference library and usually welcomes not-for-profits to conduct research at their facilities. In any city fortunate enough to have a community foundation, extensive research resources also are available. Copying machines, at modest cost, become the researcher's best friend.

The following illustrates how book research might work. Mr. J. B., from a wealthy suburb near a major tertiary care hospital, becomes a dramatic example of the cardiac surgery department's newest technology. He is near

Exhibit 17.1. Sources of Prospect Research Data on Individuals.

- Telephone directories (including yellow pages for professional listings)
- Zip-code directory
- *Who's Who in America*
- Other *Who's Who in,* . . . (thirty-four additional special areas or subjects are covered)
- The Marquis *Who's Who* books: *Who's Who in the West, Who's Who in Law, Who's Who in Finance & Industry,* and so on
- Social registers
- The *New York Times Index of Names*
- Index to *National Cyclopedia of American Biography*
- *Standard & Poors Register of Directors and Executives*
- *Dun & Bradstreet Million Dollar Directory*
- *Dun & Bradstreet Reference Book of Corporate Managements*
- *Dun & Bradstreet Middle Market Directory*
- *Walker's Manual of Western Corporations*
- Prospectuses of public corporations
- Official summary of security transactions and withholdings
- Quantas: *Compendium of Directors,* published by PC Research Services (includes salaries, stock holdings, and directorships of major corporate individuals)
- Proxy statements: Send a postcard request to a publicly held corporation for its most recent proxy statement and annual report. Proxy statements contain biographical information on a company's executives and directors, their salaries, shares of stock owned, and bonuses.
- Taft publications: *People in Philanthropy—A Guide to Philanthropic Leaders, Major Donors, and Funding Connections; The Taft Trustees of Wealth: A Biographical Directory to Private Foundation and Corporate Foundation Officers;* and *America's Wealthiest People—Their Philanthropic and Non-Profit Affiliations*
- The computer: DIALOG Information Retrieval Service, Palo Alto, CA 94304. This is only one of many information-retrieval services, but it provides immediate access to more than 100 million items of information from 180 data bases.
- City or county clerk's office or county courthouse: Probate and will information is arranged chronologically by date of death and then alphabetized.
- Tax assessment office for real and personal property values
- Local newspapers (especially the business, social and obituary sections)
- Bulletins, newsletters, magazines of organizations similar to yours or covering your constituency
- Directories and membership lists of local clubs and organizations (social, civic, political, recreational, professional, business, and so on)
- Newspaper morgues (libraries)
- Influential contacts

death from a massive viral infection of the heart muscle. In the special surgical unit, his heart is disconnected, an artificial assist device is hooked up. While his own heart is at rest and his body is maintained by artificial means, powerful antibiotics are injected. In a few days, the miracle of modern medicine has healed his heart. The artificial heart is disconnected, and his own heart resumes its natural functions. He makes a complete recovery; his usual life-style is restored. He is extremely grateful.

How is data gathered about Mr. J. B. and his family? The hospital administrator knew the patient to be a community leader. His name frequently appeared in both the business and social press. In conversations with physicians and family members during the recovery process, it is learned that

Mr. J. B. led the governing body of his church, owned a biotechnology company with several subsidiaries, lived in a gated community within the wealthy suburb, and had a private yacht. With his surgeon, he had shared his great desire to recover sufficiently to take his family on its annual spring cruise to an offshore island retreat. He also made his gratitude abundantly clear to the surgeon. He offered to help in any way he could.

The information is relayed to the development office, and a file is begun. The man and his wife have both indicated they wish to express their appreciation to the hospital and specifically to the specialized cardiac surgery unit. The challenge is not whether to open a file or not; the challenge is how best to research all of the publicly available data about Mr. J. B. and his family so that an appropriate strategy is developed.

Basic business information about Mr. J. B. can be gleaned from several resources. Check *Who's Who in America*. The Marquis books have thirty-four special areas or subjects; in this case, the most appropriate might be *Who's Who in* (the region of residence), *Who's Who in* (the industry relevant to the prospect), and others. An excellent resource could be *Standard & Poors Register of Directors and Executives*, and the *Dun & Bradstreet Reference Book of Corporate Managements*.

If the parent corporation headed by Mr. J. B. is public, write for an annual report and the most recent proxy statement, which should include biographical sketches of the company's executives and directors, their salaries, shares of stock owned, and bonuses. Visit the morgue of the local business press and review the company's file. Be prepared to take extensive notes or to make photocopies.

Most states publish a directory of corporations with fairly extensive information: annual sales, gross revenue, numbers of employees, key officials, lists of products, and parent or subsidiary companies. *Dun & Bradstreet* publishes directories within which Mr. J. B.'s corporation may be listed, such as the *Million Dollar Directory*, the *Middle Market Directory*, and the previously mentioned *Reference Book of Corporate Management*. Make the reference librarian at your main library your best friend. That individual can provide a wealth of assistance and substantially reduce book research time.

Should there be a social register for the city, a quick check will reveal Mrs. J. B.'s maiden name and provide children's names and ages. Again, a visit to the newspaper's morgue and a review of the social clippings will provide much additional and beneficial information: service on community boards; attendance at major social events; philanthropic gifts within the community; membership in various organizations such as Rotary International, the Chamber of Commerce, and so forth; affiliations as a volunteer in community agencies; membership in Junior League (for her) or other key community social organizations; and the level of involvement in various functions as an attendee, chairperson, or president of a social service agency or arts board of trustees. A check of the country club, yacht club, and other social and civic organizations' rosters frequently will add substance to the research.

The book research must include a visit to the tax assessor's office to review property holdings. These, too, are a matter of public record and can expand the prospect's profile significantly. At times it will be imperative to visit the probate courts to check the terms of a will. Although the primary focus may begin with Mr. J. B., note that very often wealth marries wealth; do as comprehensive a work-up on Mrs. J. B. as possible.

Be certain that the links to other not-for-profits within the community are explored and ascertained. It will be important to know the full extent of the family's philanthropic passions. It is evident from recent medical history that a new passion is beginning and the development director will need as much information as possible from both individual and book resources to properly evaluate the desire and the means to give. Each bit of information contributes to the overall cultivation strategy.

The Importance of Call Reports

The *call report* or *contact report*, by whatever name is used in a given development office, is a notation to the file (hard copy or computer files) of the most recent meeting, discussion, phone call, or social visit with the prospect. Within this part of the research process an assumption is made that there will be a level of selectivity about which data are placed in file.

Necessary information is that which ensures the highest level of correctness in deciding cultivation and solicitation strategies. Notes to the file after contacts with prospects can often hold the key to a successful ask.

Call reports can become quite personal and detailed. The decision about the amount and types of detail to be retained in a file rests with the development officer working within board guidelines and policies.

It is important to address the issue of confidentiality in this context. Although most information on an individual will be gathered previously from him or her, or from public sources, it is usually shared on an a "need-to-know" basis with only those who will be directly involved with cultivating and soliciting the gift. Labeling computer and hard-copy files "CONFIDENTIAL" and opening and closing all evaluation meetings with an admonishment to confidentiality is recommended. Call reports should be reviewed by the researcher and summarized or excerpted to include only essential and helpful information.

Certain sensitive and very private personal situations will come to light in the fact-gathering process. It is not uncommon to learn about a family member's drug or alcohol problem, an unknown bankruptcy, extramarital affairs, and other family secrets. It is critical to develop and adhere to strict policies and guidelines for the maintaining of files and the selecting of information to be retained within those files.

Call reports can provide excellent indicators of successful cultivation strategies. A planned giving officer from a large Midwestern arts foundation discovered that a prospect had been a jazz cornetist in his youth. Tickets to a special concert a few months later made a big hit. A community social service agency development officer on the Eastern seaboard did not play golf. He arranged, however, to accompany a major contributor on his early morning rounds to collect stray golf balls on the course adjoining his home. As a child the development director had often tagged along with his father on such forays and the activity with the prospect allowed for special bonding.

Ethical Considerations

The development officer, in concert with the board, must set forth certain basic policies for the accumulation and retention of data. What sources of information will be used? How will new information be maintained and accessed? How will secondhand or hearsay information be treated? The prospect's right to privacy must be considered. Picture this scenario: A major contributor has just joined the board and asks to see his file. Be prepared. This has happened in enough cases to make all development professionals wary.

It is essential to establish a sense of caring about the prospect. Top development professionals put the donor's needs first and foremost, and nowhere is this more appropriate than in the gathering and maintenance of research data. Leadership, whether board or staff, must conduct itself on the highest level and discourage the gossip mentality.

However, the importance of complete files, including notes of all contacts and the relevant items discussed during such meetings, cannot be overemphasized. A case in point is a large, West Coast health care system that had, over the period of six years, cultivated an eccentric widow who had no heirs. She had made frequent references to her will, which gave half of her estate to benefit a certain medical specialty. Furthermore, notes to the file indicated that she wished the use of such funds to be at the discretion of the chief of that service, as long as he was part of the organization.

Upon her death, the will was filed for probate and the organization learned that her attorney, in his naivete about charitable bequests, had written the will so that the bequest went instead to the physician's private practice group—a for-profit corporation. This was clearly not her intent. The bequest would incur a huge tax liability if it was received into the physician's private practice; yet, understandably, he desired full control over the use of the funds, whether or not he remained at the hospital where he and his group practiced. What to do? Nearly $1 million was at stake.

A friendly suit ensued, with the hospital contending that the donor had intended a charitable gift. The comprehensive call reports substantiated the deceased's intent to the satisfaction of the court. (It is of interest to note that four development directors had pursued the relationship over the six-year period, another example of the value of good record keeping.) The hospital and the physician negotiated a settlement that gave the doctor full control over the use of the funds so long as he remained with that hospital or was practicing his specialty at that facility more than 50 percent of his time. This wording accommodated the physician's need to strengthen his connection to the region's primary university to do research in his specialty. For the hospital, it retained the use of the bequest if the physician severed his relationship with the hospital entirely.

When to Stop Gathering

> He who deliberates fully before taking a step will spend his entire life standing on one leg.
>
> —Chinese proverb

There comes a time, often long before all the available information can be gathered, when the solicitation process begins. The research process has established linkage, ability, and interest, or, at the minimum, two of these ingredients. Because the ask usually is preceded by cultivation over time, which often includes direct involvement of the prospect with the institution, the accumulation of information goes on. The classic story of the insurance salesperson who studied the prospect lists and compiled mountains of information on each individual but forgot to make the calls is well known. Development officers will chuckle over the "call reluctance" syndrome, but all too often both staff and volunteer solicitation teams succumb to the malady. Good research can provide the cushion of comfort needed to begin the direct-contact process by identifying a mutual interest, a business relationship, prior attendance at social or educational events, and so on.

How to Evaluate Gift Potential

The research process will include a rating that indicates the prospect's suspected ability to give. Important indicators include a record of gifts to philanthropic activities, the location and value of residences and other real estate holdings, career position, salary and other income, and positions on corporate boards. Social clubs and other memberships, recreational interests, and stock holdings are equally important.

Every community has its strata of wealth. Usually, one country club has the "old money" membership. Look for new residential estate areas and learn who is purchasing property, what it costs to join that area's country club, and whether these are the sons and daughters of the old money group or newcomers to a growing region.

Identify who holds the key leadership positions in the area's largest corporations. In publicly held companies, salaries, benefits, and stock options of these people are a matter of record.

Learn who on the prospect list has second homes elsewhere—Florida, the Hawaiian islands, the Caribbean, or ski lodges and mountain hideaways. The wealthy frequently socialize together not only at home but also in other locales around the world. If one has bought a new ski condominium in Vail, chances are that several close friends have made similar commitments.

If navigable water is nearby, check the marina registries and yacht ownerships. Who belongs to the premier yacht club? Unless membership restrictions prohibit it, such rosters are key sources of information.

Solid research, carefully maintained and updated, and used as frequent reference for those who design cultivation and solicitation strategy is one of the most valuable tools the development offices can have. It takes an ongoing commitment to the process. The process comprises identifying the constituency, gathering the information, maintaining the information, and *using* the information. Effective results can be had from 4 × 5-inch file cards with handwritten information as well as from exhaustive and complex hard-copy or computer files.

For a development officer just coming on board, reading the key files is one of the first and most essential tasks. Successful fund raising depends on it. Maintaining files is time-consuming, so if time is short and the staff is small, consider recruiting two or three dedicated volunteers who will help build and maintain files and handle the ongoing task of clipping from the daily press and other periodicals.

The rule on research is to do it. Keep it simple and keep it up.

Corporations
as a Gift Market

Almost every not-for-profit organization that has an organized fund raising program will seek gifts from corporations for its cause. Some, of course, will do admirably well in this area, while others for various reasons, including the very nature of the organization, will either fail to attract support or only raise nominal amounts from the corporate community.

Corporations as a Source of Support

In the aggregate, corporations provide approximately only 5 percent of total giving to not-for-profits. The amount that specific not-for-profits receive from corporations in the form of contributed income can easily range from nothing to virtually 100 percent of total giving. Again, much depends on the specific nature of the organization seeking funds and the type of constituency it has established.

More than one-third of all annual corporate support goes to educational causes (*Giving USA*, 1988). Although this figure has remained fairly constant, there has been a marked shift over the past decade away from support of colleges and universities and toward more targeted support for precollege education, both at the primary and secondary level.

The second most funded category for corporate grants covers the broad area referred to as "health and human services." This category now represents 27 percent of all corporate giving each year, down from 37 percent in the mid-1970s.

Still, one area that has experienced growth in corporate giving in recent years is grants to not-for-profits working on environmental issues. This would seem consistent with a growing awareness on the part of the American public about the environment.

Religion and religious causes, however, receive virtually no support from corporations and yet receive the lion's share of total contributed income each year, almost exclusively from individuals.

A good statistical overview of corporate giving can be found in *Giving USA*, which is published annually by the American Association of Fund-Raising Counsel's Trust for Philanthropy.

Why Corporations Give

Just why do corporations give funds to charitable organizations? After all, corporations by their nature exist to make a profit, not to make charitable donations. Fortunately, many companies in the United States have decided that establishing either a formal or an informal charitable-giving program is in their best interest.

Certainly a variety of reasons and opinions are put forth for why corporations give. Some of the most common reasons are the following.

1. *Good corporate citizenship.* Many companies feel that it is important to present a positive image in the communities in which they operate. Such an image can be maintained or heightened through charitable gifts to local not-for-profits that provide community services.
2. *Enlightened self-interest.* Most fund raisers subscribe to the notion that companies make charitable gifts because it is basically in their best interest to do so. Because companies hire local employees, they want to maintain an educated and healthy work force. This often can be accomplished by supporting the work of local charities such as colleges, hospitals, and cultural organizations.
3. *Individual leadership initiative.* Companies are also likely to support not-for-profit organizations simply because of the interest and clout of those in charge. This is often the case in family businesses in which the founder may direct help to a favorite charity without a committee vote. This will also happen in large corporations where the CEO or president uses his or her clout to direct gifts to selected charities.
4. *Location.* Most often a company will restrict its support to not-for-profits in the communities in which the company operates and has an employee base.
5. *Quid pro quo interests.* Many companies use quid pro quo interest (that is, they ask, "What's in it for us?"). Such a company wants to see a tangible return on its charitable investment. Such a direct relationship between making a gift and obtaining something in return (other than general satisfaction) is not always easy to delineate. Some people, however, argue

that seeking such a connection diminishes the spirit of philanthropy. Still, many companies continue to look for such linkages.

How Corporations Give

One of the distinctions that separate company donations from those made by individuals and foundations concerns the sources from which contributions can originate within a company. Companies have several "pots" of money from which charitable donations are made. These include company foundations, direct giving, executive discretionary funds, subsidiary or individual plant budgets, marketing budgets, and research and development budgets.

Company Foundation. A fair number of large U.S. companies have established charitable foundations similar to those that exist as private foundations. Corporate foundations allow companies to maintain a fairly stable level of giving each year because foundation income usually is not subject to the ups and downs in profits that companies are subjected to each quarter.

In addition, corporate foundations, like private foundations, must file an annual report with the Internal Revenue Service (IRS Form 990-PF) that lists yearly income, grants, and current directors, and is available for public inspection.

Direct Corporate Giving. Much more commonplace than corporate foundations are direct corporate-giving programs. This simply means that a company provides grants to not-for-profit organizations directly out of its net profits. The Taft Group of Washington, D.C., has conducted a study suggesting that more than two-thirds of all corporate contributions are made through direct corporate-giving programs (*Taft Corporate Giving Directory*, 1990).

These companies are not required to report on their grant-making activities to the public. Companies that have matching-gift programs (that is, matching gifts made by their employees based on some predetermined ratio) will include these contributions as part of their direct corporate-giving programs.

Executive Discretionary Funds. Many companies, both large and small, and especially family run businesses, have "pools" of charitable funds available for contributions at the discretion of top managers, usually CEOs or presidents. Typically, these will be small grants to community-based organizations in which the top executive may sit as a board member.

Subsidiary or Individual Plant Budget. Again, quite typically, a large corporation with several subsidiaries or plant locations will set aside a portion of its annual grants budget for disbursement by individual "satellite" managers.

These budgets are often quite small, perhaps limited to several thousand dollars each year, but they are contributed almost exclusively to community agencies in cities and towns where plant operations are headquartered.

Marketing Budgets. In the past decade, a company's marketing budget has become another source of corporate funds that has played a growing role in corporate philanthropy. This source makes gifts to charities as part of what has come to be known as "cause-related marketing," a relatively new phrase that has been attributed to the American Express Company. Cause-related marketing is the process of making gifts to a not-for-profit based on the amount of products or services purchased by an organization's constituency. Although there continues to be debate in the professional fund raising community about whether cause-related marketing is a pure form of charitable giving, many not-for-profits have come to view it as a viable, and yet usually small, source of contributed income.

Companies also make grants from their marketing budgets in forms other than cause-related marketing. For example, a company may support an organization's special event by paying for tickets or tables through the company's advertising or marketing budgets. Such support, although of benefit to a charity, typically is not considered a donation and thus is not tax-deductible.

Research-and-Development Budgets. A company's research and development budget is another source of funds that is tapped primarily by educational and health causes. Companies are often quite interested in underwriting university or health-related research projects, the results of which may lead to new company products.

When investigating the scope of a corporate-giving program, it is important to review all potential pools of corporate-gift funds. It is not uncommon for some companies to support not-for-profits by supplying funds from all of the sources mentioned above, while others may give only through one avenue.

Types of Corporate Giving

Cash Gifts. Most not-for-profits need cash grants to meet operating and program costs, and this is the kind of support most typically provided by companies. An annual study of corporate giving conducted by the AAFRC's Trust for Philanthropy, *Giving USA*, reveals that more than 75 percent of all corporate giving is in the form of cash or "cash equivalents," usually as corporate bonds or stocks (1990, pp. 78–91).

Noncash Gifts. Unlike individuals and foundations, both of which make primarily cash gifts, companies have the resources and the flexibility to offer a variety of other types of assistance to nonprofit agencies. (Individuals, of course, can and do volunteer their time to charity, and many donate items other than cash.)

Corporate noncash giving can take a variety of forms and should be included in any comprehensive corporate fund raising plan. Several of the more popular examples of noncash gifts include company product donations, equipment donations (usually older equipment that has been used to manufacture the company's product line), land, loaned executives who volunteer their expertise to not-for-profits, use of corporate facilities, support of organization events (such as providing food and refreshments), free or low-cost publicity including printing services, and low- or no-interest loans, which are quite naturally popular with the banking community.

In addition, companies often encourage their top officers to accept invitations to serve on not-for-profit boards and committees. To encourage volunteering, a number of companies now make grants to not-for-profits where employees are involved as volunteers. An excellent list of companies that make such employee-volunteer grants was compiled by Vincent S. Foster (1989).

The value of a noncash gift should also be included in an organization's annual report to the extent that its fair value can be determined. In the aggregate, noncash contributions (also referred to as "in-kind" gifts) represent close to one-quarter of the value of annual corporate giving in the United States.

Several comprehensive lists have been prepared on noncash ways in which companies can support not-for-profit organizations. One of the more thorough lists was compiled by Alex Plinio (1983), former president of the Prudential Insurance Foundation.

All astute fund raisers must take into account the myriad ways in which companies can support not-for-profit organizations. Most corporate giving is a mixture of cash and noncash contributions. When approaching a company for the first time, some not-for-profits may find that it is to their advantage to pursue an in-kind gift. A request that leads to support might provide a later entrée to more significant cash contributions. In every case, it is important to know about all of the charitable-giving options available when approaching a company for support.

Trends in Corporate Giving

As with all types of giving, corporate philanthropy continually changes. Therefore, it is important to keep in mind some of the overall trends in corporate philanthropy. For example, many companies now prefer to make smaller, one-time grants to a broader range of not-for-profit organizations. This is contrary to the multiyear commitments that were more popular in previous years. Most grant making now is based on an annual competitive-application process. It is rare to find grants that are automatically renewed each year without at least an updated letter of request.

There has also been a distinct shift in the corporate community from support for "bricks-and-mortar" projects (capital requests) to more project-specific funding. Companies are devoting more of their giving resources to addressing specific problem areas in society such as poverty, illiteracy, and teenage pregnancy. Partly for this reason, unrestricted corporate giving to support an organization's operating budget is becoming an increasingly smaller share of all corporate grants.

Giving has become much more focused and tied into company objectives. Some companies attempt to tie their support to a social problem that, if solved, could lead to increased business in the future. For example, a publishing company may target its philanthropic support to helping solve illiteracy.

Many companies are also looking for ways to leverage their support. This can often be achieved by using challenge grants. Typically these grants require that a not-for-profit raise an equivalent amount from other sources before the company provides its own support. The Foundation Center provides an annual indexed list of foundations, including corporate foundations, that make challenge or matching grants.

There has also been an increase in foreign companies setting up corporate foundations in the United States. The Taft Group reports that foreign-owned companies operating in the United States contributed more than $200 million to the not-for-profit sector in 1989. This trend is likely to increase with the growth of the global economy. In response to this growing market, the Taft Group has also published *International Corporate Giving in America*, an annual directory that profiles more than three hundred of these companies. The assets of these new foreign-owned corporate foundations, and their direct-giving programs, are already well into the hundreds of millions of dollars and are having a noticeable impact on the not-for-profit community.

Some individuals in the not-for-profit sector have expressed concern about the net effect of mergers and acquisitions on corporate giving. The 1980s were almost synonymous with such corporate changes, which resulted in an overall reduction in the total number of corporate-giving programs, but it appears that the 1990s will see a slowdown in the rate of mergers and acquisitions. This should prove beneficial to those involved in corporate fund raising.

Approaching a Corporation

The mechanics of approaching a corporation for a gift are very similar to those that are effectively used to obtain support from individuals and foundations. There are, of course, slight modifications to the solicitation process that are unique to corporations.

Five steps are essential in successful corporate fund raising: (1) developing an effective and persuasive case for support, (2) conducting extensive research to determine those companies that may be interested in supporting a specific cause, (3) developing and implementing a cultivation program designed to attract the interest of potential corporate donors, (4) initiating and completing a solicitation strategy at the appropriate time, and (5) providing postgrant follow-up and additional cultivation that will encourage additional future support.

The Case for Support. An essential element in preparing any effective fund raising strategy includes the first critical step of developing a case for support. A good case will include a rationale as to why a company would want to support a specific not-for-profit organization.

The case for support must address the specific services provided by the organization, how these services are both benefitting and being used by community members, and how a grant will sustain and enhance the charity's program and services. Of course, these same elements are needed in developing an effective case to individuals and foundations. The added element required in a corporate proposal is showing how a corporate gift will not only provide support to a not-for-profit but also reap potential benefits to the company. The more powerful the linkage developed between the act of making a gift and the benefits that may accrue to the company, the more likely it will become to obtain support.

As noted earlier, corporations make gifts to not-for-profits for a variety of reasons including self-interest and community image. To develop an effective case for support, it is important to account for one or more of the elements cited in the earlier section of this chapter, "Why Corporations Give."

The Importance of Research. Perhaps the single most important step in corporate fund raising, aside from the actual ask, is research. The purpose of research is to target those companies (typically those that conduct business within an organization's service area) that can support the organization. Because time is a valuable commodity, cultivation and solicitation efforts must focus on those companies that are most likely to provide support. Time spent on effective and careful research will shorten the list of companies to approach and also reap substantial dividends because the yield of successful solicitations will be that much higher.

Research can take many forms, including personal visits to corporate funding offices, comparing notes with professional peers, attending conferences at which corporate funders speak, reviewing annual reports of other not-for-profits in the same city or community, and using written resource materials on corporate philanthropy.

The research process really has two phases. The first develops a list of likely prospects. The second phase is devoted to "fleshing out" these prospects by developing profiles based on personal communication.

List Development. Developing lists of potential corporate prospects can be accomplished in a variety of ways. One is to review commercial reference materials on the subject of corporate giving.

Many reference materials are on the market today to help narrow the search to "high-potential" corporate prospects. The scope and quality of these resources have increased considerably in the last few years as the fund raising profession continues to grow and mature.

The best sources of published information on companies that make charitable gifts include the New York–based Foundation Center, which publishes such directories as the *National Guide to Corporate Giving* and *Corporate Source Profiles*; the Taft Group, based in Rockville, Maryland, which is known for a variety of helpful resources, including *The Taft Corporate Giving Directory* and *The Taft Guide to Corporate Giving Contacts*; and the San Francisco–based Public Management Institute which also publishes an annual corporate-giving directory. An excellent list of the names and addresses of these and other organizations was compiled for a recent newsletter from the publishers of the *Corporate Philanthropy Report* (see Smith, 1990, p. 13).

In addition, many states now have their own directories of corporate funders. Sometimes these directories focus on private foundations and may only include corporate foundations and no direct corporate-giving programs. Many larger cities now have special not-for-profit resource reference centers affiliated with city or state libraries that carry information on corporate philanthropy.

Many cities have also established regional association of grant makers (RAGs) that may have representatives from large corporate funders. A more complete list of corporate-giving reference materials appears in Exhibit 18.1.

Not-for-profits can also develop lists of companies in their immediate service areas through three methods.

1. Review Chamber of Commerce directories.
2. Buy such information from a commercial data base company. Such data bases often provide the same information that can be obtained through printed resources. Because on-line searches can be expensive, it is important to define the search parameters as carefully as possible before accessing a particular data base.
3. Read the local newspaper and review lists of corporate donors who have made grants to other not-for-profits in the same service area. Many cities now have special weekly, biweekly, or monthly business newspapers that often include articles on local corporate philanthropy. It is also important to review reference materials that reveal corporate affiliations. Many local companies in a community are subsidiaries of much larger companies. In many instances, the parent organization may have a clearly defined giving program that the local subsidiary may not be aware of or participate in, or the local company may have its own set of guidelines.

Exhibit 18.1. Companies Publishing Corporate-Giving Reference Materials.

The Foundation Center
79 Fifth Avenue, 8th Floor
New York, NY 10003
(212) 620-4230

The Taft Group
12300 Twinbrook Parkway, Suite 450
Rockville, MD 20852
(800) 888-8238

American Association of Fund-Raising Counsel
Trust for Philanthropy
25 West 43rd Street
New York, NY 10036
(212) 354-5799

The Chronicle of Philanthropy
1255 23rd Street, NW, Suite 785
Washington, DC 20037
(202) 466-1050

Corporate Philanthropy Report
2727 Fairview Avenue East, Suite D
Seattle, WA 98102
(206) 329-0422

Public Management Institute
358 Brannan Street
San Francisco, CA 94105
(415) 896-1900

Creating Prospect Profiles. Once a list of potential corporate funders has been created, it becomes necessary to move to the next, more vital, step in the research process. This involves developing in-depth, accurate profiles of corporate giving. The best way to do this is to initiate direct, personal contact with the funder.

The most cost-effective way to accomplish this task is to call the funder directly to verify the names, contact persons, and addresses of each corporate prospect. Such calls also will provide much more accurate and timely information on the directions that a specific corporate-giving program may be taking.

Where feasible, personal visits to corporate-giving offices are strongly encouraged. Sometimes referred to as "cultivation calls," these visits certainly are easier to arrange in companies that have staffed corporate-giving programs. Otherwise, personal visits will be with those in charge of corporate philanthropy, who are often part-time individuals in the public relations or human resources office.

Whether telephone call or personal visit, such contacts provide not only the opportunity to ask specific questions about a company's giving program but also information for the prospective funder about the not-for-profit seeking support. In many instances, a potential corporate prospect may not be able to provide support but can direct an organization to other companies in the same service area that might be in a position to offer grants.

Personal presolicitation calls are also a valuable way to obtain information on a company's giving program that does not appear in written resource materials. Funding priorities have a way of changing rapidly and a personal visit can help to "capture" the latest information. A cultivation call can also be used to develop a profile on the personal interests of the corporate-giving executive. Tapping into these interests, especially if a not-for-profit has programs in these areas, can only increase the chances of receiving a grant.

Cultivation. Another important phase of the corporate fund raising process is to develop an effective cultivation program before making the actual request for support. Cultivation strategies vary from agency to agency and from prospect to prospect.

Cultivation may involve sending an organization's newsletter or annual report to a corporate funder. Sending other information, such as updates on a fund raising campaign or in-depth reviews of an organization's programs or services, also is recommended. Each prospective funder should be called ahead of time to determine his or her interests, because some funders may not be able to continually accept unsolicited literature.

Another effective cultivation technique is to involve the corporation's employees with the organization. This might include asking employees to volunteer for a committee assignment or participate in a special event.

One particularly effective, although long-range, technique is using what sometimes is referred to as the "rising star" phenomenon. An organizational representative meets with a high-level executive in the company to identify upwardly mobile achievers in the corporate hierarchy. The idea is to involve these high-energy people in an agency, perhaps on a committee, before they climb higher on the career ladder. Some of these early achievers will make it to the executive suite, where they will be in a position to direct grants to an organization in which they have been or are currently involved.

Solicitation. Perhaps the one phase of corporate fund raising—or any type of fund raising—that takes up the least amount of time but which is the most critical, is the actual solicitation. This is simply because most of the groundwork (that is, research and cultivation) has taken place before the ask is made.

In the ideal situation, a face-to-face appeal is the most effective form of corporate solicitation, just as it is with individuals. Such a personal visit might take place between an organization's director and a company's CEO. It might also take place between a corporate-giving officer and an organization's chief fund raiser. In every case, it is important to keep all levels of the corporate hierarchy informed about the level at which the solicitation will take place.

Although a personal solicitation may be the most effective form of fund raising, it is usually the exception to the rule in corporate giving. Like foundations, most companies have developed carefully defined proposal-review guidelines. For example, a company may have an employee committee composed of both management and labor representatives that meets at regular intervals to review proposal requests. Usually all proposals have been reviewed ahead of time by a committee member to provide other members with a brief description of each project. In this situation, a personal solicitation is virtually impossible, so the agency must rely more on cultivation and the actual written proposal.

Whatever approach is made, one of the most important factors in the solicitation process is to reach a close on the request, just as with individual and foundation fund raising or almost any successful sales program. It is always important to follow up with every company to which a proposal has been submitted to verify the status of the request. This can often be accomplished simply by phoning the company contact person as needed after the request has been received and reviewed. It is important to seek a definite *yes* or *no* answer so that future strategies can be initiated.

The Proposal. One critical component of the solicitation process that is endemic to corporate and foundation fund raising is the preparation of a written proposal. (Fund raising with individuals, on the other hand, does not usually require a written proposal, although for very large requests, one may be desired.) A proposal is most likely to succeed when it is clearly for a project of the very highest priority to the organization.

A corporate proposal does not have to be a long or elaborate affair; in fact, most companies discourage lengthy proposals. Nothing more than a two-page letter from the not-for-profit's executive director or board president to the company's CEO may be needed. The proposal will specify the project for which support is being sought, the specific amount being requested, and how the company will benefit from making such a gift (that is, the quid pro quo arrangement between donor and beneficiary).

If not in the form of a letter, most corporate proposals should still include a brief cover letter signed by the not-for-profit's executive director or board president. Letter proposals should also be signed by one or both of the same individuals. Usually the body of the proposal is written by a member of the fund raising staff or, preferably, by the not-for-profit's staffmember who is most knowledgeable about or ultimately responsible for the project needing funds.

The proposal will usually be accompanied by several appendices as required by the corporate funder. These include:

- a board of directors list,
- proof of tax-exempt status (usually, 501(c)(3) letters issued by the Internal Revenue Service), and
- the not-for-profit's audited financial statements.

In addition, the funder may request that a completed grant application accompany the proposal.

Corporate solicitations are a highly structured form of fund raising, much more so than those for individuals. Many corporations have specific proposal deadlines and funding cycles to which the fund raiser must adhere. In addition, the corporate-giving decision-making process has become much more formal. There is much less emphasis today on the traditional "old boy" network that tended to dominate grant-making policy in the past. As noted, many companies now have committees that review grant requests.

Follow-up. Following the submission of a proposal, a face-to-face solicitation, or both, it simply becomes a matter of time until the outcome of the request will be known. It is not unusual to submit a proposal to a company and wait anywhere from six to eighteen months until funds are actually received if approved. This is why careful project planning and cash-flow analysis are crucial pregrant steps when seeking support from both corporate and foundation funders.

During the period from submission to decision, the funder may call to ask questions or to obtain additional information. The not-for-profit may want to submit periodic reports to the company especially if progress has been made on the project to be funded or if large gifts have been received. Companies like to see other funders supporting a project and have historically been more likely to support not-for-profits who have garnered substantial support from their own constituencies.

The outcome of a grant request will trigger one of two responses. Either support will be granted at some level (although not necessarily at the amount requested) or it will be declined, at least for the present. Whatever the outcome, it is important to immediately thank the company and its representatives for their time in reviewing the proposal. A carefully prepared response may help lead to future funding if immediate support is not forthcoming. Also, if a grant is turned down, it is usually appropriate to inquire about how this decision was reached and if a modified request can be submitted. Regrettably, some funders will not share this information.

Follow-up will also usually include a self-assessment component. Such questions as whether the quality and timing of the solicitation were appropriate will be addressed. Leadership may also wish to review volunteer solicitor assignments to see if corporate prospects should be reassigned during a future campaign.

Postdecision follow-up is a very important element of the solicitation process and yet one that is often overlooked. Such follow-up lays the ground-work for future grant requests.

Postgrant Reporting. Over the last decade, the number of corporate funders requiring postgrant interim reports has increased substantially. These re-ports are usually prepared by the not-for-profit receiving funding on a quarterly, semiannual, or annual basis. This protects both the funder and the not-for-profit and shows that the contributed funds are being used for their intended purpose. It also helps the not-for-profit keep track of the progress being made on the project. It is likely that such grant-reporting requirements will continue to be an accepted part of corporate grant making in the future.

Tips for Success. Here are additional tips that may prove helpful in raising funds from the corporate community.

1. Plan ahead when making a corporate solicitation. Consider submitting a proposal on the first day after a deadline has passed to give the prospect ample time to review the request. Proposals received on or near a deadline typically receive less attention.
2. Always read the funding guidelines carefully. Read between the lines to determine what is not being mentioned. Guidelines usually state clearly what is and is not eligible for funding, but some programs or projects may not be specifically excluded or included, thus falling into a "grey" area. Consult with the funding prospect to determine whether a project may be of interest and thus worth a proposal submission.
3. Administrative assistants in a corporate-giving office can provide valu-able advice by telephone that sometimes is more comprehensive than what a director will provide on a company's philanthropic program.
4. When approaching a company for the first time, it might be easier to develop a long-term relationship by making an initial request for a small annual gift. A larger grant will be more likely if cultivation is successful and annual support is given each year.
5. Where possible, develop a relationship with corporate-giving consul-tants who advise corporate funders.
6. Seek out companies with new corporate-giving programs or new person-nel. In the early phases of a corporate-giving program, funding guide-lines are usually broad and unfocused. It may be easier to obtain support early in the cycle.
7. Utilize corporate employee matching-gift programs where appropriate. A good source for information on matching-gift programs is the Council for the Advancement and Support of Education in Alexandria, Virginia.
8. Determine what professional groups corporate-giving officers belong to and look for ways to become involved with those groups. A not-for-profit may wish to host a meeting for one or more of them.

9. A not-for-profit should invite corporate-giving officers to visit the organi-
    zation's facilities. Solicitation success rates jump dramatically when fun-
    ders can see firsthand what not-for-profits seek to accomplish.

Conclusion

Over the years, corporations have played an important role in American
philanthropy and can be expected to do so in the decades ahead. They
remain a viable source of support for today's not-for-profits. Although the
total amount of corporate charitable funds has increased each year, competition for these still-limited dollars also continues to increase.

    In all likelihood, corporate giving will continue to be the most volatile
type of charitable giving with companies continually entering and leaving
the philanthropic sector. In addition, companies will continue to define and
shift their charitable priorities as they adapt to society's most pressing needs.

    The most effective fund raising programs will continue to include a
corporate-giving component in their overall fund raising mix and will develop a comfortable percentage of total funds over time that can be successfully raised each year from the corporate community. This percentage will
vary from organization to organization and will depend on such factors as
the not-for-profit's size, location, and nature.

    The most successful organizations will use a careful program of re-
search, cultivation, and solicitation targeted to those companies that are
most likely to support their cause. Organizations that can adapt and work in
creative ways to meet the corporate community's concern about social needs
will be the true fund raising winners in the years ahead.

Foundations
as a Source of Support

One of the most interesting areas of philanthropy, particularly to individuals or organizations learning about fund raising for the first time, is the world of foundations. Foundations are not-for-profit entities that have been established to provide support to charitable organizations through grants. Many people who are new to fund raising find the foundation sector an exciting area to explore because they know little about foundations, why they exist, or how they operate.

Although small in comparison to the total amount contributed each year by individuals collectively, foundations nonetheless represent a major force in philanthropy. As a rule, foundation grants are significantly larger than gifts from individuals and thus have a greater impact on meeting specific needs and addressing and solving specific problems.

The Foundation Center, a New York–based repository of information on foundations, estimates that more than 27,000 foundations currently operate in the United States. These foundations have combined assets of more than $94 billion and distribute more than $7 billion each year in grants. Because total giving from all sources now exceeds $100 billion per year, foundations represent some 5 percent to 7 percent of all giving, a statistic that has remained fairly constant over time.

Perhaps what sets foundations apart from their corporate and individual brethren the most is that by law they must distribute some percentage of their assets (sometimes referred to as the "principal fund" or "endowment") each year to charitable groups. The payout rate is established by the government. Currently, foundations must annually distribute grants totaling 5 percent or more of their portfolio assets.

Foundations also represent an increasingly organized community in the philanthropic sector and have a significant voice in shaping philanthropic policy. For example, a group of foundations may pool its resources to address a specific issue of interest to the group. In this way, foundations can have a greater impact on addressing and perhaps solving a problem that other sources such as individuals, corporations, and government are either unable or unwilling to accomplish.

For most not-for-profits, foundations represent a part of the overall charitable pie that, if properly cultivated, can lead to substantial and sometimes sustained support. An excellent statistical review of foundations, including charts and graphs of trends in foundation giving, appears in the introduction to each issue of the *Foundation Directory*, which is published annually by the Foundation Center.

Types of Foundations

Current nomenclature divides philanthropic foundations into four specific types: independent foundations, company-sponsored foundations, community foundations, and operating foundations.

Independent Foundations. The Internal Revenue Service defines an independent foundation as a "private foundation" whose primary role is to meet the needs of the not-for-profit community through grants. Most private foundations are established by individuals or families and tend to be funded either by inherited wealth or by wealth accumulated through a business activity.

Grant decisions are often made directly by the donor or members of the donor's family. In some instances, the foundation's administrative functions will be turned over to a professional staff (usually one full-time or one part-time individual) hired by the donor. Some independent foundations are established as the result of a donor's will, and grants are distributed annually only to those organizations specifically mentioned in the will. As with most types of foundations, independent foundations usually restrict giving to charities within certain geographic boundaries.

Company-Sponsored Foundations. As the label implies, company-sponsored foundations are established by companies. Although these foundations may carry the company's name (for example, the BankAmerica Foundation) they run separately and independently of the company. Corporate foundation grants are often made to a broad spectrum of not-for-profit organizations. In many instances, these foundations will adapt giving philosophies that are based on the company's own mission; therefore they support not-for-profits that enhance the company's objectives. Corporate foundations also will tend to target grants to those communities in which the company operates and in which its employees reside.

As noted in Chapter 18, it is not uncommon for a company to provide support through both a direct corporate-giving program and a corporate foundation. Many companies feel that a foundation program provides for a more stable and predictable annual source of charitable funds because many company foundations are established with an endowment. Direct corporate giving is heavily dependent on economic ups and downs (and hence changes in corporate profits), which can lead to dramatic swings in the amount contributed annually. Most direct corporate-giving programs (as discussed in Chapter 18) have little or no endowment and thus make grants each year through infusions of cash from the company itself, an amount typically based on a percentage of net operating profits.

Community Foundations. Community foundations are very similar to private foundations; both are established for charitable purposes. A key difference is that community foundations represent the resources of a large number of donors rather than one individual or family. As public charities, community foundations have much more diverse board representation than do private foundations in order to reflect the various constituencies within a community. To make grants, community foundations must obtain contributions. As such, these foundations must seek out a much broader base of support, which again reflects the community that each foundation serves.

As the label implies, community foundations normally operate within a fairly distinct geographical area such as a city or region. Most major cities have community foundations, including San Francisco, New York, and Cleveland. Regional foundations are freestanding entities that both solicit gifts and provide support to not-for-profits. Most regional foundations cover several counties or entire states.

Aside from their own grant-making programs, community foundations often provide conduits through which small family foundations may make grants. Donors may establish "advised" funds to benefit selected charities, with the funds flowing through the community foundation.

Community foundations have grown in total number, assets, and annual grants in the past decade, and it is projected that this trend will continue. At present, six of the one hundred largest foundations in the United States are community foundations (as ranked by total giving). Professionals anticipate that the number of community foundations within the top one hundred foundations will continue to increase.

Although many community foundations have their own clearly defined giving programs and staff, many also provide administrative services to small family foundations. This service is extremely helpful to unstaffed foundations because of economy of scale in providing administrative needs such as bookkeeping and check-writing services to several foundations at one time.

Operating Foundations. Operating foundations are also considered to be "private foundations" by the Internal Revenue Service. However, operating foundations are established by charter to fund specific research or other programs. Although operating foundations are often listed in philanthropic reference books, few make grants to outside charitable organizations.

Researching Foundations

Of all the types of charitable giving covered in this book, fund raisers will soon discover that foundations are the easiest sector to research. This is because all foundations are required by the Internal Revenue Service to file a tax information form each year. Known as Form 990-PF (for private foundations) this annual document lists the name and address of each foundation, the names and titles of its officers, and how much the foundation distributed to not-for-profit groups for the specific fiscal year, including the names of the recipients and the amounts received.

Based in large part on these IRS forms, several companies have produced reference materials to help not-for-profits seek foundation support. The two largest providers of information on foundations are the Foundation Center, a not-for-profit organization, and the Taft Group, a for-profit company in Rockville, Maryland. Many other smaller information providers, including state and local organizations, have compiled and printed guides to foundations in specific states. All of these reference materials are available for purchase from the respective publisher or organization. The Foundation Center provides a handy reference guide to many of these state guides, and each listing gives the name and address of the supplier and the cost of the directory. This reference guide appears as an appendix to the Foundation Center's *National Data Book of Foundations*.

Many of these reference materials are also available in state and university libraries. For example, the Foundation Center maintains comprehensive reference libraries in New York, Washington, San Francisco, and Cleveland. Many of the Foundation Center's reference materials are also available at state libraries. A complete list of these locations appears in the front of the Center's *Foundation Directory*.

Most directories do not include all 27,000 of the nation's foundations. The most comprehensive profiles on foundations are, quite naturally, reserved for the largest foundations, which usually have the largest staffs and make the most grants. For quick thumbnail sketches on every U.S. foundation, the Foundation Center publishes the *National Data Book of Foundations*. This two-volume set ranks all foundations by state and total annual grant support within each state. It is accompanied by an alphabetical listing of all foundations.

The single most readily available piece of information on every foundation continues to be Form 990-PF. Although the 990-PFs contain only essential and thus minimal information, they provide a base for putting together more comprehensive profiles. The Foundation Center maintains 990-PFs on microfiche for all of the nation's foundations, and photocopies are available from Foundation Center locations for a nominal charge. Complete sets of all 990-PFs (and limited sets by geographic region) can be purchased from several organizations (including the Foundation Center) that provide this service.

Many not-for-profits conducting research on foundations have also turned to electronic data-base services to screen foundations that might make grants in support of specific projects, programs, or needs. DIALOG Information Services of Palo Alto, California, maintains several foundation data-bases, including an electronic version of the Foundation Center's *Foundation Directory* and *Foundation Grants Index* and several produced by other organizations.

Not-for-profits have been conducting electronic data-base searches for several years to screen for possible foundation support. Fortunately, newer technology and a better understanding of how to use these data bases have improved the yield from this type of research. When working with electronic data bases, it is important to clearly define the search parameters as specifically as possible before beginning. By doing so, a researcher will obtain a fairly precise list of foundations that have been known to make grants similar to those that an organization is seeking.

Analyzing Foundation Guidelines

A major part of the foundation-research function is to be able to understand and interpret foundation guidelines and other written and statistical information. The most important questions that a not-for-profit seeking funding must ask are:

1. Does the foundation support other similar "like kind" agencies?
2. Does the foundation clearly state that it provides support for the type of project for which the organization is seeking funds?
3. Does the foundation make grants in the same geographic area in which the organization is located or conducts its programs?
4. Does the foundation make grants in the same monetary range that the organization is proposing?

If the agency is able to answer *yes* to all four questions, then the chances for a successful outcome are much higher.

An organization also must keep in mind application deadlines and procedures and whether a foundation is likely to cover the full cost of a project or whether it will prefer to underwrite only a portion of the project. It is also important to determine whether a foundation is likely to provide renewal grants in the future.

Approaching a Foundation

The previous section examined ways to identify foundations that may be interested in supporting a specific not-for-profit or its programs. Once this initial research is conducted, it becomes necessary to refine and narrow the list of potential foundations to a more manageable size. The best way to proceed is by contacting the foundation directly by telephone to obtain one or more of the following items:

- grant-application guidelines,
- the foundation's annual report, and
- a grant-application form.

Not all foundations always have all three available. For example, only the largest foundations tend to print an annual report. Many foundations require that a grant-application form accompany any request for funds. However, other foundations do not use such a form. Many foundations also print application guidelines to help not-for-profits decide whether they should submit a request. Again, many smaller foundations do not publish printed guidelines.

When approaching a foundation, it is important to keep in mind that most foundations do not have staffed offices. Less than one-fourth of the nation's 27,000 foundations have staffed offices. Of these, the average size is usually one full-time or one half-time individual. Only the largest foundations with substantial asset bases have the operating funds available to provide staff to review and process grant requests.

The best initial approach that can be made to a foundation is by phone because it is possible to talk directly with a foundation representative about the foundation's interest in a specific project or program. The foundation's staff can indicate whether the not-for-profit's program fits within the guidelines of the foundation's current funding interests. A phone conversation may also reveal when the foundation's board will meet and what support documents must accompany a proposal.

In many instances, a phone call will not be possible simply because the foundation does not maintain a staffed office. In this situation a carefully written letter that summarizes the project and the interest of the not-for-profit in approaching the foundation with a grant request will suffice. Most foundations will send a reply letter that is usually written by an officer or a director. The response letter will either indicate that the proposed project is not of interest to the foundation or that it is of interest, with the not-for-profit then being invited to submit a full proposal.

Besides written reference materials and direct contacts with foundations, fund raisers will be able to obtain other information on foundations by communicating with their professional peers and meeting foundation grant makers at public forums and conferences. This type of information is usually far more accurate than information provided by printed directories simply because of the time lag inherent in any written document.

Request for Support: The Proposal

Once the research has been completed on a foundation and it appears that the nonprofit's program fits within the guidelines of the foundation's interest areas, the time will arrive to submit a proposal, particularly if the foundation has encouraged the organization to apply for a grant. Foundation proposals tend to be more comprehensive and lengthy than those prepared for individual or corporate prospects. These proposals will usually include a cover letter by the not-for-profit's executive director or board president and several appendices that include a list of the organization's board members and its latest audited financial statements.

Foundation proposals tend to follow the same general format and outline. This includes an opening statement that summarizes the project and the amount being requested, perhaps a short history of the organization, identification of the problem that the organization is seeking to solve, how a grant from the foundation will help alleviate the problem, and how the organization will evaluate the success or failure of the program in meeting or solving the problem. A comprehensive budget outline is usually included as an appendix to the formal proposal (also see Exhibit 19.1).

Many foundations will help not-for-profits that submit proposals by providing a clearly defined format for proposal submission. These guidelines help the not-for-profit shape and create the proposal. It also helps the foundation evaluate the proposal more efficiently because the foundation's program officer or officers will be better able to screen proposals that follow a similar format.

Packaging a Proposal. Many people who submit proposals for the first time wonder how a proposal should be packaged. There is no set formula, but simplicity is the most common rule of thumb. Today foundations receive numerous proposals, all of which must be read and evaluated. In most instances, extraneous packaging such as binders or covers will have little impact on whether a project is funded. In preparation for board meetings at which funding decisions are actually made, many foundations condense a request for support into one or two paragraphs (regardless of the length of the proposal!). The most effective use of time should be spent on creating a compelling case for support and following foundation guidelines when available.

Direct Personal Contacts. Many large foundations require that a request for funds follow a carefully prescribed order of events. This often means submitting a proposal by mail before a specific deadline. Then sometime after the deadline, the proposal is reviewed by the foundation's grants committee and

Exhibit 19.1. A Brief Guide for the Preparation of Proposals for Special Projects.

The main thing is to have an idea and a clearly thought out plan to accomplish something important. . . . The project or program should be concisely described in straightforward English, with a minimum of technical jargon.
— Manning P. Pattillo (1982)

Key components to an effective proposal:

1. A *cover letter* signed by the head of the organization's governing board and perhaps the CEO.
2. A *project title* (and subtitle, if necessary), usually no more than ten words.
3. A *project summary* of two hundred words or less that describes the proposal's purpose, timing, and dollar requirements and which validates the organization submitting the proposal.
4. A *problem statement* or *needs assessment* to validate the existence of unmet needs in the community, define the client group to be served, and acknowledge what has been done in the past or is currently being done to address the problem by other groups as well as by the organization submitting the proposal.
5. *Objectives* that are specific, explicit, and measurable statements of *what* the project will achieve in addressing the problems described in the previous statement. Avoid overly ambitious statements that may not be attainable.
6. *Methods* or the "how" as it relates to the "what" of the objectives. These are detailed descriptions of the activities to be implemented in providing a solution to the identified problem. Information must be included on the people who will be key in the program's implementation plus data on why the chosen methodology is superior to past or present solution attempts.
7. An *evaluation* that describes the tools and procedures to be used in determining whether the objectives have been achieved and the methods used have been appropriate.
8. *Future plans* or an analysis of how the program will continue in the future, *including* an evaluation of long-term funding requirements and sources for that support.
9. A *budget* for personnel, facilities, equipment supplies, communications, travel, dues, and subscriptions.

a letter is sent to the not-for-profit either declining to support the project or indicating that funding has been approved.

Many not-for-profits quite naturally want to improve the odds of having a project funded and will look at ways to make direct and personal contact with a foundation's board members. Because all foundations react differently and follow different procedures, it would be best to first contact the foundation's staff (if one exists) to let it know of the agency's interest in communicating directly with one of the foundation's directors. This simple and forthright act of courtesy is often very much appreciated by the foundation's staff. By keeping all levels of a foundation's hierarchy apprised of an agency's solicitation approach, the chance of offending an individual (or not following a specific foundation's procedures) is greatly minimized.

The importance of using personal contacts certainly cannot be over-emphasized. It is very likely that all not-for-profit organizations have at least one member of their constituency who is either directly related to a foundation or is at least a business or personal associate of someone who sits on a foundation board. Most of the foundation guides available today also include appendices of officers and directors of foundations. There are also several companies whose main service is to help not-for-profits identify linkages among their constituencies to the foundation world.

After a Proposal Is Submitted. Once a proposal is submitted, little remains to be done until a decision is reached. During this waiting period, an organization may wish to provide follow-up information to the foundation prospect, especially if a substantial grant has been received from another foundation for the same project in the time since the proposal was submitted. Many foundations like to see other support before committing their own resources. And many foundations prefer to work in partnership with other funders to help meet a specific need or problem.

Site Visits

Many not-for-profits achieve much greater success in receiving funding for a project if they can convince members of the foundation board to visit the organization before they submit a proposal. The odds of receiving a grant are greatly enhanced if a foundation staffmember or board member can see firsthand what the organization is seeking to accomplish.

A site visit may also take place after a proposal is submitted and before a decision is reached. This often happens when an organization's proposal clears the initial screening by the foundation's board but actual funding rests on the results of a site visit.

A site visit may also take place after a proposal has been funded. In this case, a foundation staffmember or board member may want to visit the organization to see how the grant was used and what the foundation's funds made possible.

Follow-Up Reports

As the competition for funds continues to grow and foundations become more concerned about how their funds are used, many foundations now require postgrant follow-up reports. Although these reports can place an extra burden on a not-for-profit receiving a grant (depending on the complexity of the reporting forms and procedures), it helps to reassure the foundation that the funds are being used for their intended purpose. Such reports are actually of great help to not-for-profits because they discipline an organization to monitor the project being funded.

Expressing Appreciation

Whether or not a proposal is funded, it is very important to write a thank-you letter to the foundation. Most foundations make an effort to read every proposal they receive and it is in an organization's best interests to thank a foundation executive for making this effort. Many times a proposal is turned down on a first request simply because the funds are fully committed, not because the project is not worthwhile. A simple phone call or letter follow-up may lead to funding at a future date.

Conclusion

For many years, foundations have represented a sizable pool of funds available to help meet or solve society's more pressing needs. The funding interests of foundations tend to change over time, depending on changes in public opinion and the makeup of a foundation's board and its interests. Over the years, many foundations have developed more comprehensive guidelines to help grant seekers determine more accurately whether their projects will be of interest to a particular foundation.

Sufficient written research is available on foundations to help not-for-profits identify those foundations that could be considered solid prospects for a specific project. Many of the printed research books available today are also accessible through electronic data bases.

The key to effective grantsmanship will continue to be the development of successful linkages between the interests of foundations and programs that meet those interests. Grants will be awarded to organizations that perform careful cultivation, submit clear and concise proposals, and, where possible, use personal contacts to explain the project.

Fund Raising
at the Grass Roots Level

The *Doubleday Dictionary for Home or Office* defines *grass roots* as referring to "1) ordinary people, especially those apart from the centers of political power or influence; 2) the primary source or foundation."

This definition provides an excellent starting place for understanding the difference between grass roots fund raising and mainstream fund raising. Grass roots fund raising is done by "ordinary people" rather than professionals or those close to great sources of money or power. A few people have an idea. They see a pressing social need and want to respond or have an artistic vision and wish to create a cultural vehicle for it or wish to improve an existing institution such as a school. They get together in a living room or a church basement and plan how to create change. Once they begin their activities, they find that they have also created an organization. Their plan must include raising money. They start with a garage sale; they canvass their neighborhood; they seek donations from small stores, churches, and synagogues; they send a few appeal letters; and sometimes they even ask their wealthier friends for gifts of $100 or $250. This is grass roots fund raising: the kind that ordinary people use their own skills and resources to achieve.

Grass roots fund raising does not require paid staff. It does not require technical knowledge of planned giving or proposal writing. And it does not require much, if any, front money.

After a year or more, a grass roots organization often decides to become bigger so that it can do its work more quickly and effectively. It seeks and receives foundation funding in the form of seed money to expand its response to a now-proven need; it hires staff, and gradually it may no longer be grass roots. Probably most institutions in the United States started off as grass roots efforts.

For many reasons, many groups that begin as grass roots organizations either choose to or are forced to remain grass roots. Perhaps the issues they work on lend themselves best to small-scale local organizing, or perhaps the groups have no desire to develop broader visions or mandates beyond their grass roots origins. We will explore here the impact, the importance, and some of the similarities and differences in grass roots groups' fund raising.

To understand the vast range of groups that fit the definition of grass roots, it is useful to review who gives money away. Eighty-five percent of all money provided by the private sector (that is, nongovernment sources) comes from living individuals; an additional 5 percent is given by individuals through bequests. Foundations and corporations each provide only some 5 percent of total giving. Most people are surprised at the scope of individual giving, but what is more surprising is who actually gives this money. Numerous studies over the past decade have shown that fully 85 percent of the money given away by living individuals comes from families with incomes of $50,000 and less. The middle- and working-class people of our country are not only the majority of donors, but also the bulk of donators. Furthermore, a 1981 study by INDEPENDENT SECTOR (1988, pp. 5–7) showed that families living on incomes of $5,000 gave away an average of $238 to charity (most often their religious institution). In 1986, the poverty level for a family of two was $7,500, so families of any size living on incomes of $5,000 are extremely poor. Nevertheless, they give away almost 5 percent of their gross income. The average American family, on the other hand, gives away less than 2 percent of its disposable income.

The most thorough study undertaken to date on Americans' giving patterns was done by the firm of Yankelovich, Skelly, and White. The study showed that the richer the family, the less it gave away as a percent of its income. Simply stated, then, the majority of donors to grass roots organizations are middle- and working-class people, and they also give the majority of money. This is not to negate the tremendous impact and importance of wealthy people and their gifts, without which the major institutions of our society would not exist, but to highlight the often-overlooked contributions of ordinary people (Klein, 1988, p. 5).

Grass roots organizations make up the majority of not-for-profits in the United States. They represent far more than one-half of the organizations incorporated as nonprofit [501(c)(3)] organizations with the IRS. And some experts estimate that more than 1 million other organizations have no designated tax status or operate under the fiscal sponsorship of an umbrella organization. Most of these would fit the description of *grass roots*.

What is a grass roots organization? Generally speaking, it is one with a budget of less than $500,000 (in fact, many have budgets of only $10,000 to $100,000). It is run by a team of board members or volunteers and one or two paid staffmembers (although many grass roots groups have only part-time or no staffmembers) and works in a specific and limited geographic area. The work of grass roots organizations span the gamut of political and social issues.

Grass roots groups often face one another in legal and legislative battles over environmental issues, gun control, abortion, housing, water rights, rent control, and the like, but many groups can also be found providing essential human services such as day care, running small churches and community centers, and providing shelter for the homeless and food for the hungry.

Grass roots organizations form amateur theaters, choirs, and small orchestras, as well as publish poetry, newspapers, and novels. Sometimes they work locally to help people far away, such as spontaneous relief efforts for hurricane or earthquake victims.

Grass roots fund raising reflects their organizing. It includes almost all strategies that raise money from individuals, and it does not generally include raising money from foundations, corporations, or government. Grass roots fund raising does not usually include large-scale fund raising efforts such as direct mail appeals, planned giving campaigns, phone-a-thons, or large special events such as golf tournaments, designer showcases, and charity sweepstakes. A grass roots fund raising strategy must be accomplished by volunteers without much expense and with a fairly quick return.

An integral part of the definition of grass roots is the element of volunteerism. Because these groups have little access to money, they rely heavily on volunteers and are usually started by volunteers. Thus contributions of time become integral to grass roots fund raising. This concept will become more clear as the history of grass roots organizations is discussed.

The term *grass roots* was originally an insult, one used to denigrate organizations considered to be "here today, gone tomorrow" and with roots no deeper or more lasting than the roots of grass. Like other labels meant to insult — such as *protestant, feminist,* and *liberal* — this one has been redeemed as a descriptive term used with pride by those groups who have ordinary people at the heart of their organizations.

The Historical Record

To understand the scope of grass roots organizations, it is useful to look at a few historical examples of what ordinary people, working on shoestring budgets, have been able to accomplish.

From the beginning of the colonial settlement of what would become the United States, the earliest grass roots groups were churches. As the colonies began to realize their need for independence from Great Britain, revolutionaries met secretly to discuss freedom and to write the documents that would eventually become the Constitution and the Bill of Rights. The entire Revolutionary War began as a strictly grass roots effort. Less known are other grass roots undertakings. The very first charity organized by women was begun in Philadelphia in 1778 by freed slaves. Known as the Free African Society, it was an early version of insurance. For twenty-five cents per week, members were ensured of money to tide them through emergencies.

Another of the first charities organized by women was the Society for the Relief of Poor Widows and Children, which was formed in New York City in 1797. The founder, Isabella Graham, was herself a self-supporting widow, a rarity at a time when women had no legal right to own property and little opportunity to earn money. During the first winter of the society's existence, it helped ninety-eight widows and two-hundred small children by enrolling the children in schools and teaching the women sewing as a source of income. The society raised money by charging its members (women only) $3 a year and taking contributions from men. The society was extremely well organized; in its first year, it had more than two-hundred members and had received more than $1,000 in extra donations from members and men (McCarthy, 1989, pp. 50, 60–73).

Building churches and schools, and carrying out the work of these self-help societies characterized the majority of grass roots efforts through the 1700s. Starting in 1830, however, people added to these activities by organizing around the issue of the abolition of slavery. Freed and escaped slaves formed underground networks, and whites worked in hundreds of abolition societies, which grew to more than one thousand by 1837. The abolition of slavery was always a grass roots movement rooted in churches and funded through the small contributions of thousands of members (Evans, 1989, pp. 127–30).

An activity that became important later in the nineteenth century was the temperance movement. The most famous organization to arise from that crusade was the Women's Christian Temperance Union (WCTU), which was created in 1874. Frances Willard, the charismatic president from 1879 to 1899, received no salary for her full-time work in the first ten years of her presidency. She supported herself by lecturing and passing the hat at every meeting. The WCTU itself survived primarily by using the fund raising strategy of "parlor meetings" (today's house parties). WCTU donors were almost entirely women of moderate means, and yet, in 1889, the money raised in just the Chicago chapter allowed the WCTU to run two day nurseries, two Sunday schools, an industrial school, a shelter for four thousand homeless or destitute women, a free medical dispensary that treated more than 1,600 patients, a lodging house that provided temporary housing for 50,000 men, and a low-cost restaurant. Some of these enterprises generated their own funds, but most were underwritten by hundreds of small gifts.

Between the end of the Civil War and the passage of the Nineteenth Amendment in 1920, the most important grass roots movement was that of women's suffrage. Two groups are of interest here: the all-women National Women's Suffrage Association and the American Women's Suffrage Association, which admitted men. Formed in the late 1860s, these two organizations coexisted for more than twenty years before merging to become the National

American Women's Suffrage Association, now the League of Women Voters. The money needed for this movement (which lasted more than fifty-two years and took forty-seven campaigns and state constitutional conventions, and nineteen successive congresses to endorse women's right to vote) was supplied by hundreds of thousands of women and men through small and large gifts, special events, membership fees, and bequests. It was a truly grass roots movement that became an institution.

The suffrage movement also provides a good example of how organizations move from total reliance on grass roots fund raising as they grow. By the turn of the century, Susan B. Anthony, Alice Paul, Lucy Stone, and other leaders had attracted many very wealthy women to their cause. Elizabeth Eddy left $50,000 to Anthony in a bequest, which was used to publish Anthony and Stone's *History of Women's Suffrage*. Mrs. Frank Leslie left $2 million in a bequest "for the furtherance of the cause of Women Suffrage" in 1890 after many years of moderate but steady support (Klein, 1990, pp. 3–6).

The next effective grass roots movement was that of civil rights, which many date from the U.S. Supreme Court's 1954 ruling in *Brown* v. *Board of Education*. The grass roots fund raising aspect of the civil rights movement began with the direct-action strategy of the Montgomery, Alabama, bus boycott of December 1955. For 381 days, not a single black person rode the public buses in Montgomery. The campaign cost $3,000 a week, and all of the money was raised through black churches. Every night, participants at church rallies would contribute dollars, quarters, and even pennies. Black churches continued to be a major source of funds for the various strategies of the civil rights movement through the 1960s and 1970s (Hulbert, 1978, 1980).

Many other movements and causes have demonstrated the impact of grass roots organizations on the history and development of our nation, including such major accomplishments as school lunch programs, the development of community standards for the quality of milk and water, child care centers, public kindergartens, juvenile courts, playgrounds, the passage of the Pure Food and Drug Act of 1906, much of the progress of the labor movement, and the preservation of such important natural scenic areas as Mesa Verde, the Palisades of the Hudson River, and Kings Canyon National Park. The 1980s brought victory for the anti–nuclear power movement (no new nuclear power plants have been scheduled or are being built in the United States), the rise of the prochoice debate and the phenomenal organizing of both pro- and antichoice activists, public recognition of the gay and lesbian liberation movement, and extensive organizing for advocacy and services for people infected with the AIDS virus.

The scope of these groups and the movements they represent show the vital role that grass roots organizations play in all segments of our society. These groups and the critical work they do are a tribute to the success of grass roots fund raising.

Grass Roots and Mainstream Fund Raising

The main difference between grass roots fund raising and more mainstream fund raising is in scale. Grass roots fund raising is done on a much smaller scale than mainstream fund raising and operates on small budgets, requires quick returns, and uses low technology and minimal technical skill.

Visibility is the first significant problem that grass roots organizations face. By definition, these groups are too new, too controversial, or too small to have been publicly accepted or widely known. Many lack the skills to get media attention or to be taken seriously. As a result, they have little or no name recognition. This means that much of their fund raising involves explaining their case to people, which makes their fund raising efforts much more time-consuming. As a result, grass roots groups often use strategies to raise money that do not require explanations of their work. Special events are a good example. People who like movies or dances or auctions will usually attend without knowing a great deal about the group sponsoring the event. Unfortunately, special events are not an efficient way to raise funds; in fact, they often lose money. Nevertheless, because of their lack of visibility, grass roots groups must dedicate some of their fund raising efforts strictly to building visibility.

A compounding factor for many advocacy groups is that they work on issues that are not easily summarized and that require a certain amount of background information to understand. For example, groups working to create change through legislation or litigation must explain their issues, how they plan to reach their goals, and why they feel their chosen strategies will work to address the social concerns being addressed. This is very different from grass roots or larger groups who provide direct services such as feeding the hungry or housing the homeless. Their strategy is straightforward and understandable.

The second formidable issue is that of front money. The old saying "You have to spend money to make money" points up the difficulties that grass roots groups have in getting ahead. Without front money, grass roots groups must settle for cramped offices, no clerical help, old photocopy machines, and so on. The disadvantages that come with this lack of modern equipment and adequate facilities are somewhat offset by the tendency of grass roots organizations to stay aligned with their constituencies. They are no richer than the poor on whose behalf they work. This solidarity is important for building a movement.

But such a low income level can also hinder a grass roots group in getting its work done efficiently. Without front money, a grass roots group spends a lot of time cutting corners, trying to get things donated, and doing things as cheaply as possible. For example, if a large institution needs a computer, it is likely to simply buy it. A grass roots group that needs a computer is more likely to send three volunteers out looking for a free one. Many a grass roots group has found itself the recipient of an outdated computer with failing parts that are no longer available and a difficult and archaic operating system. The computer is not used to capacity, if at all. As a result, the group decides to have a garage sale or bake sale to raise money to buy a decent computer. This whole process puts it six months behind the larger institution, which was able to fulfill its computer need immediately.

Nevertheless, grass roots groups operate at a very high level of efficiency. Fired by enthusiasm for their work and belief in their cause, a few people will do a huge amount of work and do it well, accomplishing a lot each day. The director of a grass roots organization may not only write a direct mail appeal but also be the one to fold the letters, stuff the envelopes, affix the labels, and sort the bulk mailing while answering the phone (there is no secretary), sweating through a hot summer day (there is no air conditioning), and coordinating the work of volunteers who are there to help.

A third factor that distinguishes grass roots organizations from larger institutions is in whether they have paid staff and at what sort of salaries. Grass roots groups that can afford paid staff generally pay $10,000 to $30,000 a year less for director positions than do larger not-for-profits. Their benefits packages may also be quite slim. These meager compensations have driven some people out of the world of grass roots organizing. Although some who work with grass roots groups are not skilled enough or competent enough to get jobs in larger not-for-profits and thereby justify lower wages, the vast majority of paid staffmembers in grass roots groups are highly motivated, skilled, committed, and hard-working. Furthermore, in organizations with few staffmembers, grass roots directors develop a wide range of skills— including bookkeeping, budgeting, administration, public relations, and program development and evaluation—that other agencies divide among more specialized personnel. Clearly, the movements that grass roots groups have spawned and the changes they have wrought are testimony not only to the dedication of the workers but also to their skills at accomplishing their objectives.

A fourth factor that distinguishes grass roots from mainstream fund raising is the difference in how quickly a strategy must produce dollars in the door. A university can initiate a planned giving program that will not see a return for five or more years, whereas a grass roots organization is generally raising the money it needs to operate that month or the next. Investing in large-scale direct mail is out of the question for grass roots groups because, even if the front money could be found, direct mail is rarely profitable until well into its second year. Taking the time to cultivate donors is difficult, too, because the gift is often needed immediately. As a result, a group settles for smaller gifts than it would get if it had the time to explain its case and meet with donors several times. This need for quick turnaround, on the other hand, gives a sense of urgency and immediacy to the work of board members and volunteers, which can be exciting. The constituency, too, knows that it is needed, and every donor feels empowered by knowing the importance of his or her gift.

In grass roots groups, it is quickly clear who does the work and who does not. Rarely are incompetent or nonproducing people tolerated; the budget will not allow it. If the group does not find a firm financial base, even if all of its fund raising is from grass roots strategies, the excitement will degenerate into anxiety and from there into burnout. Staffmembers and volunteers will leave as a crisis mentality takes over, one of the most endemic problems in small organizations.

The final difference between grass roots and mainstream fund raising is in the question of skill required. Good grass roots fund raising requires ingenuity, willingness to ask for money or time or in-kind donations, commitment to the cause, common sense, a love of people, and an understanding of human nature. Many important grass roots groups raise money with only those elements in place. Technical skill becomes icing on the cake. However, lack of skills and fund raising knowledge means that grass roots groups are often weak in certain key areas such as keeping records on donors, understanding prospect research, knowing how to write foundation or corporate proposals, getting money from the government, or setting up planned giving programs. The techniques of mass solicitation, such as phone-a-thons and direct mail, are not used, and sometimes a lack of basic knowledge — how and when to file forms with the government, how to renew a permit for bulk mail, how to pay social security taxes for employees — causes grass roots organizations endless trouble.

Despite all of these differences, one fundamental similarity remains between grass roots and other kinds of fund raising: the principle of asking for money. All groups, from the smallest to the largest, have trouble with this aspect of fund raising, particularly as it relates to face-to-face requests for money. The taboos against asking, the fear of rejection, and all of the cultural norms that give money its power affect us all.

However, when one looks at strong organizations, regardless of size, they usually have a strong team of people who ask prospects for money. When grass roots organizations can be made to understand that face-to-face solicitation is the fastest and most lucrative of all fund raising strategies, they will grow quickly, learn to shed less productive methods of fund raising, and get on with their very important work.

KEYS TO SUCCESS
IN FUND RAISING

Part Six examines the subject of ethics and professional standards, reviews resources that are available to practitioners to strengthen their skills, and explores the thesis of integrated fund raising as a method of coalescing needs with fund raising potential in a coordinated program.

With the growth and advancement of the fund raising profession in recent years, particularly with the development of national professional societies, much discussion has been centered on the subject of ethics. With the discussion has come enlightenment and confusion. Are we talking about ethical standards, moral standards, or professional standards? Do these words refer to the same subject from different reference points? Or do they differ in definitions? There is no question about definition in the minds of ethicists. There is a need for continuing discourse among members of the profession.

Continuing discourse is required on the subject of professional stance. What does the term *professional stance* mean? What is the hallmark of a professional: experience, academic degrees, management skills, communication and interpersonal skills, social commitment, dedication to a cause, integrity, pride in performance? Professional stance was alluded to indirectly in the chapter on philosophy at the beginning. The discussion continues in these concluding chapters.

Robert E. Fogal

Chapter 21

Standards and Ethics
in Fund Raising

Many people associated with the philanthropic sector are concerned about morality. They believe that what philanthropic organizations and institutions aim to accomplish embodies a nobility that exceeds the purposes of government and business. Those who earn their living in the sector often have a commitment to a "higher cause" that ameliorates the challenging conditions of employment. However, the morality of the philanthropic sector may not be as singular as many would like to think. Two examples belie these assumptions:

> The manager of the not-for-profit organization has had to face the fact that the organization is a business and not a charity. [From a newsletter published by a commercial fund raising consulting firm]

> I heard people [from the not-for-profit sector] repeatedly remark on the one hand that philanthropy "puts people first," and on the other that "business is only interested in the bottom line." Needless to say, it would be hard to find a business person who would not tell you that putting people first is the essence of good business management, both one's own employees and the customers one serves. [From a personal letter written by a businessman who participated in the Indiana University Center on Philanthropy's 1990 Symposium, "Taking Fund Raising Seriously."]

The tone of the first excerpt suggests that not-for-profits have been characterized by some people-oriented "do-good" syndrome that, while laudable, ought to be replaced by more hard-nosed, bottom-line management. The second excerpt challenges the simple dichotomy of people versus profits by implying that sound business practice involves both in relationship to each other.

Questioning the Profession

Both statements lead fund raisers to think about *why* they do what they do. Furthermore, the rhetoric of noble-sounding purposes, the pressure to meet bottom-line demands, and the daily demands of fund raising all lead to a variety of impulses, emotions, and ideas that may be incongruent, if not actually in conflict, with one another. Reflective practitioners can find themselves considering perplexing questions: Why does our profession exist? How do fund raisers contribute to the common good? To what collegial standards do fund raisers adhere? How does self-interest influence the performance of fund raisers and their organizations? What incentives motivate fund raisers?

The lack of widely established performance standards and ethical norms in fund raising is especially critical, given the centrality of philanthropic contributions to the existence of the not-for-profit sector. Voluntary association, voluntary service, and voluntary giving are the defining dimensions of the philanthropic sector. Most of the goods and services that are delivered by not-for-profit organizations could also be, and in many cases are, delivered by governmental agencies or for-profit enterprises. The products produced by not-for-profit organizations and institutions do not determine philanthropic character. Rather, it is the resources that are shared voluntarily with these organizations and institutions that determine their place in the philanthropic sector. Thus, the standards and ethics that are applied to and surround the fund raising practice reflect and reinforce the purpose and style of any philanthropic entity. In other words, *how* a not-for-profit organization or institution conducts fund raising says a great deal about and may actually determine the organization's character.

"Rights and wrongs" and "oughts and shoulds" are discussed only occasionally in the fund raising field. Discourse about such topics is made even more difficult by the lack of an accepted vocabulary that reflects common assumptions. People's experiences, emotions, and thoughts are too diverse to provide meaningful structure to conversations about "why we do what we do" in fund raising. Performance standards and ethical norms commonly result from individual practitioners drawing upon their own backgrounds and histories as singular resources for the moral justification for what they do. Whatever performance standards there are for the field, they are controlled by persons external to actual fund raising such as accountants, tax authorities, and attorneys general. The few ethical norms that may exist are based upon the oral traditions of established fund raising executives whose perspectives mostly demonstrate the subjectivity of "what's right is what works."

Such ad hoc traditions are not necessarily wrong or bad. In fact, the opposite is usually true. Most people live most of the time according to the traditions and customs that surround them. Their behavior and habits are developed under the leadership of individuals and institutions that are significant to their social formation and growth. Not following normal expectations of behavior causes what many identify as moral rebellion and anarchy. Accepted traditions and customs usually determine the ends for which we live (Dewey, 1960, p. 29).

The increased prominence of the not-for-profit sector in American society (along with the growth of nongovernmental organizations worldwide) raises many questions about voluntary support for which there are inadequate answers. Individualized perspectives that have characterized the fund raising practice no longer provide a sound basis for what the profession does. Organizations and the people who lead them are increasingly expected to respond to public demands for accountability. And the increased use of technology in fund raising highlights new issues about responsibility and relationships.

Ethical Dimensions

Thinking and talking about what is done in fund raising and why leads to what is known as *moral discourse*. According to Dewey, ethicists broadly agree that there is "no such thing as reflective morality except where men seriously ask by what purposes they should direct their conduct and why they should do so: what it is that makes their purposes good. This intellectual search for ends is bound to arise when customs fail to give required guidance. And this failure happens when old institutions break down; when invasions from without and inventions and innovations from within radically alter the course of life" (1960, pp. 29–30).

Three main points seem clear thus far:

1. Fund raising can be accomplished less and less on a "business as usual" basis.
2. The challenge to many fund raising habits comes from changes in not-for-profit organizations themselves, from changes in the public's assumptions about not-for-profits, and from technological shifts in how fund raising is done.
3. Being responsive to changing circumstances and conditions leads not-for-profit leaders and managers to consider moral issues that pertain to their organizations.

Sensitivity to moral questions does not mean that all activities in not-for-profit organizations must be examined in terms of what is right and good.

The contrary is often true. "There is no better evidence of a well formed moral character than knowledge of when to raise the moral issue and when not. . . . Many persons are so callous or so careless that they do not raise the moral issue often enough. But there are others so unbalanced that they hamper and paralyze conduct by indulging in what approaches a mania of doubt" (Dewey, 1960, pp. 12–13).

Most people make dozens of decisions each day. Not-for-profit managers, including fund raising executives, work within a frame of reference that enables them to accomplish the tasks for which they are responsible. If they become victims of "paralysis by ethical analysis," they will be asked to earn their livelihood elsewhere. Not viewing everything they do in moral terms does not imply immorality, however. Many management functions are simply nonmoral in character. That is, management decisions and actions simply relate to matters other than universal moral duties and obligations.

With these perspectives in mind, it is possible to look at several types of fund raising norms and evaluate their presence in fund raising practice.

Broad Professional Standards

Standards typically define established practices in a field of human activity. Through rules and regulations, norms of right and wrong are declared and enforced by the authorities who govern a given field. Those who do not respect standards may be subject to peer-imposed discipline ranging from warnings to loss of privilege, or to legally imposed sanctions such as fines, imprisonment, or loss of licenses. The key to recognizing and understanding standards is that they are usually "givens"; that is, they are followed by practitioners who accept the standards as the way things are done without any particular regard to the morality or ethics that may be reflected in the standards.

One set of norms for certain fund raising practices is the *Management Reporting Standards for Educational Institutions: Fund Raising and Related Activities* prepared by the Council for Advancement and Support of Education (CASE) and the National Association of College and University Business Officers (NACUBO). A central part of the *Standards* details practices to be followed for gift evaluation (see Exhibit 21.1). The original standards define how philanthropically contributed dollars in higher education ought to be counted. Other sections outline how to track costs for fund raising and related functions in public relations and constituent development.

Many experienced fund raising executives recognize these standards and adhere to them. Persons new to the field must learn them. No practitioner considers them to be moral statements. Whether or not they are followed, however, may reflect the ethical perspectives of a fund raising professional.

The CASE/NACUBO *Standards* were developed in the early 1980s at the

Exhibit 21.1. Guidelines: Gift Valuation.*

Gift Valuation.

Gifts should be valued by the organization on the date the donor relinquished control of the assets in favor of the organization. The amounts reported in this summary should be arrived at without regard to a donor's personal estimation of the gift's value, the worth and date of the gift as reported by the donor to the IRS, or the value placed on it by the IRS in reference to the individual's personal income tax liability. In cases where gifts are made in cash, the valuation should not pose a problem. In cases where gifts are made with securities, real and personal property, in trust, through insurance policies, or bearing some real or implied obligation on the part of the institution, the following guidelines should be observed.

Securities: An organization should report gifts of securities at market value on the date the donor relinquished control of the assets in favor of the organization. Neither losses nor gains realized by the organization's sale of the securities after their receipt nor brokerage fees or other expenses associated with this transaction should affect the value reported.

Real and Personal Property: Major gifts of real and personal property—such as land, houses, paintings, antiques, and rare books—should be reported at the fair market value placed on them by an independent, expert appraiser. Small gifts of real and personal property with an apparent worth of less than $5,000 may be valued by an organization staffmember who has some expertise. The informal valuation may be used for organizational reporting purposes.

Charitable Remainder Trusts, Pooled Income Funds, and Gift Annuities: Gifts made to establish charitable remainder trusts, contributions to pooled income funds, and gift annuities should generally be credited at fair market value, that is, the full amount of the assets given. In those instances where it is anticipated that a portion of the principal will be returned to the beneficiary to meet a payout obligation, the gift should be credited at its net realizable value, that is, the remainder interest as calculated by the organization for financial statement purposes.

Charitable Lead Trusts: In reporting the value of a charitable lead trust, only the income received from it each year during the period of operation of the trust should be included in an organization's gift totals.

Trusts Administered by Others: The value of the assets of gifts in trust that the organization or the donor has chosen to have administered by others should be included in the organization's gift totals for the year—provided the organization has an irrevocable right to all or a predetermined portion of the income or remainder interest.

Insurance: An organization must be named as both beneficiary and irrevocable owner of an insurance policy before a policy can be recorded as a gift. The organization should report the cash surrender value of the policy, rather than its face value, as the amount of the gift. If the donor pays further premiums on the policy, the organization should include the entire amount of the premium payment in its gift totals. If the organization elects to pay the premiums, it should consider those payments as operating expenditures and not report increases in the cash surrender value as gifts. Regardless of whether the donor or the organization pays the premiums on a policy it owns, the difference between the cash value and the insurance company's settlement after the donor's death should be reported not as a gift but as a gain on the disposition of assets. In those cases where an organization receives the proceeds of an insurance policy for which it was named beneficiary but not owner, the full amount received should be reported as a gift on the date delivered.

Nongovernmental Grants and Contracts: Grant income from private, nongovernmental sources should be included in an organization's gift totals; contract revenue should *not* be included. A private grant, such as a gift, is bestowed voluntarily and without expectation of any tangible compensation; it is donative in nature. A contract is a written agreement, often negotiated, between the organization and the awarding agency and is enforceable by law.

---

*Reprinted with permission of the Council for Advancement and Support of Education (CASE) and National Association of College and University Business Officers (NACUBO). *Management Reporting Standards for Educational Institutions*, cosponsored by CASE and NACUBO and supported by a grant from the Exxon Educational Foundation. 1982, pp. 3–4.

urging of Lilly Endowment, Exxon Educational Foundation, and other foundations who were distressed by the abuses of corporate matching-gift programs by colleges and universities. Business and financial officers worked with higher education fund raisers to define practices that were congruent with established accounting methods. Such methods had been used to one degree or another by many organizations for many years and drew on the knowledge of authorities outside of fund raising such as accountants, attorneys, and tax experts. The standards were not intrinsic to fund raising itself. Through their acceptance and use, however, they have become norms for fund raisers or fund raising standards.

The process that created the CASE/NACUBO standards involved taking norms from outside the field of fund raising and internalizing them so that they became the norms within higher education fund raising. The practical consequences of this process—integrating fund raising into the general financial management of a college or university—also embody the symbolic value of having fund raising accepted as a legitimate part of the institutional enterprise. Fund raising standards had to agree with and be part of the entire management function; fund raising standards enabled management to accept fund raising as something that belonged to the institution (White, 1989).

The CASE/NACUBO *Standards* determine what data are collected about fund raising in higher education and how they are to be organized. Professional association awards are based on these data; such recognition positively reinforces the use of such standards. However, there is no mechanism for applying sanctions to those who do not follow the norms.

This type of norm can be viewed from three different perspectives. Organizationally, their acceptance represents a willingness to follow conventional practices of financial management. Professionally, fund raisers who follow such norms accept the responsibility of ensuring that their organizations respond to accepted practices. Personally, fund raisers who have internalized such practices carry them into any employment situation that calls for their use.

Other Professional Standards

Another kind of performance standard involves a process-oriented dimension of fund raising practice. In an essay originally prepared for the instructional materials of The Fund Raising School, Henry A. Rosso defined the "cycle" of fund raising as "a discipline of gift development that progresses in logical order from preparation to planning to program execution to control" (see Chapter 2). The steps of the cycle are:

1. Prepare the case statement that identifies the social needs central to the organization's concern and that outlines the organization's response to those needs.

2. Define objectives that can measure how the organization plans to meet the social needs.
3. Prepare a statement of financial needs that will support the programs designed to fulfill the objectives.
4. Analyze the requirements of the market to which the programs will be aimed.
5. Involve volunteers, usually board leaders, whose commitment is essential to fund raising success.
6. Validate the financial needs required for program support through the thoughtful consideration of the organization's lay leadership.
7. Evaluate the gift markets with the aim of achieving a diverse resource base that will contribute to a resilient organization.
8. Select the fund raising vehicles that are appropriate to each fund raising market (or segments of each market) and that result in appropriate cost–benefit ratios.
9. Identify prospective donors in each market segment and analyze their potential for giving as determined by their linkage to the organization, their interest in its mission, and their ability to give.
10. Prepare the fund raising plan, drawing on the facts and their analyses gleaned thus far.
11. Prepare the communications plan that will meaningfully relate the case to each market segment or donor prospect.
12. Expand the volunteer corps with persons who are committed to the cause, who are willing to contribute, and who want to involve others in that commitment.
13. Solicit the gift in a way that communicates the importance of the cause and the dignity of the donor.
14. Renew the gift, building the donor's sense of involvement and the organization's sense of a trust obligation.

These statements are standards in that they articulate what many consider to be established practices for effective fund raising; they outline norms of what is done by respected leaders in the field. They differ from the CASE/NACUBO *Standards* in at least two respects.

First, they do not depend upon any external authority. Whether or not they are followed depends upon the desire of an organization and its leadership, including the fund raising executive, to respect the established management standard of "analyze, plan, execute, and control." The acceptance of fund raising as a management function will reflect the sense of internal self-regulation that exists within the organization.

Second, the statements may lead to reflection about the values that guide the life of a not-for-profit organization. If they do not serve as a norm for an organization's fund raising practice, their consideration should at least provoke lively discussion among professionals and lay leaders about why things ought to be done a certain way. For example:

- How important is it to an organization to periodically evaluate its mission against the social needs that it purportedly serves?
- What role does the governing board play in defining those social needs?
- To what extent does the organization fulfill a sense of public trust by addressing needs that serve the common good?
- Does the professional staff perform in a way that demonstrates a desire to live *for* philanthropy or to live *off* of philanthropy?
- What respect is accorded to people who voluntarily share their time, knowledge, and money with the organization?

Discussion of these and similar questions requires that people reflect together about the purposes that pull them into a common cause. Such conversations almost inevitably involve words such as "We ought to do . . ." or "What we should do is. . . ." These are phrases of moral and ethical content. In the best case, they introduce rational perspectives about the good that is anticipated through the organization's policies and procedures. For an organization to pursue moral purposes, it must do more than simply "carry on" as it always has; it must know what it is doing and consciously choose to do it. A process such as the fund raising cycle provides a discipline for an organization's moral discourse.

Another kind of baseline for ethical reflection is provided by the Josephson Institute's *Ethical Values and Principles for Foundation and Non-Profit Executives* (see Exhibit 21.2). These principles use terms that are traditionally heard in conversations about personal ethics: *honesty, integrity, promise keeping,* and so on. Few volunteers or professionals in not-for-profit organizations would argue with these values. In fact, it is precisely for this reason that most people want to be part of a philanthropic organization.

It is important to recognize that neither the organizational discipline represented by the fund raising cycle nor the Josephson Institute's personalized *Ethical Values and Principles* will necessarily be applied prescriptively to particular situations. The religious, cultural, or political orientations of different people can result in genuine disagreement about the common good that policies aim to achieve or the procedures for achieving the common good. Differences over what should be done and how it should be done may also reflect contrasting preferences in individuals' styles and approaches to problem solving. Or those differences may result from discord in the actual value assumptions that reflect dissimilarities in peoples' life histories.

How fund raisers view performance standards and ethical norms has been documented by Carbone (1989), who enumerated six characteristics that are commonly associated with professional behavior (p. 27):

1. autonomy of decision making
2. a systematic body of knowledge and skills
3. self-regulation and collegial standard setting

Exhibit 21.2. Ethical Values and Principles for Foundation and NonProfit Executives.*

1. *Honesty.* Honest people are truthful, sincere, forthright, straightforward, frank, and candid. They do not cheat, steal, lie, deceive, or act deviously. Not-for-profit executives should be scrupulously honest in their dealings with donors and grant makers, beneficiaries and grantees, employees and volunteers, board members, the public, and the government.
2. *Integrity.* People and organizations with integrity are principled, honorable, and upright. They are courageous and act on convictions. They will fight for their beliefs and will not adopt an "ends justifies the means" philosophy that ignores principle or is expedient at the expense of principle. Not-for-profit executives and foundation trustees respect the integrity of the mission established by their organization's board.
3. *Promise Keeping.* People worthy of trust keep promises, fulfill commitments, abide by the spirit as well as the letter of an agreement. They do not interpret agreements in an unreasonably technical or legalistic manner to rationalize noncompliance or to create justifications for escaping their commitments.
4. *Fidelity.* People worthy of trust demonstrate fidelity and loyalty to other people and to organizations by friendship in adversity, support, and devotion to duty. They do not use or disclose information that is learned in confidence for personal or professional advantage. Executives and board members should safeguard their ability to make independent professional judgments by scrupulously avoiding undue influence and conflicts of interest.
5. *Fairness.* Fair people manifest a commitment to justice, the equal treatment of individuals, and tolerance for and acceptance of diversity. They are open-minded, willing to admit they are wrong, and, where appropriate, change their positions and beliefs. They do not overreach or take undue advantage of another's mistakes or difficulties.
6. *Caring.* Concern for the well-being of others manifests itself in compassion, giving, kindness, and serving. It requires that one attempts to help those in need and avoids harming others.
7. *Respect.* Ethical people demonstrate respect for human dignity, privacy, and the right to self-determination of all competent adults. They are courteous and decent. They provide others with the information they need to make informed decisions about their own lives. Executives in the not-for-profit community should provide as much relevant information to the public as is reasonably possible to permit intelligent assessment of goals, means, and results as they relate to the organization's mission.
8. *Citizenship.* Responsible citizenship involves lawfulness, participation (by voting and expressing informal views), social consciousness, and public service. Not-for-profit organizations must be especially careful to obey all relevant regulations and laws, including tax laws.
9. *Excellence.* Ethical people are concerned with the quality of their work. They pursue excellence and are diligent, reliable, industrious, and committed.
10. *Accountability.* Ethical people accept responsibility for their decisions, for the foreseeable consequences of their actions and inactions, and for setting an example for others.
11. *Safeguard Public Trust.* People in organized philanthropy have special obligations to lead by example, to safeguard and advance the integrity and reputation of all organizations that depend on voluntary support and public trust, to avoid even the appearance of impropriety, and to take whatever actions are necessary to correct or prevent the inappropriate conduct of others.

*Adapted from The Josephson Institute, 1990. Reprinted by permission.

4. commitment to and identification with the profession
5. altruism and dedication to service
6. a code of ethics with accompanying sanctions.

These characteristics resulted from a survey of more than 750 fund raisers, all of whom are members of one or more of three main professional associations for the field: the National Association of Fund Raising Executives, the Council for the Advancement and Support of Education, and the Association for Healthcare Philanthropy.

Characteristics 3, 5, and 6 address issues of standards and ethics. The respondents showed a certain ambivalence about these characteristics: 62 percent said that self-regulation and standard setting was important, but only one-third supported peer judgment. "When asked about 'primary satisfaction' [fund raisers] cite 'knowledge that their work benefits people'; [but] when asked about incentives, salary is mentioned five times as often as any other factor." While "nearly nine out of ten fund raisers say it is important to be aware of ethical standards and use them as guides," only one-third "agree that fund raisers know the [professional association] codes and follow them" (Carbone, 1989, pp. 27, 32, 39, 40).

The lack of consensus about these issues among fund raising professionals both reflects and contributes to the lack of clarity within the not-for-profit sector about philanthropy. Like all surveys, Carbone's provides a snapshot of where fund raisers are now.

The Code of Ethics and Professional Practices of the National Society of Fund Raising Executives (NSFRE) (Exhibit 21.3) is an effort to provide ethical leadership to both the field of fund raising and the philanthropic sector. From Carbone's survey, the NSFRE code clearly has not achieved the status of a standard: It is not customarily known and accepted, and it possesses no power of enforcement through sanction. However, it shares with the fund raising cycle and the Josephson Institute's *Ethical Values* the character of a frame of reference that can lead to insights on policies and procedures based upon enduring principles. It supports the CASE/NACUBO *Standards* by affirming the use of established fiduciary controls, including the regulations of the Internal Revenue Service.

A Case Study

The principles and norms outlined in the three exhibits ought to inform the behavior of fund raising executives by helping them to distinguish right from wrong, and propriety from impropriety. As the NSFRE code states, however, fund raising professionals are likely to "write their own code of ethics every day." The following hypothetical case may help illustrate that reality.

A community agency located in a metropolitan area of 450,000 provides health services and emotional support to youth and young adults who experience a controversial medical condition. The seven-year-old agency initially grew rapidly and has functioned on a rather constant level the last three years. Operating on an $800,000 budget that is 40 percent supported with voluntary contributions, the agency is suffering from a major decline in unrestricted operating support. Jane, the executive director, informed the

Exhibit 21.3. National Society of Fund Raising Executives Code of Ethical Principles.*

The National Society of Fund Raising Executives exists to foster the development and growth of fund raising professionals and the profession, to preserve and enhance philanthropy and volunteerism, and to promote high ethical standards in the fund raising profession.
To these ends, this code declares the ethical values which NSFRE members embrace and which they strive to uphold in their professional activities.

Members of the National Society of Fund Raising Executives are motivated by an inner drive to improve the quality of life through the causes they serve. They seek to inspire others through their own sense of dedication and high purpose. They are committed to the improvement of their professional knowledge and skills in order that their performance will better serve others. They recognize their stewardship responsibility to assure that needed resources are vigorously and ethically sought and that the intent of the donor is honestly fulfilled. Such individuals practice their profession with integrity, honesty, truthfulness and adherence to the absolute obligation to safeguard the public trust.

Furthermore, NSFRE members

- serve the ideal of philanthropy, are committed to the preservation and enhancement of volunteerism, and hold stewardship of these concepts as the overriding principle of professional life;
- foster cultural diversity and pluralistic values and treat all people with dignity and respect;
- affirm, through personal giving, a commitment to philanthropy and its role in society;
- adhere to the spirit as well as the letter of all applicable laws and regulations;
- bring credit to the fund raising profession by their public demeanor;
- recognize their individual boundaries of competence and are forthcoming about their professional qualifications and credentials;
- value the privacy, freedom of choice, and interests of all those affected by their actions;
- disclose all relationships which might constitute, or appear to constitute, conflicts of interest;
- actively encourage their colleagues to embrace and practice these ethical principles.

*_NSFRE Journal_, Spring 1991, 16 (1), p. 62. Reprinted by permission.

senior management that programs will have to be eliminated and staff reduced if the $50,000 shortfall in unrestricted gifts is not met during the last two months of the fiscal year. Neither earned income nor government support is likely to increase enough to meet this need, and the organization's cash reserves are inadequate to cover the anticipated deficit.

Jane has instructed Harry, the development director, to do everything possible to obtain the needed $50,000 as quickly as possible. Harry has worked at the agency for some eighteen months, becoming the agency's chief development officer after serving in a fund raising position at a large cultural organization in the same city. He believes that the services provided by the agency are very important.

Harry wants to be a successful fund raiser, and he has demonstrated considerable skill by already reaching the total $320,000 fund raising goal. Although restricted gifts for specified programs have exceeded their individual goals, unrestricted giving has dropped.

Jane has directed the management staff to keep the fiscal situation confidential, telling neither the board nor the program staff about the problem.

The next day, Harry asked Jane to review with him several fund raising possibilities that he is considering. She responded that she would get back to him; she had an appointment in a few minutes with the board member who chairs the personnel committee. Two days later, Jane still had not answered Harry's request to review options.

Harry was considering the following possibilities:

1. Solicit the board in a special appeal based upon the agency's emergency needs.
2. Prepare a direct mail appeal that focuses on an extreme but seldom encountered case of care the agency provided.
3. Redirect miscellaneous amounts from several restricted gifts to make up the difference in unrestricted support.
4. Quietly reinterpret some restricted gifts so they could be used for general purposes.
5. Approach certain donors of restricted gifts (including a few board members) to ask for their permission to redirect their contributions.
6. Solicit a major gift from a person in the city known to be wealthy but viewed by many as having obtained that wealth through questionable means.
7. Contact a leading contributor to the cultural organization where Harry worked previously and who Harry knows has a family member who benefitted from the services the agency provides.

Several issues can be noted.

-   In what ways should the CASE/NACUBO *Standards* be applied to the options being considered?
-   If Rosso's fund raising cycle had governed the agency's planning and management of philanthropic support, would the situation have developed as it did? Were fund raising goals properly determined? Is there a clear sense that the board shares a fiduciary responsibility for the agency?
-   To what extent do the Josephson Institute's *Ethical Values* contribute to a climate of trust at the agency?
-   What conflicts of "greater good" may exist between the benefits of services delivered and the means of obtaining support to deliver those services?
-   What values motivate Harry's performance as a fund raiser? What professional risks might he experience?
-   Do any of the options exclude ethical considerations?

The moral content of the philanthropic sector is not an established or static dimension of its identity. To be philanthropic, however, requires a continuing consideration of the common good and the voluntary actions of people to achieve what they perceive to be the common good. Ethical decisions assign values to human behavior and organizational outcomes. Ethical decisions temper self-interest with the needs of human community.

Fund raising thrusts leaders and managers of not-for-profit organizations into the center of the philanthropic agenda. The standards and ethics that govern fund raising practices play a defining role in what philanthropic organizations contribute to the common good.

Resources for Strengthening Fund Raising Skills

Development is a rapidly changing profession. Fund raising executives need to stay current with trends in funding, laws governing giving and not-for-profits, new strategies for researching prospects, local and regional demographics, economic indicators, and other information that influences the development process. Fortunately, courses, workshops, publications, and professional associations can provide information vital for professional and institutional advancement.

Planning for Professional Development

In spite of an acknowledged need to consult resources that can sharpen skills and expand awareness of the issues surrounding fund raising, the development officer's work schedule often prohibits taking an afternoon for a workshop or a morning to read current professional journals. Although there are certain times when it is difficult to focus on professional growth, development officers should try to set aside regular time for these activities. Individuals who are determined to take a workshop or read their backlog of publications make appointments with themselves by blocking out an afternoon or morning so that no outside appointments can be scheduled.

In addition to time pressures, there is the challenge of selecting from the vast array of course announcements, publication promotions, and other materials that are directed to the development officer. It is easier to make decisions about professional development and to obtain institutional funding and support for time away from the office or money for publications, when a personal growth plan has been drafted in which goals and objectives are clearly stated (perhaps as part of the development plan). In this plan, goals, objectives, and time lines for acquiring additional skills or increasing expertise are outlined. The plan should become part of the annual performance-review process between the development professional and his or her supervisor.

There are many ways to expand professional knowledge, a few of which are described as follows.

Courses and Workshops. At least once a year, development professionals should take a course or workshop that will enhance skills, increase expertise, or expand professional affiliations. In the application to become a certified fund raising executive (CFRE), candidates are asked to summarize their course work and must have taken a specified number of continuing education units (CEUs) to qualify. This certification program, which is sponsored by the National Society of Fund Raising Executives, recognizes those individuals who have performed service to their employers and to their profession for a period of at least five years and have successfully passed a written examination that covers the basic principles of fund raising and philanthropic service. The CFRE and the Advanced CFRE symbolize professional achievement and commitment. A strong indicator of that commitment is continual professional growth. Other certification programs, such as that sponsored by the Association for Healthcare Philanthropy, also require evidence of continuing education.

Fund raising executives considering advanced degrees may find that local colleges or universities offer master's or Ph.D. programs in areas related to philanthropy, not-for-profit management, and fund raising. These are increasing in number and should be evaluated carefully for cost, academic value, and potential for career enhancement.

Many course announcements are directed to the development professional's office. They come from colleges and and universities, private consulting and training companies, and from organizations such as The Fund Raising School, a program of the Center on Philanthropy at Indiana University, or The Grantsmanship Center in Los Angeles. Courses are specific (planned giving, accounting for not-for-profit executives, successful marketing of your not-for-profit, and so on) or general (basic comprehensive courses from The Fund Raising School or The Grantsmanship Center). Sessions can be short (one-half day) or long (one week or longer). Costs range from $35 for a half-day session sponsored by the United Way or other community organization to more than $1,000 for a several-day course offered by a private consulting or training company. Locations vary from a hotel or other facility in the community to a college or university center at a distant location. Deciding which course to take involves a number of considerations:

1. Does the course support professional growth objectives?
2. Is it within the budget (including travel)?
3. What is known about the sponsoring organization?
4. Who are the faculty members and what are their reputations?
5. Are there others who have taken this course who can be consulted for recommendations?
6. In what ways will the organization benefit from the information gained in the class?
7. Would there be other or better courses in this area?

If it is necessary to prepare a proposal for the board or executive director to take a workshop or course, these questions can serve as the basis for that request. Funding for courses should be part of the institutional budget and be related to a professional development plan.

When returning from a course or a workshop, the information should be as widely shared as possible. If it is a specific course in an area of fund raising or management, an informal meeting can be held with those who share your interest and would benefit from the information. If it is a comprehensive course such as those at The Fund Raising School or The Grantsmanship Center, the full board or development committee should receive a report. If undertaking a degree program, whether or not it is funded by the organization, occasional reports that summarize on-the-job application of new knowledge may be valued by the executive director or the board. By conveying the directly applicable benefits gained from educational experiences, fund raising executives can effectively leverage any investment the organization has made and help to ensure future support for continuing education.

Professional and Business Journals. Development professionals should regularly read publications that focus on fund raising, not-for-profit management, trends in philanthropy, and local or national news that affects the environment for fund raising. There are numerous publications from which to choose, including those published especially for the not-for-profit sector and those designed for a broader audience. The following is a small sampling of available publications.

Two tabloid-size newspapers are specifically for our sector: *NonProfit Times* and *Chronicle of Philanthropy*. The *Times*, which is published monthly, provides sections on preparing fund raising letters, aspects of data-base management and computers, and general management issues and fund raising. In addition, it has timely articles about specific aspects of the sector (corporate giving, foundation trends, and so on) that affect its subscribers. The *Chronicle*, which is published biweekly, features more current news and fewer in-depth "how-to" articles. Items that summarize developments in the philanthropic sector are balanced with articles and interviews about people and issues. A widely consulted feature is the classified advertising of job openings from around the country and overseas.

Magazines such as *Fund Raising Management, Philanthropy Monthly, Philanthropy Digest*, and *Foundation News* are also available by subscription or at local libraries. Although some publish information that is meant to be used immediately (such as listings of current foundation grants or funding opportunities), these journals also have a timeless quality that permits their intentional (or accidental) accumulation for later reading.

There are also two quarterly journals to which fund raising professionals can subscribe: *Nonprofit and Voluntary Sector Quarterly* and *Nonprofit Management and Leadership*. The latter began publication recently and contains articles by scholars and practitioners.

When making the decision to subscribe to a particular publication, it is wise to review several issues and to evaluate them against the criteria of relevance and information value, the usefulness of the how-to articles, and the circulation the journal can have to others within the organization.

Reading about the not-for-profit sector exclusively will provide only a limited view of professional issues. In fund raising, the marketplace is as important as the institution. Development professionals should read the business section of their local newspaper and any community business journals, browse the *Wall Street Journal* whenever possible, and skim such magazines as *Business Week, Fortune, Forbes, Harvard Business Review*, and *Inc.* for relevant articles. The credibility of our sector is enhanced by development professionals who are knowledgeable about the environment in which they operate. To have discourse on issues that are important to potential donors requires an understanding of the business, social, and professional worlds.

Because of the pressures of development jobs, managers often apologize when they are "caught" reading. Instead, they should apologize for *not* taking time to read. It is a critical component of professional growth.

Occasional Publications. Organizations such as INDEPENDENT SECTOR, the National Society of Fund Raising Executives (NSFRE), the Association for Healthcare Philanthropy, the American Association of Fund-Raising Counsel (AAFRC), and the Council for Advancement and Support of Education (CASE) publish occasional brochures, newsletters, and memos on pertinent issues. These publications are benefits of membership. INDEPENDENT SECTOR's quarterly publication *State Tax Trends for Nonprofits* summarizes state rulings and regulations that affect not-for-profits. Another INDEPENDENT SECTOR publication comes from the National Forum to Encourage Giving, Volunteering and Not-for-Profit Initiative. It also focuses on current issues, principally aspects of tax legislation.

A typical independent newsletter is the small publication *Nonprofit Issues* published monthly by the Health, Education, and Nonprofit Law Department of Montgomery, McCracken, Walker & Rhoads, a Philadelphia law firm. Not-for-profits can subscribe at a reduced rate.

Another source of current information is the Foundation Center, which has two national collections. One is located at 79 Fifth Avenue, New York, NY, 10003; the other is at 1001 Connecticut Avenue, NW, Suite 938, Washington, DC 20036. The Foundation Center also has field offices in San Francisco and Cleveland and a network of more than 175 cooperating libraries in every U.S. state as well as abroad. The center has regular mailings that describe its many practical funding guides and services.

An additional national resource is the computer-based bibliography of publications in the area of philanthropy that has been compiled and cataloged by Indiana University's Center on Philanthropy. The bibliography is divided into sections such as "Volunteers" and "Fund Raising," and the listings are available on request for a modest fee. The center is located at 550 West North Street, Suite 301, Indianapolis, IN 46202-3162.

Books, Videotapes, and Audiotapes. Books, videotapes, and audiotapes are an additional resource for the development professional. Books may be specific (for example, capital campaigns, direct mail, and leadership issues) or general (how to fund raise), and audio and videotapes may be produced on a single subject or as a series. The selection of these materials should be related to plans for institutional and professional advancement and budgeted as a developmental expense. For those organizations without financial resources for these items, the development officer may wish to make acquisitions for a personal library of materials.

INDEPENDENT SECTOR and the Foundation Center offer mail-order catalogs of books, audiotapes, and videotapes. Another source of helpful publications is the National Center for Nonprofit Boards (Publications Department, 2000 L Street, NW, Suite 411, Washington DC 20036).

Some publishers market directly by mail. Such catalogs are worth reviewing, and books and tapes can often be sent on approval. The *Harvard Business Review* also offers reading, listening, and viewing materials on areas of management and leadership.

In addition to publications offered by catalog, many bookstores have large sections that feature books on management and leadership. The number of these books has grown considerably in recent years, and these publications should be reviewed if the professional is to stay current. Critical evaluations of many of these books are offered in the fund raising and business periodicals cited above, and some are noted in the *New York Times Book Review, The New York Review of Books*, and the book review sections of local newspapers.

Fund Raising as a Multidisciplinary Function

In considering the resources for strengthening the fund raising process, emphasis has been placed on those that relate most directly to the fund raising process or the constituency with which development professionals must be familiar. But another key aspect of the development function deserves mention: Fund raising is a multidisciplinary function.

Effective fund raising requires (1) sensitivity to the donor's interests and needs, (2) awareness of the environment in which the donor is functioning, and (3) appreciation for the role that organizational values and mission play relative to the donor's values and needs. These skills require more than just fund raising training: They require a knowledge of social sciences, the humanities, and other disciplines *and* their application. The development officer must be part psychologist, sociologist, anthropologist, economist, and historian, as well as familiar with the principles of values transmission.

Advanced degree programs in not-for-profit management, organizational development or behavior, public policy management or other fields related to the not-for-profit sector are increasingly interdisciplinary. The following are some of the ways in which various disciplines can enhance the development professional's ability to manage the fund raising process.

Psychology. The study of human behavior provides an excellent background for the development practitioner. Of special interest is motivational theory. It is extremely helpful to understand why someone will give to an organization or why a staffmember's productivity is declining. When motivations are understood and respected, stronger relationships are developed with staffmembers, volunteers, and donors. Although intuition may serve most people well during challenging or sensitive transactions, a background in psychological principles can improve interactions with various constituencies.

Sociology. This science of society, social institutions, and social relationships is also basic to fund raising. The study of sociology enhances the development professional's ability to work effectively with community institutions and to summarize community needs. Because fund raising focuses on relationship building, understanding the styles, configurations, and dynamics of social relationships is very important. Familiarity with broader sociological interpretations for the societal problems that not-for-profits are trying to solve provides a dimension to the development process that cannot be found in resources that focus only on fund raising.

Anthropology. Aspects of culture and environment profoundly affect the fund raising process and the perception of the organization within the community. Ignorance of the cultural basis for behavior can distort the response to that behavior and lead to actions that may be inappropriate. For those who have not explored the anthropological framework in which they live and work, new insights await. This fresh perspective can provide new approaches to old problems with satisfying results.

History. Contemporary culture largely ignores history, particularly its lessons. Not-for-profit organizations exist to meet the human or societal needs in the community, and as such they are helped by the development practitioner who knows and respects the historical context of the problems that must be solved. A sense of order can be derived from studying the history and growth of all societies, the knowledge from which can be applied to a community's cycles of change. The study of history can provide a context for interpreting current conditions as well as a stronger basis for evaluating alternatives.

Values Transmission. An outgrowth of cultural anthropology, the study of values transmission is another interesting area for development practitioners. Academic courses are offered in this subject, and they are provocative and fascinating. For development professionals, the study can be particularly valuable. Fund raising is a marketing or exchange process based on the notion of a *values exchange*. Its premise rests in the knowledge that people invest in organizations that maintain and transmit their values. An understanding of the dynamics of values transmission in our society offers exciting insights into the potential for increasing the effectiveness of organizational marketing and fund raising.

Economics. No discussion of the interdisciplinary framework that guides the fund raising process would be complete without mentioning economics. To be successful at raising and managing funds requires a knowledge of current and historical issues in economics: sources of money, stock and bond markets, inflationary trends and factors, tax laws, principles of accounting, investment strategies, and other related areas. In an era of increasing demands for financial accountability, fund raising executives should equip themselves with a broad understanding of these economic principles.

A Fund Raising Curriculum. A growing number of colleges and universities are offering majors in fund raising or fund raising management. The danger of overconcentrating on fund raising and management techniques is the potential loss of comprehensive instruction in the social sciences and humanities. Those who are responsible for the development of these curricula must be diligent in keeping the course offerings broadly inclusive. Otherwise, the humane education that comes from the liberal arts and which is translated into not-for-profit policies, practices, and programs may be in jeopardy.

Professional Associations

Professional societies for fund raising executives offer networking and continuing education, and they provide professional standards. Affiliation with one or more of these organizations provides publications (for example, the NSFRE *Journal* or CASE *Currents*) and opportunities to take courses or attend regional, national, or international conferences. For many, however, the greatest benefit of joining such a group is the professional association with other professionals.

These professional organizations include the following.

National Society of Fund Raising Executives. The NSFRE is the largest professional society of fund raising practitioners in the world, with a 1991 membership of more than eleven-thousand individuals in more than one-hundred chapters. For more than thirty years, NSFRE has been committed to fostering the development and growth of fund raising executives and the fund raising profession. Five membership categories are offered to cover all levels of experience.

NSFRE offers a variety of services for its members, including educational seminars and publications. The society also promotes ethical standards and serves as a resource on fund raising and philanthropy. The NSFRE *Journal* is a comprehensive quarterly publication. The society also publishes an annual membership directory, *Who's Who In Fund Raising.* A National Fund Raising Library and Resource Center is at NSFRE's headquarters in Alexandria, Virginia, and offers books, periodicals, cassette tapes, speeches, pamphlets, and brochures. The NSFRE's International Conference on Fund Raising is held annually each spring and is attended by more than two-thousand fund raising professionals.

The NSFRE administers the Executive Leadership Institute (ELI) in cooperation with the Center on Philanthropy at Indiana University. This three-day seminar focuses on leadership and management issues. The NSFRE was the driving force behind the certified fund raising executive (CFRE) program, which it sponsors. Becoming a CFRE requires a minimum of five years of continuous experience in the not-for-profit sector, a track record in raising money, evidence of continuing education, and contribution to the profession. An advanced certification program also is available.

Many NSFRE chapters sponsor "Fund Raising Days" in cities across the nation. These one-day sessions offer affordable workshops and an opportunity to network with others from the same city or region. National Philanthropy Day, which occurs annually in mid-November, has also become a regular observance for many chapters. Inaugurated by Congress and the president in 1986, National Philanthropy Day is an opportunity to pay tribute to Americans for their efforts in support of the not-for-profit community. Awards presented at these celebrations include those that honor philanthropists, volunteer fund raisers, corporate grant makers, professional fund raisers, and foundation grant makers.

Further information may be obtained from the National Society of Fund Raising Executives, 1111 King Street, Suite 3000, Alexandria, VA 22314.

The Association for Healthcare Philanthropy. Formerly the National Association for Hospital Development this not-for-profit organization of nearly two-thousand hospital and health care executives was established to strengthen the performance of professionals who advance philanthropy and manage resource development programs for the nation's hospitals. Its members include development professionals from the United States and Canada, and its International Educational Conference has been held annually for almost twenty-five years. AHP has an extensive training program for its members and offers regional as well as national educational programs. Its fellowship program recognizes "veterans" in hospital development and has provided mentoring for those entering the profession or those who have little experience. AHP also provides services and publications to its members. Its national headquarters are located at 313 Park Avenue, Suite 400, Falls Church, VA 22046.

The Council for the Advancement and Support of Education. CASE serves administrative and development professionals in independent schools, private and public colleges, and universities. Its broad area of service includes recruitment, alumni relations, admissions, publications, promotion, and development. It has an extensive awards program. More than 3,200 colleges, universities, independent schools, educational associations, and subscribers from the United States, Canada, Mexico, and eighteen other countries belong to CASE. In the United States there are eight geographical districts, each of which has its own member activities.

Annually, CASE updates and publishes its "Double Your Dollars" matching-gift brochures that are available for purchase by all not-for-profit organizations. Originally developed to serve educational institutions, these brochures are now produced for arts and health and human services organizations as well. "Double Your Dollars" lists corporations that will match employee gifts to organizations. Designed to fit in a standard letter-sized envelope, the brochures can be included in institutional mailings. The annual and comprehensive *Matching Gift Details* book lists all corporations that match gifts and the areas they will match, such as education, arts, and health.

Regional CASE conferences are held regularly at locations throughout the United States, and a national conference is held annually. *Currents*, the council's quarterly publication, is widely read by development and administration professionals. It carries articles on fund raising, admissions, publications, and a wide array of other issues of interest to professionals working in the field of education.

CASE is headquartered at 80 South Early Street, Alexandria, VA 22304.

For specific disciplines and practices within the fund raising profession, other associations provide professional publications and services. They include the following.

The American Society for Training and Development. The ASTD comprise staffpeople or consultants who provide regular training and program development for organizations. "Development" in the ASTD name refers not to fund raising but to management or leadership development. Many trainers who serve the not-for-profit sector are affiliated with ASTD. Local chapters can be found in major cities across the United States. The national office is located at 1630 Duke Street, Box 1443, Alexandria, VA 22313.

American Association of Fund-Raising Counsel. The AAFRC is another organization of consultants. Its annual publication *Giving USA* is another good resource for development offices. AAFRC also has other occasional publications available to its members. AAFRC is located at 25 West 43rd Street, New York, NY 10036.

In addition to these associations, there are local and national organizations for those working in prospect research, planned giving, and other specialized areas within the development profession.

Conclusion

In a rapidly changing environment and a fast-growing profession, increased demands are placed on development professionals to remain current, informed, and energized. The array of resources available—courses, periodicals, books, audiotapes, videotapes, interdisciplinary studies, and professional societies—should be sampled by fund raising practitioners as a way of responding to the challenges of their profession. As the not-for-profit sector matures, performance expectations for its leaders are increasing. Successful fund raising executives will meet those expectations through the establishment of personal and professional growth goals that are fulfilled through reading, course work, and association with other professionals.

Putting It All Together:
The Integrated Development Plan

Fund raising is a delicate fabric of tightly woven threads, each of which is endowed with a distinct integrity, each of which contributes a vitality to the total strength, and each of which confers a dignity upon the whole. As has been stated before in this text, fund raising is a discipline that draws its purpose, its excitement, and its vigor from all of its parts. By understanding their interrelations, the fund raising planner can make judicious use of each to better fulfill the organization's revenue-production requirements.

Previous chapters have characterized each of the parts that make up the complete structure of fund raising. This chapter will assimilate the various concepts into the whole fabric that is referred to frequently as *the integrated development plan* or *the total development plan*. Several concepts emerge from this type of fund raising. One captures all of the organization's financial needs in an overall goal for a slower-paced fund raising program that can be extended over a number of years. The second applies the full development plan as an ongoing strategy that uses four specific forms of fund raising to meet financial needs. This level of fund raising has several distinct advantages; these will be delineated in this chapter.

Not-for-profit organizations that are not schooled in the overall potential of disciplined fund raising begin their efforts by asking for money to meet budget requirements and by occasionally conducting a capital campaign. For the most part, the fund raising methods used to raise this money are simple and basic: events such as "benefits" or "fund raisers," direct mail appeals, and more primitive forms of grantsmanship directed to foundations and corporations. Little effort is made to secure the truly large gift that is required by the capital campaign.

These methods may be appropriate in the early stages of an organization's fund raising experience, but they are too rudimentary to raise the level of funds required for adequate program, capital, and endowment support. Mature fund raising demands the broader resource development program that includes all of the elements that make up the process. These elements are an essential part of an integrated program, and they apply equally to fund raising programs initiated apart from the more comprehensive development format.

The critical elements of fund raising are the institutional plan with a clear statement of external and internal needs, fund raising goals that reflect these needs, fund raising plans, case definition, constituency identification and involvement, gift history, communications plan, leadership development, fund raising staff, office support, and adequate budget. Each element can exert a positive or negative influence on the overall process of fund raising. Any one element's failure can affect the organization's ability to serve its mission properly and to function effectively in fund raising.

Organizations of the independent sector serve a multiplicity of human and societal needs. The strategies devised to address the *external* needs create four distinct areas of *internal* financial needs: current program support, special-purpose needs, major and minor capital needs, and endowment needs. The full or total development concept is the result of an institutional strategic plan that seeks to identify the entire range of financial requirements. Everything that can be interpreted as an internal need can be gathered under the rubric of a total development program. These needs, reviewed and approved by the board of trustees, will serve as the fund raising goal of separate unrelated programs, or as a part of the fully integrated total development plan.

Fund Raising Programs

There are four areas of financial needs and four fund raising methods or programs that can be used to raise the funds that will resolve these needs.

The Annual Fund. (See Chapter 6.) The annual fund has current program support as one of its primary objectives. By building a base of recurring gifts, the fund can ensure a level of income that will support current operating programs and by doing so will support the annual operating budget. Few contributors will give to meet operating-budget requirements. They will give to programs that are responsive to the external needs that are identified in the organization's statement of mission because programs can be construed as solutions to problems. Contributors want to give to solve problems, not to balance an operating budget.

Another and important objective of the annual fund is to attract recurring gifts to build a base of contributors. The guiding strategy is to "get the gift, get it to repeat, and get it to upgrade." Building and nurturing a base of contributors develops a giving history that will bond the contributor to the organization and thus enhance opportunities for multiple gifts and for gifts that will increase in value in response to special appeals.

The Special-Purpose Gift. (See Chapter 10.) A thoughtfully conceived, comprehensive plan will often identify a broad array of special-purpose needs. These needs can be related to programs, minor or major capital requirements, the acquisition of sophisticated equipment to support program activity, or perhaps personnel additions. In each case, the need will open up opportunities to involve and solicit annual contributors with a special interest in the organization or to approach foundations and corporations for this type of gift. The special-purpose gift is a "sight-lifting" device, a method to invite contributors to increase the value of their support by giving for a special purpose or to meet a special need or by helping the organization to do a better job in serving its mission. Invariably, the special gift will be larger than the gift that is made to the annual fund, which "lifts" the contributor's sights.

The Capital or Asset-Building Gift. (See Chapter 8.) This level of fund raising is intended to meet the capital or asset-building needs of the not-for-profit organization. Gifts can be paid in cash or made in the form of a pledge payable over several years. Or it may constitute a transfer of assets, generally property in the form of land or in the form of stock holdings that have appreciated in value. Capital fund raising can take several forms. It can be an intensive campaign to attain a specified goal within a relatively short period of perhaps nine to eighteen months. It can be a strategically designed major-gift effort directed to the interests of a limited number of donors capable of making large gifts. It can be just one part of the total development plan that will be accomplished over a period of two, three, or more years.

The Planned Gift. (See Chapter 9.) A planned-gift solicitation seeks gifts from current asset holdings or from the contributor's estate. The gift is committed at the conclusion of a solicitation, although its actual value is not available to the organization until the gift's maturity, generally at the death of the primary contributor or a surviving beneficiary or at the end of a term. Planned gifts are made in the form of revocable or irrevocable trusts, gift annuities, pooled income funds, charitable lead trusts, bequests, and insurance. Planned giving is an ideal fund raising method to attract gifts for endowment purposes.

Philip S. Brain Jr., a respected sage of the profession, explains that these four methods hold certain implications for all of fund raising:

- All parts—annual fund, special gifts, capital campaigns, and planned giving—are interrelated; success cannot be achieved in isolation.

- Each part plays a significant role in support of the others.
- Each part must be fully developed and in relationship with the others.
- There is a logical progression from one part to another.

Fund Raising Prerequisites

Certain requisites will command the attention of the governing board and the senior management team before this broader program of fund raising can be implemented.

Governance. The statement of the overall needs, internal and external, and the plan to raise the funds that will address the internal needs must be reviewed, accepted, and approved by the governing board. It is essential that board members place their full support behind the plan by contributing to the best of their ability and by urging others to do so.

Management. The chief executive must serve as the principal advocate for the mission, the primary architect of the vision, and the inspirational force for the continuing advancement of the organization into the future. The senior management group, with the full participation of the board of trustees, must articulate the values for the organization and participate in communicating these values to the constituency. The chief executive—as the primary link to the governing board and through the board to the larger constituency—must constantly champion the development program and the goals that it seeks to serve.

Programs and Services Staff. Program accomplishments, not budget requirements, will attract generous gift support to the organization. The competence and the commitment of the program staff will provide the motivation for people to give and for individuals to involve themselves as volunteers. Program specialists make excellent "expert witnesses." As members of a soliciting team, they can effectively articulate the scope and worth of the programs. Key program staffmembers should team with board members and other volunteers to explain the organization's accomplishments to potential contributors.

Fund Raising Staff. The ability of this staff to plan, organize, and administer programs will determine the outcome of the fund raising effort. However, administration is not the single factor that is most conducive to effective production. Other compelling factors are adequate budget, proper office space, competent support staff, and sincere acknowledgment by program and management staff that fund raising is an integral part of the total organization.

All four of the factors that contribute to the success of a total development program are interrelated and must not remain in bureaucratic isolation. None should be seen as weaker than or subservient to any of the others. All four are integral parts of the organization's structure and therefore interdependent.

Supporting Elements

Several elements must support the organization and its mission. These include the following.

1. Responsible trusteeship, competent management, quality services, concern for the individual, valid needs, and stewardship through open accountability will justify the case for philanthropic generosity.
2. The statement of mission, the very foundation of the organization's case position, must be a statement of shared values or a philosophical expression of the human or societal needs that the organization is endeavoring to serve. The mission is a statement of the organization's reason for being.
3. Proper communication methods require an acknowledgment of the constituents' needs and wants, an awareness of their perceptions and their requirements, and a readiness to design the public relations plan that will respond to these needs.
4. Acceptance of fund raising as a management function and as a management process requires the acceptance of the chief fund raising officer as an important member of the senior management team.
5. The involvement of trustees, administrators, and program staffmembers with the development function is essential to ensure that key people become fully conversant with and supportive of the development objectives, policies, strategies, plans, and programs.
6. The need to institutionalize the development function by weaving it into the fabric and endowing it with the power and the dignity of the organization is a fact of reality in a complex, somewhat turbulent, and always challenging environment. Fund raising must bear the mantle of the institutional mission as its symbol of honor.

Prerequisites for Full Funding: An Outline

I. The Institutional Plan
   A. Create plans that reach at least three to five years forward as a design of the organization's strategy for addressing its mission, goals, and objectives.
   B. An imperative: The plan should set forth details of program support, special purpose, and capital and endowment needs for the period of

the plan. The dollar requirements can serve as a guide to fund raising programs for each year of the plan, as well as for the total period.

II. Full Board Involvement

A. A sense of personal "ownership" is an important motivating force to induce board members, volunteers, and staffmembers to give and to work for the success of the program. Ownership can be generated by encouraging people to assist in determining needs, identifying prospects, and helping with solicitation.

B. The board is the constituency's energy center. It can mirror the constituency's interest. It should serve as a sounding board to receive and to reflect the constituency's feelings about the program and about the organization's readiness for major fund raising. It can and should present and represent the organization to its constituency.

III. Case and Cases: The Primary Document

A. Each request for gifts must have a case of its own drawn from the organization's larger case.

B. Each case must be exciting, compelling, and responsive to the prospective donor's interests and requirements for information.

C. The case must describe valid needs, and it must offer various gift options that will be suitable to the contributor's situation to facilitate the donor's gift-making capabilities.

D. The case must be renewed regularly if it is to have merit and if it is to have pertinence for prospective contributors.

IV. Volunteers for Fund Raising

A. Volunteers will play many roles willingly in the fund raising program once their commitment to the organization has been confirmed.

B. To encourage this commitment, volunteers must be meaningfully involved, properly recognized, and given a sense of importance. They must be made to feel that they are an important part of a worthwhile team serving a worthwhile program. Their involvement is making a difference.

C. Training for volunteers must have a major place in this transaction.

V. Planning

A. The total development program is a full-circle approach to the organization. It examines every aspect of an organization's being. The plan's final draft must be converted into a living document with meaning for each trustee, each member of any advisory body, and each staffmember, as well as for strategically important leaders in the organization's service area.

B. To be effective, the plan for total development should be prepared, evaluated, refined, and accepted by those people who possess the power to put it into action.

Integrated Development

The integrated development concept operates from a primary focus: a thoughtfully defined, well-organized plan that is unyielding in its discipline to earn the respect of those who will be associated with it. It will be capable of providing the human and financial capital that the organization requires to support its program outreach into the community and for the fund raising that will make that outreach possible.

Again, it must be emphasized that there are many facets to the total development concept, each offering opportunities for different approaches and different interpretations. Two models pertain.

Model 1. The total development concept can be a totally integrated program operating with a single goal that encompasses annual program support needs, special-purpose needs, capital needs, and endowment needs. All needs are part of the total fabric. The all-inclusive goal becomes a megagoal relative to the organization's size, and gifts are sought against the requirements of this goal. All fund raising programs serve the larger goal, all function at the same time, and all are carefully coordinated to comply with the stiff requirements of the overarching goal and strategy.

If Model 1 of the totally integrated program is to succeed, then it must be a working model of clear communications, sensitive cooperation, and tightly disciplined coordination that involves all of the working divisions of the plan. Communications, cooperation, and coordination must be the message.

Model 2. The total development program is not under a single umbrella. The fund raising goal is not a single goal. Each of the four fund raising programs function independently with their own goals, and yet all are coordinated by the master plan for fund raising that is controlled by the chief development officer and coordinated through the board's development committee. The four methods — annual fund, special-purpose gifts, capital fund raising, and planned giving — function at the same time, with the administrator of each program understanding and respecting the wisdom that each program contributes significantly to the strength and long-term values of the others.

Conclusion

Fund raising must function in a competitive environment that is becoming more complex with the passing of each year. The simple, uncoordinated forms of fund raising that pertained during the first six or seven decades of the twentieth century are inappropriate for the most part to the demands of not-for-profit organizations reaching for the twenty-first century. A dependency on single sources of funding — foundations, corporations, or government — is too risky for any but the smallest of agencies, and even these must understand that the playing field provided by the dominant funding source is "tilted" to the funding source's advantage.

Diversity of funding is the secret of financial stability. Diversity of fund raising methods adds to that security. Organizations that depend on limited action in fund raising by confining their activity just to grantsmanship, direct mail, or special events or just to an anxious and unrewarding pursuit of endowment through planned giving are building a weakness in their structure. The chances are quite likely that these organizations are not involving themselves in the long-term planning that compels continual assessments of the human or societal needs that are germane to their missions. The chances are equally likely that these organizations are not communicating properly with their constituencies or are not devoting much time to case renewal. They are not building a base of informed, involved, and supportive contributors who give because they are informed, involved, and committed to the organization and to all that it endeavors to accomplish.

Broad-based, diversified fund raising requires responsible governance, effective management, responsive programs, proper stewardship of funds, and full accountability to the constituency that is being served. Broad-based and diversified fund raising is an unrelenting and demanding taskmaster. Broad-based fund raising also raises a lot of money to satisfy diverse program support and the special-purpose, capital, and endowment needs of not-for-profit organizations.

RESOURCES

The resources that follow were developed by Arthur C. Frantzreb and are referred to in Chapter 10, "Seeking the Big Gift."

Seeking the Big Gift: Why People Do Not Give

1. Absence of powerful authenticators on the governing board, which is legally responsible for management
2. Absence of a reasonable plan for the organization's future and related costs of that future
3. Absence of gift, grant, and investment policies and experienced counselors
4. Inadequate communications about the organization's dynamics, promises, and productive services
5. Not being impressed by the solicitors or the agenda for solicitation
6. Premature determination of readiness to give
7. Failure to ask for a specific gift or gift range that complements prospect research data
8. Failure to ask for a gift commensurate with urgency or case motivation
9. Failure to recommend the use of multiple resources rather than checkbook balance
10. Failure to include spouse or associates in the cultivation and solicitation sessions
11. Mechanical, impersonal, and premature requests
12. Failure to suggest a specific gift objective

Seeking the Big Gift: Prevailing Assumptions

1. Assume that people want to belong, to be part of a success.
2. Each person must be convinced of his or her importance in that success.
3. Each person evaluates the logic of the plan, program, cultivation, and solicitation.
4. People quietly assess their confidence in governance, management, planning, administration, and services.
5. People are complimented by being asked to give at a level and at a time that compliments their capacity, leadership, and financial impact.
6. Potential donors are the only ones who will decide the amount, methods, and timing of their commitments.
7. People who are not asked to give according to their own estimate of their capacity know:
    a. homework has not been done,
    b. a studied plan does not exist,
    c. their value has not been assessed,
    d. solicitors have not given personally, or
    e. this is just a test, and is not serious.
8. People determine their commitment relative to the goal sought.
9. People respond to goals and deadlines.
10. People resent begging, appeals, pressure, and deficits.

Seeking the Big Gift: Deterrents to Success

1. Incomplete or inaccurate research and study of the personal interests, concerns, and nuances of the prospect
2. Little knowledge or understanding of the prospect's needs for appreciation, self-esteem, self-realization, goals, and desires
3. Insensitive, mundane, speedy cultivation for the organization's needs rather than the prospect's needs for personal satisfaction
4. Failure, reluctance, or disinclination to ask prospect for support that compliments his or her estimate of personal capacity to give
5. Assumption of the prospect's predilections to give just because of previous gifts or the presumption of evidence of capacity regardless of priority interest
6. Failure to rehearse the solicitation process before the actual meeting
7. Eager willingness to accept a token gift offer for mere numerical fund raising purposes rather than to build a substantial philanthropic financial commitment
8. Inadequate or unfortunate "body language" during the presentation interview: sloppy posture, inappropriate use of gestures, poor vocal qualities, clothing disarray, and so on
9. Pressing for consideration on emotional grounds rather than on logical grounds: budget deficits, little or no endowment, poverty problems, memorializing oneself, and so on
10. Communication of the solicitor's personal commitment
11. Disinclination to suggest gift opportunities for current fund, special

project, and planned giving simultaneously to motivate maximum philanthropic impact of the prospect's total investment

12. Failure to suggest specific gift ranges or personal gift goals rather than techniques on how to do it

13. Presenting the case without a cosolicitor

14. Talking too much

15. Listening too little

16. Overuse of names and experiences rather than analogy

17. Failure to get prospect talking about him- or herself and dreams, hopes, and concerns

18. Failure to ask what the solicitor or the organization can do for the prospect; facility visit, participation in program, service as host, create special funds, meet special persons, and so on.

Seeking the Big Gift:
What the Prospect Thinks

1. Is the request reasonable to consider at all?
2. Did the presentation seem reasonable — persuasive yet without pressure?
3. Is the organization really doing the job professed? Do I agree with it? Am I truly grateful for services rendered to me?
4. Do I respect the organization's management, leadership, and staff?
5. Is the organization well managed?
6. Does the organization have a plan for its future that ensures that my support will be tantamount to an investment rather than a plug for a hole in a leaky vessel?
7. What should be my role in financial support — minimal, merely testing the efficacy of the organization's case? Average, supportive, but not philanthropic? Generous — a gift of confidence in the integrity, purpose, and future of the organization?
8. What are my priorities? Family security, current financial and imminent obligations, church, hospital, retirement center, career investments, social responsibilities — or none of these?
9. With whom should I "invest" voluntary resources to ensure society's and my neighbor's security, health, and opportunities as they may be provided for me?
10. Should I invest in our institutions and organizations for the future as others in the past have provided for me today?
11. What is the record of support by others of the organization?
12. Will my participation really count? Do I want it to truly count?

13. Should this organization be one of my top priorities in view of all of the above considerations?

14. Should I just make a token gift and see what happens to it and to me?

15. Did the presenters say what they were giving? Did they before they saw me? Were they sincerely committed or were they just soliciting because they did it last year?

16. What about those club gifts — which one is best for us now? Are all those "benefits" really necessary? Do I really want to get that involved? How much do those benefits cost?

17. What did they say about endowing our annual support? I haven't looked at my will in years. I didn't know that the state has a will for me.

18. Why should I decide now? Why am I a leadership gift donor?

19. They mentioned monthly payment opportunities. That would be a much easier way to do what I ought to do, but how will I remember each month?

20. I could make a large gift because IRS says I can "carry over" my gift averages each year for a while.

21. If the gift commitment is too large, how would it look? Maybe it should be anonymous.

22. What would my spouse think about all of this?

23. What about his or her interests and involvements?

24. Should this be *Mr. and Mrs.*?

25. What are the spouse's priorities?

26. Small gifts really don't add up to what I should really do. But how much would?

27. I really have never been a large donor to anything. Maybe I ought to start now. After all, those committee people were really persuasive about the organization and my importance to it. I could provide $100 ($1,000, $10,000) a month if I put my mind to it and still take care of other obligations.

Seeking the Big Gift: Solicitation Strategy

I.   Strategies to Consider
  A.   Introduce prospect to the organization
    1.   Frequent, attractive, sharp newsletter
    2.   Special-status letter from the CEO
    3.   Invitation to organization facilities for
      a.   meetings
      b.   special events
      c.   academic, health care, planned-gift seminars
      d.   open house
      e.   CEO meal
    4.   Trustee- or volunteer-hosted luncheons, dinners, and so on to meet CEO
    5.   CEO consultation sessions to market test the case
  B.   Invite to special council or committee for public relations or special-purpose involvement (*never* use advisory committee)
  C.   Cold call by CEO "to get acquainted"
  D.   Rapid sequence of impelling (but not soliciting) communications
  E.   Inculcate desire for generous philanthropy
  F.   Create desire for personal achievement through personal gift objectives
II.   Techniques for Solicitation
  A.   Person-to-person, 1:1; *no* printed presentation
  B.   Two persons (never more), 2:1; *no* printed presentation
  C.   Verbal presentation, letter follow-up

    D.   Special printed presentation with personal letter and letter follow-up

    E.   Present range of gift options—high first, then intermediate—to compliment the prospect's capacity; never lowest level first

    F.   Suggest multiple financial resources available to initiate gift objective and to consummate with prospect's interest and desires

    G.   Listen for clues to prospect's interests; if favorable, proceed; if not, sell; if enthusiastic, reconsider and raise request for support commensurate with prospect's interests and desires

    H.   Enlist in associates program at highest possible gift level and select capital gift objective

III.   Forms for Solicitation

    A.   Place for solicitation

       1.   neutral environment preferred

       2.   organization environment

       3.   prospect's environment

    B.   Statement of intent

       1.   pick gift objective to provide by cash or other assets

       2.   commit income plus assets for gift objective

       3.   suggest term-payment plan

       4.   bind by codicil addition to will or estate plan

    C.   Suggest underwriting

       1.   people

       2.   programs and services

       3.   physical facilities

       4.   endowment for security and stability

    D.   Methods of giving

       1.   cash, one-time

       2.   cash on term basis, 3–5 years

       3.   cash on term basis plus bequest

       4.   cash plus some asset

          a.   securities

          b.   life insurance

          c.   real property

          d.   personal property

       5.   cash plus some asset plus one or more deferred gift devices

          a.   annuity

          b.   wealth-replacement trust

          c.   unitrust

    E.   Memorial or tribute fund

References

American Association of Fund-Raising Counsel. *Giving USA: The Annual Report of Philanthropy*. New York: American Association of Fund-Raising Counsel, annual publication.

Batten, J. D. *Tough-Minded Leadership*. New York: AMACOM, 1989.

Bennis, W. G. *On Becoming a Leader*. Reading, Mass.: Addison-Wesley, 1989a.

Bennis, W. G. *Why Leaders Can't Lead: The Unconscious Conspiracy Continues*. San Francisco: Jossey-Bass, 1989b.

Bennis, W. G., and Nanus, B. *Leaders: The Strategies for Taking Charge*. New York: HarperCollins, 1985.

Blanchard, K., and Johnson, S. *The One Minute Manager*. New York: Morrow, 1982.

Burns, J. M. *Leadership*. New York: HarperCollins, 1978.

Carbone, R. F. *Fund Raising as a Profession*. College Park, Md.: Clearinghouse for Research on Fund Raising, 1989.

Chronicle of Philanthropy, July 24, 1990.

Conger, J. A. *The Charismatic Leader*. San Francisco: Jossey-Bass, 1989.

Corporate Philanthropy Report. Seattle, Wash.: Craig Smith (editor and publisher). 2727 Fairview Avenue, E, Suite D, Seattle, WA 98102.

Council for Advancement and Support of Education [CASE]. *National Clearinghouse for Corporate Matching Gift Information*. Washington, D.C.: CASE.

Council for Advancement and Support of Education [CASE] and the National Association of Colleges and University Business Officers [NACUBO]. *Management Reporting Standards for Educational Institutions: Fund Raising and Related Activities*. Washington, D.C.: CASE and NACUBO, 1982.

Dewey, J. *Theory of the Moral Life*. New York: Holt, Rinehart and Winston, 1960.

Directory of International Corporate Giving in America. Rockville, Md.: Taft Group, 1991.

Drucker, P. *Managing the Non-Profit Organization: Principles and Practices.* New York: HarperCollins, 1990.

Evans, S. M. *Born for Liberty: A History of Women in America.* New York: Free Press, 1989.

Fisher, J., and Quehl, G. *The President and Fund Raising.* ACE/Macmillan, 1989.

Flanagan, J. *The Grassroots Fundraising Book.* Chicago: Contemporary Books, 1982.

Foster, V.S. *Fund Raising Management,* June 1989, pp. 16, 18, and 55.

Foundation Center. *Foundation Report.* New York: Foundation Center, annual publication.

Gardner, J. W. *Self-Renewal.* (Rev. ed.) New York: Norton, 1981.

Gardner, J. W. *On Leadership.* New York: Free Press, 1990.

Greene, E. "Development Chiefs Found More Likely Than CEO's to Insist on Experience in Fund Raisers." *Chronicle of Philanthropy,* July 24, 1990, p. 24.

Hayes, J. L. *Memos for Management.* New York: AMACOM, 1983.

Heltne, L. D. "The Charity Hires a Fund Raiser." *Insight,* 1989.

Hersey, P. *The Situational Leader.* New York: Warner, 1984.

Hersey, P., and Blanchard, K. *Management of Organizational Behavior.* Englewood Cliffs, N.J.: Prentice-Hall, 1982.

Houle, C. O. *Governing Boards: Their Nature and Nurture.* San Francisco: Jossey-Bass, 1989.

Hulbert, J. "From Politics to Protest." *Just Economics,* 1978, *5* (3).

Hulbert, J. *Self Sufficiency and Black Organizations.* Washington D.C.: Youth Project, 1980.

INDEPENDENT SECTOR. *Giving and Volunteering in the United States: A Summary of Findings.* Washington, D.C.: INDEPENDENT SECTOR, 1988.

Iowa Humanities Board. *Meeting the Challenge of Change, 1971–1986.* Iowa City: Iowa Humanities Board, 1987.

Josephson Institute. *Ethical Issues and Opportunities in Philanthropy and Fund Raising.* Oakbrook, Ill.: American Prospect Research Association, 1990.

Klein, K. "Stop Looking for Wealth." *Grassroots Fundraising Journal,* 1988, 7 (8), p. 5.

Klein, K. "Women and Philanthropy, Part One." *Grassroots Fundraising Journal,* 1990, *9* (2), pp. 3–6.

Kotler, P., and Andreasen, A. R. *Strategic Marketing for Nonprofit Organizations.* Englewood Cliffs, N.J.: Prentice-Hall, 1987.

Kouzes, J. M., and Posner, B. Z. *The Leadership Challenge: How to Get Extraordinary Things Done in Organizations.* San Francisco: Jossey-Bass, 1987.

Lautman, K. *Dear Friend: Mastering the Art of Direct Mail Fundraising.* Rockville, Md.: Taft Group, 1984.

Lundy, J. L. *Lead, Follow or Get Out of the Way.* San Diego, Calif.: Avant Books, 1986.

McCarthy, K. *Parallel Power Structures: Women and the Voluntary Sphere*. New Brunswick, N.J.: Rutgers University Press, 1989.

National Association of Attorneys General. *A Model Act Concerning the Solicitation of Funds for Charitable Purposes*. Washington, D.C.: National Association of Attorneys General, 1986.

National Society of Fund Raising Executives. *Who's Who in Fund Raising: 1990–1991*. Alexandria, Va.: National Society of Fund Raising Executives, 1990.

Northwest Area Foundation. *The Deferred Gifts Program: Future Funding for Private Colleges*. St. Paul, Minn.: Northwest Arts Foundation, 1980.

Panas, J. *MegaGifts: Who Gives Them, Who Gets Them*. Chicago, Pluribus Press, 1984.

Pattillo, M. P. *Foundation News*, Nov. 12, 1982.

Payton, R. L. *Philanthropy, Voluntary Action for the Public Good*. New York: ACE/Macmillan, 1988.

Plinio, A. "Art Collections Can Showcase Nonprofits." *Fund Raising Management*, June 1983, pp. 76–77.

Raybin, A. D. *How to Hire the Right Fund Raising Consultant*. Rockville, Md.: Taft Group, 1985.

Seymour, H. J. *Designs for Fund-Raising*. Rockville, Md.: Taft Group, 1966.

Smith, C. *Corporate Philanthropy Report*. Seattle, Wash.: Craig Smith, 1990.

Sproul, R. D., Jr. *Money Matters*. Wheaton, Ill.: Tyndale House, 1985.

Stehle, V. "Median Salaries of Non-Profit Chief Executives Rose 9% in a Year to $42,000." *Chronicle of Philanthropy*, July 24, 1990, p. 24.

Taft Group. *Taft Corporate Giving Directory, 1990*. Rockville, Md.: Taft Group, 1991.

Warwick, M. *Revolution in the Mailbox: How Direct Mail Fundraising Is Changing the Face of American Society and How Your Organization Can Benefit*. Berkeley, Calif.: Strathmoor Press, 1990.

Waterman, R. H., Jr. *The Renewal Factor*. New York: Bantam, 1987.

White, D. E. "Donor Recognition in Planned Giving: Myth vs. Reality." Presented at the Second Annual Conference of the National Committee on Planned Giving, Indianapolis, Indiana, October 22–24, 1989.

Wisdom, P. E. "Another Look at Costs." *The President and Fund Raising*. Washington, D.C.: ACE/Macmillan, 1989.

Other Sources

American Association of Fund-Raising Counsel, 25 West 43rd St., New York, NY 10036

American Society for Training and Development, 1630 Duke St., Box 1443, Alexandria, VA 22313

Association for Healthcare Philanthropy, 112-B East Broad St., Falls Church, VA 22046

Center on Philanthropy, 550 West North St., Suite 301, Indianapolis, IN 46202-3162

Chronicle of Philanthropy, The, 1255 23rd St., NW, Suite 785, Washington, DC 20037

Compendium of Directors, PC Research Services, P.O. Box 7444, Trenton, N. J., 08628

Conservative Digest, National Press Building, Suite 1210, Washington, DC 20045

Corporate Philanthropy Report, 2727 Fairview Ave. East, Suite D, Seattle, WA 98102

Council for Advancement and Support of Education, 80 South Early St., Alexandria, VA 22304

Dear Friend, Fund Raising Institute, 12300 Twinbrook Parkway, Suite 450, Rockville, MD 20852

DIALOG Information Services, Inc., 3460 Hillview Ave., Palo Alto, CA 94304

Direct Marketing Association, 6 East 43rd St., New York, NY 10017

Direct Marketing Magazine, 224 7th St., Garden City, NY 11530-5771

Dun & Bradstreet, 3 Sylvan Way, Parsippany, NJ 07054-3896: *Million Dollar Directory; Middle Market Directory*

Dun & Bradstreet, 99 Church St., New York, NY 10007: *Reference Book of Corporate Managements*

Foundation Center, 79 5th Ave., 8th Floor, New York, NY 10003: *Corporate Source Profiles*; *Foundation Grants Index*; *National Data Book of Foundations*; *Foundation Directory*; *Foundation News*

Grantsmanship Center, P.O. Box 6210, Los Angeles, CA 90014

Harvard Business Review, P.O. Box 52623, Boulder, CO 80322-2623

Hoke Communications, Inc., 224 7th St., Garden City, NY 11530-5771: *Fund Raising Management*

INDEPENDENT SECTOR, 1828 L St. NW, Suite 1200, Washington DC 20036

Management Center, 944 Market St., Suite 700, San Francisco, CA 94102

Marquis Who's Who, Inc., 200 East Ohio St., Chicago, IL 60611: *Who's Who in America*; *Who's Who in the West*; *Who's Who in Law*; *Who's Who in Finance & Industry* (and 34 additional special areas)

Master Software, 8604 Allisonville Road, Suite 309, Indianapolis, IN 46250

The Nation, 72 5th Ave., New York, NY 10011

National Center for Non-Profit Boards, 2000 L St., NW, Suite 411, Washington, DC 20036-4907

National Cyclopedia of American Biography, T. White, Clifton, NJ

The National Review, 150 East 35th St., New York, NY 10016

National Society of Fund Raising Executives, 1101 King St., Suite 3000, Alexandria, VA 22314: *NSFRE Journal*; *Who's Who in Fund Raising*

The New Republic, 1220 19th St., NW, Washington, DC 20036

The New York Review of Books, 250 West 57th St., New York, NY 10107

New York Times Book Review, and *New York Times Index of Names*: University Microfilms International, 300 North Zeeb Road, Ann Arbor, MI 48106

Nonprofit Issues: Health, Education, and Nonprofit Law Department of Montgomery, McCracken, Walker & Rhoads, Attorneys-at-Law, Three Parkway, Philadelphia, PA 19102

NonProfit Times, P.O. Box 408, Hopewell, NJ 08525

Philanthropic Digest, Inc., Box 7059, Wilton, CT 06897

The Philanthropy Monthly, P.O. Box 989, New Milford, CT 06776

Public Management Institute, 358 Brannan St., San Francisco, CA 94105

Revolution in the Mailbox, Mal Warwick & Associates, Inc., 2550 9th St., Suite 103, Berkeley, CA 94710

Society for Nonprofit Organizations, 63144 Odana Road, Suite 1, Madison, WI 53719: *Nonprofit World*

Standard & Poors Register of Directors & Executives, 25 Broadway, New York, NY 10004

Standard Rate and Data Service, 3004 Glenview Road, Wilmette, IL 60091

Taft Group, 12300 Twinbrook Parkway, Suite 450, Rockville, MD 20852: *America's Wealthiest People—Their Philanthropic and Non-Profit Affiliations*; *Directory of International Corporate Giving in America*; *People in Philanthropy—A Guide to Philanthropic Leaders, Major Donors, and Funding Connections*; *The Taft Trustees of Wealth: A Biographical Directory to Private Foundation and Corporate Foundation Officers*

United Way of America, 95 M St. SW, Washington, DC 20024

Walker's Manual of Western Corporations, 1200 Quince Orchard Boulevard, Gaithersburg, MD 20878

Index

ISBN 1-55542-387-6

90000

9 781555 423872